i

Uncle John's
Colossal
Collection of
Quotable
Quotes

By the
Bathroom Readers'
Institute

Bathroom Readers' Press
Ashland, Oregon

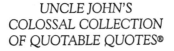
UNCLE JOHN'S
COLOSSAL COLLECTION
OF QUOTABLE QUOTES®

For information, write
The Bathroom Readers' Institute,
P.O. Box 1117, Ashland, OR 97520
www.bathroomreader.com
888-488-4642

Cover design by Michael Brunsfeld,
San Rafael, CA (*Brunsfeldo@comcast.net*)

Uncle John's
Colossal Collection of Quotable Quotes®
by The Bathroom Readers' Institute
ISBN: 1-59223-266-3
Library of Congress Catalog Card Number:
2004110246

Printed in the United States of America

Second Printing, March 2005
11 10 9 8 7 6 5 4 3

*   *   *

"For those who like this sort of thing, this is the sort of thing they
will like."
                                                    —Abraham Lincoln

THANK YOU!

The Bathroom Readers' Institute sincerely thanks the people whose advice and assistance made this book possible.

Gordon Javna
Jay Newman
John Dollison
Jeff Altemus
Brian Boone
Julia Papps
Angela Kern
John Gaffey
Laura BlackFeather
Thom Little
Raingirl Thering
Michael Brunsfeld
Raina Sanderson
Lori Larson
Sydney Stanley

Allen Orso
Paul Stanley
Jenny Baldwin
Nancy Toeppler
Scarab Media
Joe Diehl
Mustard Press
Steven Style Group
Barb Porsche
Paula Leith
Chris Olsen
Our A-Team: JoAnn & Amy
Porter the Wonder Dog
Samuel Clemens
Thomas Crapper

Extra special thanks to our family of "quote herders:"
Debbie Thornton, Sara and Zena, Christy and Tigerlily
Collins, Annie McIntyre, Jennifer and Rhys, Catie, Adam
DeRose, Dena Berliner, Leslie Weishar, Larry Newman,
Mommy and Daddy Newman, Eric Stahlman, Jessica Lee,
Kathy Balogh, Amanda Wilson, Tara Gingerich, Chris
O'Rourke, Joel and Wendy Macneil, Neil Reed, Jeremy
Holmes, and our biggest celebrity fan, Eddie Deezen

*   *   *

"Fantasy is a necessary ingredient in living. It's a way of looking at life through the wrong end of a telescope...and that enables you to laugh at all of life's realities."

—**Dr. Seuss**

CONTENTS

v

*   *   *

OOPS!

"Your food stamps will be stopped effective March,
1992, because we received notice that you passed away.
May God bless you. You may reapply if there is a
change in your circumstances."

**—A letter sent out by the
South Carolina Dept. of Social Services**

INTRODUCTION

*Greetings from the Bathroom Readers' Institute
in the peaceful hamlet of Ashland, Oregon.*

About a year ago, while putting together quote pages for our 16th annual edition of the *Uncle John's Bathroom Reader*, we realized that making quote pages is a lot of fun! So we got an idea (*"Ideas won't keep; something must be done about them." –Alfred North Whitehead*): why not make an entire book of quotations, *Bathroom Reader* style.

So we immediately began working on it—using the same approach that has made our *Bathroom Reader* series so successful: Include a wide range of topics, tidbits of obscure trivia, and a healthy dose of humor. (*"Humor is a reminder that no matter how high the throne one sits on, one sits on one's bottom." –Taki*) And we must admit, we're pleased with what we've created. (*"Creativity is the central source of meaning in our lives." –Mihaly Csikszentmihalyi*)

Result: **Uncle John's Colossal Collection of Quotable Quotes**

This is like no other book of quotations ever produced. You'll find deep thoughts (*"It takes a big man to cry, but it takes a bigger man to laugh at that man." –Jack Handy*), celebrity secrets (*"The embarrassing thing is that the salad dressing is outgrossing my films." –Paul Newman*), goofs (*"I go to lots of overseas places, like Canada." –Britney Spears*), wisdom (*"With the new day comes new strength and new thoughts." –Eleanor Roosevelt*), political quips, insults, free advice, and much, much more.

We collected more than 4,000 quotations from 1,600 speakers and writers. Some of them are household names, and some of them are obscure (like Mihaly Csikszentmihalyi). But they all had something important to say—something that we wanted to share with you. So happy reading...

And as always, Go with the Flow!

—Uncle John, the BRI Staff, and Porter the Wonder Dog

TOILET TALK

*We begin this quote book where
else but…in the bathroom.*

"Education is so important
when it comes to domesticity.
I don't know why no one ever
thought to paste a label on
the toilet tissue spindle giving
1-2-3 directions for replacing
the tissue on it. Then everyone in the house would know
what Mama knows."
—**Erma Bombeck**

"I am sitting in the smallest
room of my house. I have your
review before me. Soon it will
be behind me."
—**Max Reger,
German composer, in
a letter to a music critic**

"Men are never so serious,
thoughtful, and intent, as
when they are at stool."
—**Jonathan Swift**

"I grew up with six brothers.
That's how I learned to
dance—waiting for the bathroom."
—**Bob Hope**

To Robert Mitchum: "You're
like a pay toilet, aren't you?
You don't give a sh*t for nothing."
—**Howard Hughes**

"I found out why cats drink
out of the toilet. My mother
told me it's because it's cold in
there. And I'm like: 'How did
my mother know that?'"
—**Wendy Liebman**

"How about the guys that
stand there grabbing the urinal for balance? I watch in
amazement. They come up
and say, 'I'm a big fan, can I
shake your hand?' And I'm a
bad guy for saying, 'Excuse
me!' They were just holding
the big wonger, and they want
to shake your hand."
—**Donald Trump**

"Posterity will ne'er survey
A nobler grave than this:
Here lies the bones of
Castlereagh
Stop, traveler, and piss."
—**Epitaph of Viscount
Castlereagh (1769–1822)**

"I don't know if I want a fuzzy
cover on my toilet seat, but I
want to meet whoever invented them. Who lifted a toilet
seat and thought, 'That needs
a hat?'"
—**Rita Rudner**

If you're average, you'll visit the bathroom 2,500 times this year. Happy reading!

QUOTES ON QUOTES

"This is a page of quotes about quotes." —Uncle John

"It is better to be quotable than honest."
—Tom Stoppard

"What's the use of a good quotation if you can't change it?"
—Dr. Who

"I never know how much of what I say is true."
—Bette Midler

"The point of quotations is that one can use another's words to be insulting."
—Amanda Cross

"When I'm talking to people I like to stop and quote myself. My quotes have a way of spicing up conversation."
—Brendan Behan

"I don't want to be quoted, and don't quote that I don't want to be quoted."
—Winston Burdett

"One original thought is worth a thousand mindless quotings."
—Diogenes

"I hate quotations. Tell me what you know."
—Ralph Waldo Emerson

"The trouble with words is that you never know whose mouths they've been in."
—Dennis Potter

"Nothing that can be said is so absurd that some philosopher has not already said it."
—Cicero

"Famous remarks are seldom quoted correctly."
—Simeon Strunsky

"Most people are other people. Their thoughts are someone else's opinions, their lives a mimicry, their passions a quotation."
—Oscar Wilde

"An aphorism is never exactly true. It is either a half-truth or a truth-and-a-half."
—Karl Kraus

"The surest way to make a monkey of a man is to quote him."
—Robert Benchley

"Children seldom misquote you. In fact, they usually repeat word for word what you shouldn't have said."
—Unknown

"Without tenderness, a man is uninteresting." —Marlene Dietrich

"It is a good thing for an uneducated man to read books of quotations."
—**Winston Churchill**

"A fine quotation is a diamond on the finger of a witty person, but a pebble in the hands of a fool."
—**Colette**

"The ability to quote is a serviceable substitute for wit."
—**W. Somerset Maugham**

"I often quote myself. It adds spice to my conversation."
—**George Bernard Shaw**

"Hanging is too good for a man who makes puns; he should be drawn and quoted."
—**Fred Allen**

"Quote me as saying I was mis-quoted."
—**Groucho Marx**

*   *   *

CELEBRITY WORKOUT ADVICE

"There's something sexy about a gut. Not a 400-pound beer gut, but a little paunch. I love that."
—**Sandra Bullock**

"The only reason I would take up jogging again is that I could hear heavy breathing again."
—**Erma Bombeck**

"If my hangover isn't too bad I do sit ups."
—**Hugh Grant**

"The only exercise I take is walking behind the coffins of friends who took exercise."
—**Peter O'Toole**

"When your arms are bigger than your head, something is wrong."
—**Steve Reeves, movie muscleman**

"Passing the vodka bottle. And playing the guitar."
—**Keith Richards,
on what he does to stay fit**

TWO KINDS OF PEOPLE...

*There are two types of people in the world: people who
read in the bathroom, and...make that one type.*

"There are two types of people in this world, good and bad. The good sleep better, but the bad seem to enjoy the waking hours much more."
—**Woody Allen**

"There are two types of people: Those who come into a room and say, 'Well, here I am!' and those who say, 'Ah, there you are.' "
—**Frederick L. Collins**

"But in truth there are only three types of people in the world: people who work, people who are not allowed to, and people who don't have to."
—**Elvis Costello**

"There are two types of people: those who divide people into two types, and those who don't."
—**Anonymous**

"Mankind is divisible into two great classes: hosts and guests."
—**Max Beerbohm**

"There are two types of people: those who are forgetful..."
—**Anonymous**

"There are only two kinds of people who are really fascinating—people who know absolutely everything, and people who know absolutely nothing."
—**Oscar Wilde**

"Artillerymen believe the world consists of two types of people: other Artillerymen and targets."
—**military saying**

"There are two kinds of people: those who say to God, 'Thy will be done,' and those to whom God says, 'All right, then, have it your way.' "
—**C. S. Lewis**

"There are two kinds of women: those who want power in the world, and those who want power in bed."
—**Jacqueline Kennedy Onassis**

"Half the world is composed of people who have something to say and can't, and the other half who have nothing to say and keep on saying it."
—**Robert Frost**

"We must believe in free will. We have no choice." —Isaac Bashevis Singer

My grandfather once told me that there were two kinds of people: those who do the work and those who take the credit. He told me to try to be in the first group; there was much less competition.

—**Indira Gandhi**

BALD TO THE BONE

Don't think of it as baldness—think of it as "follicle deficit disorder."

"The truth is that balding African-American men look cool when they shave their heads, whereas balding white men look like giant thumbs."
—Dave Barry

"The most delightful advantage to being bald—one can hear snowflakes."
—R. G. Daniels

"Balding is God's way of showing you are only human.... He takes the hair off your head and puts it in your ears."
—Bruce Willis

"Being baldplate is an unfailing sex magnet."
—Telly Savalas

"I've always wanted to be bald. I mean it, completely bald. Wouldn't it be great to be bald in the rain?"
—Harrison Ford

"Grass doesn't grow on a busy street."
—William Hague

"The tenderest spot in a man's makeup is sometimes the bald spot on top of his head."
—Helen Rowland

"I am not the archetypal leading man. This is mainly for one reason: as you may have noticed, I have no hair."
—Patrick Stewart

"People get real comfortable with their features. Nobody gets comfortable with their hair. Hair trauma. It's the universal thing."
—Jamie Lee Curtis

"There's one thing about baldness, it's neat."
—Don Herold

"I don't consider myself bald, I'm just taller than my hair."
—Lucius Annaeus Seneca

"A man can be short and dumpy and getting bald—but if he has fire, women will like him."
—Mae West

"Better a bald head than no head at all."
—Seamus MacManus

"Baldness may indicate masculinity, but it diminishes one's opportunity to find out."
—Cecil Hardwicke

STEVEN WRIGHT

He speaks in a slow monotone but he's anything but slow or monotonous. In fact, he's one of the funniest comics in the business.

"I planted some birdseed. A bird came up. Now I don't know what to feed it."

"I saw this guy hitchhiking with a sign that said 'Heaven.' So I hit him."

"I used to be a narrator for bad mimes."

"I bought a dog the other day...I named him Stay. It's fun to call him...'Come here, Stay! Come here, Stay!' He went insane."

"Ever notice how it's a penny for your thoughts, yet you put in your two cents? Someone is making a penny on the deal!"

"My apartment was robbed and everything was replaced with exact replicas...I told my roommate and he said, 'Do I know you?'"

"Once I tried to kill myself with a bungee cord. I kept almost dying."

"Curiosity killed the cat, but for a while I was a suspect."

"You know when you put a stick in water and it looks bent? That's why I never take baths."

"I bought some batteries, but they weren't included."

"I used to work in a fire hydrant factory. You couldn't park anywhere near the place."

"It's a small world...but I wouldn't want to paint it."

"Last night I stayed up late playing poker with Tarot cards. I got a full house and four people died."

"One time I went to a drive-in in a taxi cab. The movie cost me $95."

"My grandfather invented *Cliff's Notes*. It all started back in 1912. Well, to make a long story short..."

"I had a friend who was a clown. When he died, all his friends went to the funeral in one car."

"Show me a thoroughly satisfied man and I will show you a failure." —Thomas Edison

ROCK 'N' ROLL: A PASSING FAD

Here are a few "expert" predictions about rock 'n' roll.

"Maybe next year it will be Hawaiian music."
　　　　　—Jerry Marshall, New York DJ (1955)

"I never knew a guitar player worth a damn."
　　　　　—Vernon Presley, to his son Elvis (1954)

"I tell you, rock 'n' roll can't last."
　　　　　—Jackie Gleason (1956)

"[Rock 'n' roll] is sung and written, for the most part, by cretinous goons; and by means of its almost imbecile reiterations and sly, lewd—in plain fact, dirty—lyrics, it manages to be the martial music of every sideburned delinquent on the face of the earth. This rancid-smelling aphrodisiac I deplore."
　　　　　—Frank Sinatra (1957)

"The Beatles are a passing phase. They are the symptoms of the uncertainties of the times. I hope, when they get older, they'll get a haircut."
　　　　　—Billy Graham (1964)

"It will be gone by June."
　　　　　—*Variety* (1955)

Real newspaper headline: "Bland Music Competition Scheduled"

OFF THEIR ROCKERS?

Some rock stars have brilliant minds...
and others have rocks in their heads.

"I think I'm a fairly loyal person. Although there's probably a few girlfriends who would disagree with me."
—**Rod Stewart**

"I'm still equally as pissed off about the things that made me pissed off a few years ago. It's people doing evil things to other people for no reason. And I just want to beat the shit out of them. That's the bottom line. And all I can do is scream into a microphone instead."
—**Kurt Cobain**

"I smash guitars because I like them."
—**Pete Townshend**

"I don't know what real childbirth is like, but writing songs seems as close as I'm going to come."
—**Billy Joel**

"It's amazing to go to sports arenas and hear people sing 'We Will Rock You.' It's very gratifying to find that it has become part of folklore. I'll die happy because of that."
—**Brian May, Queen**

"I say no to drugs, but they don't listen."
—**Marilyn Manson**

"When you play from your heart, all of a sudden there's no gravity. You don't feel the weight of the world, of bills, of anything. That's why people love it. Your so-called insurmountable problems disappear, and instead of problems you get possibilities."
—**Carlos Santana**

"I'm the type of guy who'd sell you a rat's asshole for a wedding ring."
—**Tom Waits**

"Of course I've been in bed with several women at once. I'm a rock star, after all."
—**Sting**

"What am I here for? What is my purpose in life? This is horrible. I'm the butt end of every joke."
—**Vanilla Ice**

"All I ever wanted to do was sin and make a lot of money."
—**Mick Jagger**

"Is it boasting to say that I don't need Viagra?" —**Larry King**

LOVE...AND MARRIAGE

*Words of wisdom from people who know
the true meaning of "wedded bliss."*

"The best way to remember your wife's birthday is to forget it once."
—E. Joseph Cossman

"You may marry the man of your dreams, ladies, but 14 years later you're married to a couch that burps."
—Roseanne

"Getting married is very special. I only want to do it once. Getting married is like—it's like meeting Elvis."
—Tanya Tucker

"The biggest cause of divorce is marriage."
—Travis Tritt

"I got married when Christ died. Wasn't he 33 when he died? We both died."
—James Woods

"I think a man can have two, maybe three affairs, while he is married. But three is the absolute maximum. After that, you're cheating."
—Yves Montand

"I think marriage is a custom brought about by women who then proceed to live off men and destroy them, completely enveloping the man in a destructive cocoon or eating them away like a poisonous fungus."
—Richard Harris

"Even hooligans marry, though they know that marriage is but for a little while. It is alimony that is forever."
—Quentin Crisp

"A husband is what's left over once the nerve has been extracted."
—Helen Rowland

"A woman who takes her husband about with her everywhere is like a cat that goes on playing with a mouse long after she's killed it."
—Saki

"He marries best who puts it off until it is too late."
—H. L. Mencken

"It's time for the human race to enter the solar system." —Dan Quayle

GA-GA FOR GANDHI

Mahatma Gandhi defeated the British in India through non-violence. Ironically, he died a violent death—murdered by an assassin's gun. Here are a few of his words of wisdom.

"When I despair, I remember that all through history the ways of truth and love have always won. There have been tyrants, and murderers, and for a time, they can seem invincible, but in the end, they always fall. Think of it—always."

"Civil disobedience becomes a sacred duty when the State becomes lawless or, which is the same thing, corrupt."

"The golden rule of conduct...is mutual toleration, seeing that we will never all think alike and we shall see Truth in fragments and from different angles of vision. Conscience is not the same thing for all. Whilst, therefore, it is a good guide for individual conduct, imposition of that conduct upon all will be an insufferable interference with everybody's freedom of conscience."

"In matters of conscience, the law of the majority has no place."

"Democracy is not a state in which people act like sheep."

"Truth resides in every human heart, and one has to search for it there, and to be guided by truth as one sees it. But no one has a right to coerce others to act according to his own view of truth."

"I think it would be a good idea."
                    **—when asked what
                    he thought of
                    Western civilization**

IT'S LIKE...A SIMILE

A simile is a figure of speech in which two dissimilar elements are compared using the words "like" or "as."

"Speeches are like steer horns—a point here, a point there, and a lot of bull in between."
—**Evelyn Anderson**

"Old age is like flying a plane through a storm—once you're aboard there is nothing you can do."
—**Golda Meir**

"I often feel like the director of a cemetery—I have a lot of people under me, but nobody listens."
—**General John Gavin**

"I feel about New York as a child who's father is a bank robber—not perfect, but I still love him."
—**Woody Allen**

"Cleaning your house while your children are still growing is like shoveling the walk before it stops snowing."
—**Phyllis Diller**

"Ideas are like rabbits. You get a couple and learn how to handle them, and pretty soon you have a dozen."
—**John Steinbeck**

"Love is like the measles. The older you get it, the worse the attack."
—**Mary Roberts Rinehart**

"Marriage is like a violin. After the beautiful music is over, the strings are still attached."
—**Jacob Braude**

"A woman is like a teabag—only in hot water do you realize how strong she is."
—**Nancy Reagan**

"Slumps are like soft beds—easy to get into and hard to get out of."
—**Johnny Bench**

"Speeches are like babies—easy to conceive and hard to deliver."
—**Pat O'Malley**

"Kids are like husbands—they're fine as long as they're someone else's."
—**Marsha Warfield**

"Being married to an entertainer is like dog years—for every year of marriage, it must feel like seven."
—**Garth Brooks**

DUH!

*The funny thing about stating the
obvious is that it's so…so…obvious.*

"People who have the most
birthdays live the longest."
—**Jean Bucher**

"We hate critics….They
criticize."
—**Milli Vanilli**

"If you have intercourse,
you run the risk of dying
and the ramifications of
death are final."
—**Cyndi Lauper**

"I owe a lot to my parents,
especially my mother and
father."
—**Greg Norman**

"I know that if you leave
dishes in the sink, they get
sticky and hard to wash the
next day."
—**Arnold Schwarzenegger**

"I feel my best when I'm
happy."
—**Winona Ryder**

"There's no stopping the
future."
—**Yogi Berra**

"For NASA, space is still a
high priority."
—**Dan Quayle**

"It's no exaggeration to say
that the undecideds could
go one way or another."
—**George H. W. Bush**

"It's clearly a budget. It's
got a lot of numbers in it."
—**George W. Bush**

"Traditionally, most of
Australia's imports come
from overseas."
—**Keppel Enderbery,
former Australian
Cabinet minister**

"When more and more
people are thrown out of
work, unemployment
results."
—**Calvin Coolidge**

"The receivers are an integral part of the passing
game."
—**Hank Stram,
TV sportscaster**

REEL FUNNY

Some funny lines from some great (and not so great) movies.

"She makes me feel kinda funny, like when we used to climb the rope in gym class."
—**Dana Carvey,**
Wayne's World

"I never gave a ticket to no nun before. I gave a ticket to a guy from the IRS one time. Got audited the next year. Tell you what, Sister, I'm going let this one slide."
—**Clancy Brown,**
Dead Man Walking

Melissa: "You really love animals, don't you?"
Ace: "If it gets cold enough."
—**Courteney Cox and Jim Carrey,** ***Ace Ventura: Pet Detective***

Sandy: "Carl, I want you to kill all the gophers on the golf course."
Carl: "Correct me if I'm wrong, Sandy, but if I kill all the golfers, they'll lock me up and throw away the key."
—**Thomas Carlin and Bill Murray,** ***Caddyshack***

"I'm a mawg: half man, half dog. I'm my own best friend!"
—**John Candy,** ***Spaceballs***

"I live in a neighborhood so bad, you can get shot while ya gettin' shot."
—**Chris Rock,** ***Head of State***

History Teacher: "Who was Joan of Arc?"
Ted: "Noah's wife?"
—**Bernie Casey and Keanu Reeves,** ***Bill and Ted's Excellent Adventure***

Sookie: "What kind of name is 'Igby'?"
Igby: "The kind of name that someone named 'Sookie' is in no position to question."
—**Claire Danes and Kieran Culkin,** ***Igby Goes Down***

"These men have a supreme vow of celibacy, like their fathers, and their fathers before them."
—**Charlie Sheen,**
Hot Shots, Part Deux

Inside a phone booth...
Raymond: "Uh-oh fart. Uh-oh fart."
Charlie: "What? Raymond, did you just fart? Did you just f**king fart?!"
Raymond: "Uh-oh fart."
—***Rain Man***

"The future is made of the same stuff as the present." —Simone Weil

EPITAPHS

Uncle John's not dead, but he's already
written his epitaph: "Don't forget to flush."

Nothing in
Moderation
—Ernie Kovacs

The Body of
B. Franklin, Printer,
Like the Cover of an old Book
Its Contents turn out
And Stript of its Lettering &
Guilding
Lies here. Food for Worms
For, it will as he believed
appear once more
In a new and more
elegant Edition
corrected and improved
By the Author
—Benjamin Franklin

Even amidst fierce
flames the golden lotus
can be planted
—Sylvia Plath

I had A Lover's Quarrel
with the World
—Robert Frost

Real newspaper headline: "Dead Man Remains Dead"

THE TRUTH ABOUT LYING

Hey, there's some snew on your back.

"One who deceives will always find those who allow themselves to be deceived."
—Niccolo Machiavelli

"A little inaccuracy sometimes saves tons of explanation."
—Saki (H. H. Munroe)

"A lie is an abomination unto the Lord and a very present help in time of trouble."
—Adlai Stevenson

"If you want to be thought a liar always tell the truth."
—Logan Pearsall Smith

"It does not require many words to speak the truth."
—Chief Joseph, Nez Perce

"Nobody speaks the truth when there is something they must have."
—Elizabeth Bowen

Spock: "In 24 hours, we'll agree this conversation did not take place."
Valeris: "A lie?"
Spock: "An omission."
—*Star Trek VI*

"The opposite of a fact is falsehood, but the opposite of one profound truth may very well be another profound truth."
—Niels Bohr

"The only people who make love all the time are liars."
—Telly Savalas

"There is nothing about which men lie so much as their sexual powers. In this at least every man is, what in his heart he would like to be, a Casanova."
—W. Somerset Maugham

"Truth is stranger than fiction—but it is because fiction is obliged to stick to possibilities; truth isn't."
—Mark Twain

"He who is not very strong in memory should not meddle with lying."
—Michel de Montaigne

"Three things cannot be long hidden: the sun, the moon, and the truth."
—Buddha

VOLTAIRE

A few thoughts from the French playwright and philosopher, Francois Marie Arouet (1694-1778), better known by his pen name...Voltaire.

"We use ideas merely to justify our evil, and speech merely to conceal our ideas."

"It is dangerous to be right when the government is wrong."

"Man is free the moment he chooses to be."

"Pleasure is the object, the duty, the goal of all rational creatures."

"Life is a shipwreck, but we must not forget to sing in the lifeboats."

"Anything that is too stupid to be spoken is sung."

"Every man is guilty of all the good he didn't do."

"My prayer to God is a very short one: 'O Lord, make my enemies ridiculous.' God has granted it."

Voltaire drank between 50 and 70 cups of coffee every day.

THE WINNING QUOTE QUIZ

You can leave off your thinking caps for this one.

Speaker: Ronaldo, Brazilian soccer star
Quote: "We lost because we didn't…"
    a. "win" **b.** "show up" **c.** "cheat"

Speaker: Tony LaRussa, baseball manager
Quote: "When you're not winning, it's tough to…"
  a. "win a game" **b.** "remember your name" **c.** "place the blame"

Speaker: Chuck Knox, football coach
Quote: "Football players win…"
    a. "football games"   **b.** "baseball games"   **c.** "the lottery"

Speaker: David Garcia, baseball manager
Quote: "The only reason we're 7-0 is because we've…"
  a. "won all seven of our games" **b.** "lost all seven of our games"
        c. "won all twelve of our games"

Speaker: Jimmy Hill, soccer announcer
Quote: "If England is to win this game, they are going to have to…"
a. "score a goal" **b.** "not score a goal" **c.** "not score two goals"

Speaker: Alexander Haig, pundit
Quote: "The only way the Republican Party can hold the White House is to nominate a candidate who can…"
    a. "win"   **b.** "lose"   **c.** "seduce an intern"

Speaker: Isiah Thomas, basketball analyst
Quote: "A lot is said about defense, but at the end of the game, the team with the most points…"
    a. "wins" **b.** "loses" **c.** "seduces an intern"

All the answers are "a," of course.

"We've got to ask ourselves: How much clean air do we need?" —Lee Iacocca

BATTLE OF THE SEXES: ROUND 1

It's hard to imagine a quote book without a little bit of "he said, she said." Here's our first installment.

"Women say they have sexual thoughts, too. They have no idea. It's the difference between shooting a bullet and throwing it. If they knew what we were really thinking, they'd never stop slapping us."
—**Larry Miller**

"If men knew what women laughed about, they would never sleep with us."
—**Erica Jong**

"Women are never disarmed by compliments. Men always are. That is the difference between the two sexes."
—**Oscar Wilde**

"If you want anything said, ask a man; if you want anything done, ask a woman."
—**Margaret Thatcher**

"Men need sexual fulfillment in order to respond to a woman emotionally; women need emotional fulfillment in order to respond to a man sexually."
—**Ellen King**

"Men play the game; women know the score."
—**Roger Woddis**

"Women fake orgasms. But men can fake a whole relationship."
—**Sharon Stone**

"A historic operation occurred in Boston. Doctors successfully transplanted tissue from a pig's brain to a man's brain, and the man's brain did not reject it. That pretty much confirms what women have been saying about men."
—**Jay Leno**

"Calling women the weaker sex makes about as much sense as calling men the stronger one."
—**Gladiola Montana**

"Women can't complain about men anymore until they start getting better taste in them."
—**Bill Maher**

"There is more difference within the sexes than between them."
—**Dame Ivy Compton-Burnett**

Men and women are a lot alike in certain situations. Like when they're both on fire, they're exactly alike.

—Dave Attell

WHAT IS LIFE?

Life isn't really as bad as these folks say it is, but the "Life Is Great" quotes were kind of boring, so we used these.

"The trouble with life in the fast lane is that you get to the other end in an awful hurry."
—John Jensen

"My philosophy? Life is this beautiful buffet, but you get just one trip through the line, and only one plate. And there's no room on my plate for green Jell-O."
—Daniel Liebert

"Life is like a dogsled team. If you ain't the lead dog, the scenery never changes."
—Lewis Grizzard

"What is life? It is the flash of a firefly in the night. It is the breath of a buffalo in the wintertime. It is the little shadow which runs across the grass and loses itself in the sunset."
—Crowfoot

"There is no cure for birth and death save to enjoy the interval."
—George Santayana

"If everything is under control, you are going too slow."
—Mario Andretti

"A life spent making mistakes is not only more honorable but more useful than a life spent doing nothing."
—George Bernard Shaw

"What would I do if I had only six months left to live? I'd type faster."
—Isaac Asimov

"There is no perfection...this is a broken world and we live with broken hearts, but still that is no alibi for anything. On the contrary, you have to stand up and say hallelujah under those circumstances."
—Leonard Cohen

"To live is to suffer; to survive is to find some meaning in the suffering."
—Roberta Flack

"Life is like a very short visit to a toy shop between birth and death."
—Desmond Morris

"As a well-spent day brings happy sleep, so a life well spent brings happy death."
—Leonardo da Vinci

HOW INSULTING!

*This page of insults is too good for you.
Go read the want ads instead.*

"Don't be humble. You're not that great."
—**Golda Meir**

"You remind me of my brother Bosco—only he had a human head."
—**Judy Tenuta**

"If you can't be a good example, then you'll just have to be a horrible warning."
—**Catherine Aird**

"He looks like an explosion in a pubic hair factory."
—**Jonathan Miller, about journalist Paul Johnson**

"So boring you fall asleep halfway through her name."
—**Alan Bennett, speaking about Greek writer Arianna Stassinopolous**

"Your manuscript is both good and original; but the part that is good is not original, and the part that is original is not good."
—**Samuel Johnson**

"You're a good example of why some animals eat their young."
—**Jim Samuels**

"You have Van Gogh's ear for music."
—**Billy Wilder**

"I'm old? When you were young, the Dead Sea was only sick!"
—**Milton Berle**

"He's so old his social security number is two digits."
—**Brian Morgan**

"She had lost the art of conversation, but not, unfortunately, the power of speech."
—**George Bernard Shaw**

Moe: "What are you eating?"
Curly: "Fish. You know, fish is brain food."
Moe: "You know, you should eat a whale."
—***The Three Stooges***

"She looked as if she had been poured into her clothes and had forgotten to say 'when'."
—**P. G. Wodehouse**

"She was so ugly that one time she tried to enter an ugly contest. They told her, 'Sorry, no professionals allowed.'"
—**Redd Foxx**

PRIMETIME PROVERBS

Looking for words of wisdom about life and love? Turn on your TV.

ON LIFE...

"You know, life's a real bumpy road. What you've got to develop are good shock absorbers."
—**Uncle Charlie,**
My Three Sons

ON DEATH...

Farrah: "A swordsman does not fear death if he dies with honor."
Doctor Who: "Then he's an idiot."
—***Doctor Who***

ON COPS...

Lt. Fancy: "Keep me posted."
Det. Andy Sipowicz: "Any cases you don't want us to keep you posted on? What's the point in saying that?"
Lt. Arthur Fancy: "OK, then, get outta my office."
—***NYPD Blue***

"If you really want to study police methods, do what I do: watch television."
—**Officer Gunther Toody,**
Car 54, Where Are You?

ON TELEVISION...

Brian: "Do you get *Sesame Street* where you live?"

ALF: "No, and frankly I don't get it here either."
—**ALF**

"For a long time it gave me nightmares—witnessing an injustice like that. It's a constant reminder of just how unfair this world can be. I can still hear them taunting him: 'Silly rabbit, Trix are for kids!' I mean, why couldn't they just give him some cereal!?"
—**Carlton, *The Fresh Prince of Bel-Air***

ON SEX...

"One person's always disappointed. So far, I've been lucky; it's always been the woman."
—**Lewis,**
The Drew Carey Show

"Men don't like to cuddle. We only like it if it leads to, you know, lower cuddling."
—**Ray, *Everybody Loves Raymond***

ON RELATIONSHIPS...

"Once the trust goes out of a relationship, it's really no fun lying to 'em anymore."
—**Norm Peterson, *Cheers***

The purr-fect life: Cats sleep an average of 16 hours per day.

Brenda: "I don't want any children."

Nate: "Whoa. Hey. Who said anything about children?"

Brenda: "I was referring to you."
—*Six Feet Under*

Katie: "Benson, what's a broken heart?"

Benson: "Oh, there's no such thing, Katie. It's just a term we use to describe one of life's little disappointments that comes close to killing you."
—*Benson*

ON THE HEALING ARTS...

Doctor: "The trouble with psychologists is that we're stuck in a rut. All we do is repeat ourselves."

Bob Hartley: "Repeat ourselves?"

Doctor: "Repeat ourselves."

Bob: "How?"

Doctor: "How?"

Bob: "Yeah, how?"

Doctor: "By using the same old methods, over and over and over again and again and again and again."

Bob: "I see what you mean."
—*The Bob Newhart Show*

ON DREAMS...

Chandler: "Hey, you guys in the living room all know what you want to do. You know, you have goals. You have dreams. I don't have a dream."

Ross: "Ah, the lesser known 'I *Don't* Have a Dream' speech."
—*Friends*

ON TOLERANCE...

"All I know is, I hate racists. I hate everything about them, their music, their food, their so-called religion, the way their men are so skinny, and their wives are all so fat, but mostly, I hate the way they judge people based on tired stereotypes."
—Byron, *Andy Richter Controls the Universe*

ON RULES...

Robin: "Batgirl! What took you so long?"

Batgirl: "You wouldn't believe the traffic, and the lights were all against me. Besides, you wouldn't want me to speed, would you?"

Robin: "Your good driving habits almost cost us our lives!"

Batman: "No Robin, she's right. Rules are rules."
—*Batman*

"Without rules, we all might as well be up in a tree flinging our crap at each other."
—Red Foreman, *That '70s Show*

TO OUR FRIENDS ACROSS THE POND

There's nothing like picking on the French...
except maybe picking on the British.

"The English public, as a mass, takes no interest in a work of art until it is told that work in question is immoral."
—**Oscar Wilde**

"The cold of the polar regions was nothing to the chill of an English bedroom."
—**Fridtjof Nansen**

"No one can be as calculatedly rude as the British, which amazes Americans, who do not understand studied insult and can only offer abuse as a substitute."
—**Paul Gallico**

"Being English, I always laugh at anything to do with the lavatory or bottoms."
—**Elizabeth Hurley**

"If an Englishman gets run down by a truck, he apologizes to the truck."
—**Jackie Mason**

The average British adult drinks 228 pints of beer per year.

WILDE MAN

*Oscar Wilde (1854–1900) was one of the
most controversial authors of his day. Now he's
considered one of the greatest authors of all time.*

"When I was young, I thought money was the most important thing in life. Now that I'm old— I know it is."

"To be good, according to the vulgar standard of goodness, is obviously quite easy. It merely requires a certain amount of sordid terror, a certain lack of imaginative thought, and a certain low passion for middle-class respectability."

"When one is in love one always begins by deceiving oneself, and one always ends by deceiving others. This is what the world calls romance."

"I am the only person in the world I should like to know thoroughly."

"The pure and simple truth is rarely pure and simple."

"Life is far too important a thing to ever talk seriously about."

"We should treat all trivial things of life very seriously, and all the serious things of life with sincere and studied triviality."

"The true mystery of the world is the visible, not the invisible."

"The only way to get rid of a temptation is to yield to it. Resist it, and your soul grows sick with longing for the things it has forbidden to itself."

"It is absurd to divide people into good and bad. People are either charming or tedious."

"A thing is not necessarily true because a man dies for it."

QUOTES AND THEIR CONSEQUENCES

*Think being famous is fun? When folks like us put our foot
in our mouths, only a few people ever hear about it. But
for these public figures, the audience is much larger,
and the consequences oftentimes much greater.*

Speaker: John Lennon
Quote: "Christianity will go. It will vanish and
shrink....We're more popular than Jesus now. I don't know
which will go first—rock 'n' roll or Christianity. Jesus was all
right, but his disciples were thick and ordinary. It's them twisting
it that ruins it for me."

Background: The line that almost killed the Beatles originally
appeared in a British newspaper called *The Evening Standard.* In
March 1966, reporter Maureen Cleave spent a day with Lennon at
his mansion while he rambled on about books, music, politics, and
religion. The interview was printed in full and the statement—
taken in context—reveals that Lennon was lamenting the sad
state of modern religion, and not trying to deify the Beatles. There
was no reaction to it whatsoever in England.

Consequences: In July, an American teen magazine called *Date-
book* ran a cover story called "The Ten Adults You Dig/Hate the
Most." In the section on John Lennon, they reprinted the quote
by itself, without the rest of the interview. The result was quick
and severe: Christians denounced the Beatles and began a
campaign to destroy everything associated with the Fab Four.
Many radio stations, especially in the South and Midwest, stopped
playing their records and even organized Beatles bonfires. Some
churches threatened to excommunicate members who listened to
the Beatles. George, Paul, and Ringo received death threats. And
all this went down while the Beatles were on an American tour
that took them right through the Bible Belt. The KKK even tried
to set up a barrier and stop an August 13 concert in Memphis, to
no avail.

Lennon, for his part, was shocked that such a seemingly

innocuous statement he said four months before could have created such havoc. He held a press conference in Chicago to try to put things right. "I'm not saying that we're better or greater, or comparing us with Jesus Christ as a person or God as a thing or whatever it is. I wasn't saying whatever they're saying I was saying. I'm sorry I said it really. I never meant it to be a lousy anti-religious thing. I apologize if that will make you happy. I still don't know quite what I've done. I've tried to tell you what I did do, but if you want me to apologize, if that will make you happy, then OK, I'm sorry."

The apology did make some people happy and the fervor eventually died down, but many never forgave Lennon, and the bubblegum image of the early Beatles was all but gone. As were their U.S. touring days—the Beatles never played another concert in the United States after that tumultuous tour.

Speaker: George W. Bush

Quote: "[The Japanese prime minister and I] placed equal emphasis on nonperforming loans, the devaluation issue, and regulatory reform."

Background: In February 2002, President Bush traveled to the Far East to discuss Japan's economic future. Bush made the comment during a press conference following the meeting, but he got one word wrong: "devaluation." He had meant to say "deflation."

Consequences: That one-word gaffe nearly crashed the Japanese stock market. Devaluation is a touchy subject in Asia; if Japan were to devalue the yen against the dollar, it could potentially make Japan's exports more competitive and give them an unfair advantage over their neighbors. And although the prospect had been floating around for years, no one took it seriously until the American president used the "d-word" after meeting with the Japanese prime minister.

Shortly after the comment, the value of the yen started falling—and kept falling—until a White House spokesman explained later that day that it was nothing more than the a slip of the tongue on the president's part, and that the United States sincerely apologized for the mistake.

THE PRESIDENCY

It's important for the president to take his job seriously—after all it's the most important job in the world. But the rest of us don't have to.

"When I was a boy, I was told that anybody could become president. I'm beginning to believe it."
—Clarence Darrow

"In the United States, anybody can become president. That's the problem."
—George Carlin

"Anybody that wants the presidency so much that he'll spend two years organizing and campaigning for it is not to be trusted with the office."
—David Broder

"A female president—maybe they'd start calling it the 'Ova Office.'"
—Brett Butler

"Any man who wants to be president is either an egomaniac or crazy."
—Dwight D. Eisenhower

"The only reason I'm not running for president is I'm afraid no woman would come forth and say she's slept with me."
—Garry Shandling

"The office of the presidency is such a bastardizing thing—half royalty, half democracy—that nobody knows whether to genuflect or spit."
—Jimmy Breslin

"Take our politicians: they're a bunch of yo-yos. The presidency is now a cross between a popularity contest and a high school debate, with an encyclopedia of clichés the first prize."
—Saul Bellow

"Anyone who is capable of getting themselves made president should on no account be allowed to do the job."
—Douglas Adams

"If you were to go back in history and take every president, you'll find that the numerical value of each letter in their name was equally divisible into the year in which they were elected. By my calculations, our next president has to be named Yellnick McWawa."
—Cliff Claven, *Cheers*

THE BIRDS AND THE BEES

Why is this page called "The Birds and the Bees?"
No time for that—let's talk about sex.

"The pleasure is momentary, the position ridiculous, and the expense damnable."
—Lord Chesterfield

"Why should we take sex advice from the Pope? If he knows anything about it, he shouldn't."
—George Bernard Shaw

"Everybody lies about sex. People lie during sex. If it weren't for lies, there'd be no sex."
—Jerry Seinfeld

"You know that look women get when they want sex? Me neither."
—Drew Carey

"He thought he had to be celibate to maintain the purity of his instrument whereas I like to play mine from time to time."
—Nicole Kidman, on why she and Tom Cruise divorced

"There's nothing better than good sex. But bad sex? A peanut butter and jelly sandwich is better than bad sex."
—Billy Joel

"The closest I ever came to a menage-a-trois was when I dated a schizophrenic."
—Rita Rudner

"Sex is power and sex leaves you powerless."
**—Axl Rose,
Guns N' Roses**

"He just kept rushing through the lovemaking—which is the part I like, the beginning part. Most women are like that. We need time to warm up. Why is this hard for you guys to understand? You're the first people to tell us not to gun a cold engine. You want us to go from zero to sixty in a minute. We're not built like that. We stall."
—Anita Wise

"Sex is one of the nine reasons for reincarnation. The other eight are unimportant."
—Henry Miller

"Sex without love is an empty experience. But as empty experiences go, it's one of the best."
—Woody Allen

The first sex manuals were published in China more than 5,000 years ago.

BY GOLLY, IT'S DOLLY

Some thoughts from Dolly Parton, a country music legend.

"I think everything starts with a dream, and it was always my dream to be a star. I just think you always have to continue to dream, and I wake up in a new world every day—sort of like a goose."

"I put the hurtful things in my songs. It's better than a psychiatrist."

"I have little feet because nothing grows in the shade."

"I still like to pee off the porch every now and then. There's nothing like peeing on those snobs in Beverly Hills."

"I never left country music. I just took it with me."

"God and I have a great relationship, but we both see other people."

"Lots of women buy just as many wigs and makeup things as I do. The difference is they just don't wear them all at the same time."

"Bluegrass is the music I would have been doing all along if I could have made a living at it. It's like I had to get rich in order to sing like I was poor."

"I feel good and I don't look bad for my age. I look like a cartoon anyway, so what difference does it make? I'm always gonna look like Dolly, like a freak. But I'm the best freak I've ever been."

"I was looking up at the big sign that says Hollywood, and I thought, 'Wouldn't it be great if someday I could jerk that big ol' H down and put a D there to make it Dollywood?'"

"Yes, I've had several little things done...and several big ones." —*On plastic surgery*

"I know myself and what I want, and what I don't want is to go out to pasture. I have agreed to pose nude for Penthouse on my 100th birthday."

"God is dead." —Nietzsche, 1885 "Nietzsche is dead." —God, 1900

REEL STUPID

It seems like for every one good movie out there, there are about ten bad ones. They may not be fun to watch, but finding the dumbest of the dumbest lines makes for great reading.

"The dead look so terribly dead when they're dead."
——**Tyrone Power,** *The Razor's Edge* **(1946)**

"This is like looking for a needle in a haystack full of needles."
——**Ron Silver,** *The Arrival* **(1996)**

"You goddamned chauvinist pig ape!…You want to eat me? Then go ahead!"
——**Jessica Lange,** *King Kong* **(1976)**

"Decrucify the angel or I'll melt your face."
——**Jane Fonda,** *Barbarella* **(1968)**

"Some people may think you're cute, Babe. But to me, you're one very large baked potato!"
——**Sylvester Stallone,** *Death Race 2000*

"Satan was an acid head, so let's freak out!"
——**Alan Ormsby,** *Children Shouldn't Play with Dead Things* **(1972)**

"I've had it with cheap sex. It leaves me feeling cheap."
——**John Travolta,** *Moment by Moment* **(1978)**

"Words are plentiful; deeds are precious." —Lech Walesa

IT'S THE LAW

You don't like this page? So sue us.

"There is no such thing as an impartial jury because there are no impartial people. There are people that argue on the Web for hours about who their favorite character on *Friends* is."

—Jon Stewart

"The law is a ass. A idiot."

—Charles Dickens

"Law is a bottomless pit; it is a cormorant, a harpy that devours everything."

—Jonathan Swift

"For certain people, after 50, litigation takes the place of sex."

—Gore Vidal

"Laws do not persuade just because they threaten."

—Seneca

"If you like laws and sausages, you should never watch either one being made."

—Otto von Bismarck

"Juries scare me. I don't want to put my fate in the hands of 12 people who weren't even smart enough to get out of jury duty."

—Caryn Leschen

"The goal of all life is death." —Sigmund Freud

UNCLE JOHN'S QUOTATIONARY

Quotable people have a knack for coming up with new and clever definitions for everyday words. We've compiled our favorites into this quotationary.

ABILITY: a poor man's wealth. (Matthew Wren)

ABSTAINER: a person who yields to the temptation of denying himself a pleasure. (Ambrose Bierce)

ACTING: farting about in disguises. (Peter O'Toole)

ADOLESCENCE: a period in a kid's life when parents become difficult. (Ryan O'Neal)

ADULTERY: the application of democracy to love. (H. L. Mencken)

ADVERTISING: the rattling of a stick inside a swill bucket. (George Orwell)

ADVICE: what we ask for that we already know the answer to but wish we didn't. (Erica Jong)

AGE: something that doesn't matter unless you're a cheese. (Billie Burke)

AGREEABLE PERSON: a person who agrees with me. (Benjamin Disraeli)

AMBASSADOR: an honest man sent abroad to lie for his country. (Henry Wotten)

AMBITION: A way of working yourself to death to live better. (Brendan Behan)

ANIMAL: something invented by plants to move seeds around. (Terrence McKenna)

ANTHROPOLOGY: the science which tells us that people are the same the world over—except when they are different. (Nancy Banks-Smith)

ANTIQUE: something that has been useless so long, it's still in good shape. (Franklin P. Jones)

APOLOGY: the only thing that will allow you to get the last word with a woman. (Danny Cummins)

APPLAUSE: the custom of showing one's pleasure at beautiful music by immediately following it with ugly noise. (Percy Scholes)

ARCHITECT: someone who

"I hate definitions." —Benjamin Disraeli

forgets to put in the staircase. (Gustave Flaubert)

ARCHITECTURE: the art of how to waste space. (Philip Johnson)

ART: making something out of nothing and selling it. (Frank Zappa)

ARTIST: a receptacle for emotions that come from all over the place: from the sky, from the Earth, from a scrap of paper, from a passing shape, from a spider's web. (Pablo Picasso)

ASKING: polite demanding. (Max Headroom)

ASSASSINATION: the extreme form of censorship. (George Bernard Shaw)

ATHEIST: a man who has no invisible means of support. (John Buchan)

AUTOBIOGRAPHY: a book that suggests the only thing wrong with the author is his memory. (Franklin P. Jones)

AVARICE: the spur of industry. (David Hume)

BABY: a loud voice at one end and no sense of responsibility at the other. (Ronald Knox)

BALLET: men wearing pants so tight that you can tell what religion they are. (Robin Williams)

BANKER: a fellow who lends you his umbrella when the sun is shining and wants it back the minute it begins to rain. (Mark Twain)

BASKETBALL PLAYER: a person who plays on court and pays in court. (Joseph Martino)

BEAUTY: what a woman has when she looks the same after washing her face. (Hal Roach)

BEER: propellant of situations. (Willa Bandler)

BIGOT: one who is obstinately and zealously attached to an opinion that you do not entertain. (Ambrose Bierce)

BLUES (THE): An autobiographical chronicle of catastrophe, expressed lyrically. (Ralph Ellison)

BORE: a man who spends so much time talking about himself that you can't talk about yourself. (Melville London)

BORN LEADER: someone who's afraid to go anywhere by himself. (Clifford Hanley)

BOOKS: the carriers of civilization. Without books, history is silent, literature dumb, science crippled, thought and speculation a standstill. (Barbara Tuchman)

BOXING: a lot of white men watching two black men beat each other up. (Muhammad Ali)

BRAIN: an apparatus with which we think we think. (Ambrose Bierce)

BRAVERY: being the only one who knows you're afraid. (Franklin P. Jones)

BUFFET: a French word that means 'get up and get it yourself.' (Ron Dentinger)

BUREAUCRACY: an execution chamber in which the condemned are alternately strangled by rules, clubbed with paper, and starved in lines. (Alexander Yarrowville)

BUSINESS: the combination of sport and war. (André Maurois)

For more, see page 84.

*   *   *

ELLEN ENLIGHTENS
Ellen DeGeneres has some funny things to say about the world.

"In the beginning there was nothing. God said, 'Let there be light!' And there was light. There was still nothing, but you could see it a whole lot better."

"Human beings only use ten percent of their brains. Can you imagine how much we could accomplish if we used the other sixty percent?"

"It's so weird all the different names they have for groups of animals. They have pride of lions, school of fish, rack of lamb..."

"My grandmother started walking five miles a day when she was sixty. She's ninety-seven now, and we don't know where the hell she is."

"People always ask me, 'Were you funny as a child?' Well, no, I was an accountant."

WHY ASK WHY?

Sometimes answers are irrelevant—it's the question that counts. Take a moment to ponder these cosmic queries.

"How come aspirins are packed in childproof containers, but bullets just come in a box?"
—Jay Leno

"Why do they bother saying raw sewage? Do some people cook the stuff?"
—George Carlin

"Why do they call it rush hour when nothing moves?"
—Robins Williams (as Mork)

"Do Lipton employees take coffee breaks?"
—Steven Wright

"Why can we remember the tiniest detail that has happened to us, and not remember how many times we have told it to the same person."
—Francois, Duc de la Rochefoucauld

"Should not the Society of Indexers be known as 'Indexers, Society of, The'?"
—Keith Waterhouse

"If women can sleep their way to the top, how come they aren't there?"
—Ellen Goodman

"Why does a slight tax increase cost you $200 and a substantial tax cut save you 38¢?"
—Peg Bracken

"Can a blue man sing the whites?"
—Algis Juodikis

"What are perfect strangers? Do they have perfect hair? Do they dress perfectly?"
—Ellen Degeneres

"If sex is such a natural phenomenon, how come there are so many books on how to do it?"
—Bette Midler

"Murder is a crime. Writing about it isn't. Sex is not a crime, but writing about it is. Why?"
—Larry Flynt

"At the ballet you see girls dancing on their tiptoes. Why don't they just get taller girls?"
—Greg Ray

"If bankers can count, how come they always have ten windows and two tellers?"
—Milton Berle

"Death would be a beautiful place if it looks like Brad Pitt." —Carmen Electra

ALWAYS...

Uncle John's credo: always follow the advice of experts.

"Always forgive your enemies....Nothing annoys them so much."
—Oscar Wilde

"Always do sober what you said you'd do drunk. That will teach you to keep your mouth shut."
—Ernest Hemingway

"Always remember before going on stage, wipe your nose and check your fly."
—Alec Guinness

"Always remember that you are absolutely unique. Just like everyone else."
—Margaret Mead

"Always hold your head up, but be careful to keep your nose at a friendly level."
—Max L. Forman

"Always read stuff that will make you look good if you die in the middle of it."
—P. J. O'Rourke

"Always take hold of things by the smooth handle."
—Thomas Jefferson

"Always dream and shoot higher than you know you can do. Don't bother just to be better than your contemporaries or predecessors. Try to be better than yourself."
—William Faulkner

"Always give a word or a sign of salute when meeting or passing a friend, even a stranger."
—Tecumseh, Shawnee

"Always listen to experts. They'll tell you what can't be done and why. Then do it."
—Robert Heinlein

"Always be nice to people on the way up; because you'll meet the same people on the way down."
—Wilson Mizner

"Always do what you are afraid to do."
—Ralph Waldo Emerson

"Always do right. This will gratify some people and astonish the rest."
—Mark Twain

"Always and never are two words you should...

NEVER...

Uncle John's credo: never follow the advice of experts.

"Never hire a cleaning lady named Dusty."
—**David Corrado**

"Never trust the advice of a man in difficulties."
—**Aesop**

"Never assume the obvious is true."
—**William Safire**

"Never play peekaboo with a child on a long plane trip. There's no end to the game. Finally, I grabbed him by the bib and said, 'Look, it's always gonna be me!'"
—**Rita Rudner**

"Never pet a porcupine."
—**Kid on *Sesame Street***

"Never send a man to do a horse's job."
—**Mr. Ed**

"Never trust a wolf's tameness, a horse's health, or an enemy's smile."
—**Isreal Boone, *Daniel Boone***

"Never trouble trouble till trouble troubles you."
—**John Adams**

"Never give in, never give in, never, never, never, never—in nothing, great or small, large or petty—never give in except to convictions of honor and good sense."
—**Winston Churchill**

"Never spend your money before you have it."
—**Thomas Jefferson**

"Never miss a good chance to shut up."
—**Will Rogers**

"Never get married in the morning, 'cause you may never know who you'll meet that night."
—**Paul Hornung**

"Never explain—your friends do not need it and your enemies will not believe you anyway."
—**Elbert Hubbard**

"Never believe in mirrors or newspapers."
—**Tom Stoppard**

"Never eat more than you can lift."
—**Miss Piggy**

YOU ARE WHAT YOU EAT

Miscellaneous quotations about the stuff you put down your pie hole.

"Food is an important part of a balanced diet."
—**Fran Lebowitz**

"I want to keep fighting because it is the only thing that keeps me out of hamburger joints. If I don't fight, I'll eat this planet."
—**George Foreman**

"Americans can eat garbage, provided you sprinkle it liberally with ketchup, mustard, chili sauce, Tabasco sauce, cayenne pepper, or any other condiment which destroys the original flavor of the dish."
—**Henry Miller**

"Conversation is the enemy of good wine and food."
—**Alfred Hitchcock**

"Who was the first person to drink milk, and what were they thinking? 'Ooh boy, I can't wait till those calves get done so I can get me a shot of that.' "
—**Jerry Seinfeld**

"There is no sincerer love than the love of food."
—**George Bernard Shaw**

"You are what you eat. Which makes me cheap, quick, and easy."
—**Dave Thomas**

Oscar Madison: "You want brown juice or green juice?"
Felix Unger: "What's the difference?"
Oscar Madison: "Two weeks."
—*The Odd Couple*

"Red meat is not bad for you. Now blue-green meat, that's bad for you."
—**Tommy Smothers**

"You can tell a lot about a fellow's character by his way of eating jelly beans."
—**Ronald Reagan**

"It's so beautifully arranged on the plate—you just know someone's fingers have been all over it."
—**Julia Child**

"The perfect lover is one who turns into a pizza at 4:00 a.m."
—**Charles Pierce**

"As for butter versus margarine, I trust cows more than chemists."
—**Joan Gussow**

"French fries. I love them. Some people are chocolate and sweets people. I love French fries. That and caviar."

—**Cameron Diaz**

"He was a bold man that first eat an oyster."

—**Jonathan Swift**

"The noblest of all dogs is the hot dog. It feeds the hand that bites it."

—**Laurence J. Peter**

FRACTURED PHRASES

Writers and comedians get a lot of mileage out of taking an expression like "The early bird gets the worm" and tweaking it to get a laugh.

"Is the glass half full... or half empty?"

"If you say the glass is half full, you're an optimist. If you say the glass is half empty, you're Ted Kennedy."
—David Letterman

"Most people look at the glass as half empty or half full. I look at it as too big."
—George Carlin

"The early bird gets the worm."

Art Linkletter: "What do you think of the phrase, 'The early bird gets the worm'?"
Kid: "He's welcome to it. I tried it once and it tasted like cold spaghetti."
—*Art Linkletter's House Party*

"Necessity is the mother of invention."

"Boredom, like necessity, is very often the mother of invention."
—Dr. Smith, *Lost in Space*

"It is better to have loved and lost than to never have loved at all."
—St. Augustine

"It's better to have loved and lost than never to have seen *Lost in Space* at all."
—Kelly Bundy, *Married...with Children*

"Tomorrow is the first day of the rest of your life."

"The day after tomorrow is the third day of the rest of your life."
—George Carlin

"I HAVE A DREAM"

Some thoughts from civil rights leader Dr. Martin Luther King, Jr.

"He who passively accepts evil is as much involved in it as he who helps to perpetuate it."

"The ultimate measure of a man is not where he stands in moments of comfort, but where he stands at times of challenge and controversy."

"There is nothing more dangerous than to build a society, with a large segment of people in that society, who feel that they have no stake in it; who feel that they have nothing to lose. People who have a stake in their society protect that society, but when they don't have it, they unconsciously want to destroy it."

"It is important to see there are times when a manmade law is out of harmony with the moral law of the universe."

"There comes a time when a moral man can't obey a law, which his conscience tells him is unjust."

"Forgiveness is not an occasional act; it is a permanent attitude."

"The next thing we must be concerned about if we are to have peace on Earth and good will toward men is the nonviolent affirmation of the sacredness of all human life. Every man is somebody because he is a child of God."

"Hatred and bitterness can never cure the disease of fear; only love can do that. Hatred paralyzes life; love releases it. Hatred confuses life; love harmonizes it. Hatred darkens life; love illuminates it."

"We must develop and maintain the capacity to forgive. He who is devoid of the power to forgive is devoid of the power to love. There is some good in the worst of us and some evil in the best of us. When we discover this, we are less prone to hate our enemies."

"Our scientific power has outrun our spiritual power. We have guided missiles and misguided men."

"The time is always right to do what is right."

"HE'S LOST BOTH RIGHT FRONT TIRES"

*British motorsport commentator Murray Walker is
reknowned for his silly—and hilarious—vocal flubs.*

"The young Ralph Schumacher has been upstaged by the teenager, Jensen Button, who is twenty."

"Only a few more laps to go and then the action will begin, unless this is the action, which it is."

"There's nothing wrong with the car except that it's on fire."

"Just under ten seconds…call it nine point five in round figures."

"I imagine the conditions in those cars are totally unimaginable."

"Either that car is stationary, or it is on the move."

"With the race half gone there is still half the race to go."

"And I interrupt myself to bring you this.…"

"Mansell is slowing it down, taking it easy. Oh no he isn't! It's a lap record."

"He is shedding buckets of adrenalin in that car."

"Mansell can see him in his earphone."

"And he's lost both right front tires!"

"A sad ending, albeit a happy one."

SUPER EGOS

There's a fine line between having high self-esteem and being an egomaniac. These celebs may have crossed that line.

"When I'm really hot, I can walk into a room and if a man doesn't look at me, he's probably gay."
—**Kathleen Turner**

"The longer I live, the more I see that I am never wrong about anything, and that all the pains that I have so humbly taken to verify my notions have only wasted my time."
—**George Bernard Shaw**

"Johnny Cash sent me a letter that said he was proud of me for…walking with integrity and for always giving thanks to the good lord. He said, 'I once had a close friend that you remind me of. He was Elvis Presley.'"
—**Billy Ray Cyrus**

"I feel like I'm the best, but you're never going to get me to say that."
—**Jerry Rice**

"If I'd have made the army, we wouldn't have had all that trouble in Vietnam, 'cause I would have won it in a year."
—**Ted Nugent**

"There are many dying children whose last wish is to see me."
—**David Hasselhoff**

"I never read any novels except my own. When I feel worried, agitated, or upset, I read one and find the last pages soothe me and leave me happy. I quite understand why I am so popular in hospitals."
—**Barbara Cartland**

"I believe my music is the healin' music. I believe my music can make the blind see, the lame walk, the deaf and dumb hear and talk, because it inspires and uplifts people. It regenerates the ears, makes the liver quiver, the bladder splatter, and the knees freeze. I'm not conceited, either."
—**Little Richard**

"If it was 1965, and we'd just put out our second album, we'd absolutely be the pop kings of the world."
—**Noel Gallagher, of Oasis**

"Modesty is not a word that applies to me in any way."
—**Arnold Schwarzenegger**

"I am the Fred Astaire of karate." —Jean-Claude Van Damme

AH-H-NOLD

We really hate to pick on Governor
Schwarzenegger, but he makes it so easy.

"By the time I was thirteen I realized I'd be more successful at something physical rather than mental."

"It's the most difficult [decision] I've made in my entire life, except the one I made in 1978 when I decided to get a bikini wax."

—announcing his gubernatorial candidacy on the *Tonight Show*

"When I was 15 years old, I took off my clothes and looked in the mirror. When I stared at myself naked, I realized that to be perfectly proportioned I would need 20-inch arms to match the rest of me."

"My relationship to power and authority is that I'm all for it. People need somebody to watch over them. Ninety-five percent of the people in the world need to be told what to do and how to behave."

"Why do people treat me with fun just because I am the biggest, strongest, and most beautiful man in the world?"

"The worst thing I can be is the same as everybody else. I hate that."

Arnold has a Labrador retriever named Conan.

ON ARNOLD

"Don't think of him as a Republican, think of him as the man I love. And if that doesn't work, think of him as the man who can crush you."

—Maria Shriver, when she introduced Arnold to her uncle, Sen. Ted Kennedy

"Arnold Schwarzenegger looks like a condom full of walnuts."

—Clive James

GLASS HALF-EMPTY…

*If you don't have anything nice to
say, we'll put it on this page.*

"The nature of men and women—their essential nature—is so vile and despicable that if you were to portray a person as he really is, no one would believe you."
    **—W. Somerset
    Maugham**

"I have found little that is 'good' about human beings on the whole. In my experience, most of them are trash."
    —Sigmund Freud

"Things are going to get worse before they get worse."
    —Lily Tomlin

"Man is the only animal that can remain on friendly terms with the victim he intends to eat until he eats them."
    —Samuel Butler

"Man was made at the end of a week's work when God was tired."
    —Mark Twain

"It's silly to go on pretending that under the skin we are all brothers. The truth is more likely that under the skin we are all cannibals, assassins, traitors, liars, hypocrites, poltroons."
    —Henry Miller

"We are all serving a life sentence in the dungeon of life."
    —Cyril Connolly

"The last sound on the worthless Earth will be two human beings trying to launch a homemade spaceship and already quarreling about where they are going next."
    —William Faulkner

...GLASS HALF-FULL

Read this page and think happy thoughts!

"I don't think of all the misery, but of all the beauty that still remains."
—**Anne Frank**

"When you cannot get a compliment any other way, pay yourself one."
—**Mark Twain**

"We are all dependent on one another, every soul of us on Earth."
—**George Bernard Shaw**

"One doesn't discover new lands without consenting to lose sight of the shore."
—**Andre Gide**

"The fragrance always remains in the hand that gives the rose."
—**Heda Bejar**

"Birds sing after a storm, why shouldn't we?"
—**Rose Fitzgerald Kennedy**

"Either you decide to stay in the shallow end of the pool or you go out in the ocean."
—**Christopher Reeve**

"No matter how old you are, there's always something good to look forward to."
—**Lynn Johnston**

"The things we have in common far outnumber and outweigh those that divide us."
—**Walt Disney**

"With all its sham, drudgery, and broken dreams, it is still a beautiful world. Be cheerful. Strive to be happy."
—**Max Ehrmann**

"This moment is a gift; that is why this moment is called the present; enjoy it."
—**Allan Johnson**

SAY WHAT?

Occasionally we'll read a quote and have no idea what the speaker is talking about, so we'll read it again, hoping that the meaning will reveal itself. We're still hoping.

"I used to be very hands-on, but lately I've been more hands-off and I plan to become more hands-on and less hands-off and hope that hands-on will become better than hands-off, the way hands-on used to be."
—**George Steinbrenner**

"Concentration-wise, we're having trouble crossing the line mentally from a toughness standpoint."
—**Bill Parcels,
football coach**

"I would not live forever, because we should not live forever, because if were supposed to live forever, then we would live forever, but we cannot live forever, which is why I would not live forever."
—**Miss Alabama in the
1994 Miss USA contest.
(The question was: "If
you could live forever,
would you and why?")**

"Most critics write critiques which are by the authors they write critiques about. That would not be so bad, but then most authors write works which are by the critics who write critiques about them."
—**Karl Kraus**

"I would be batting the big feller if they wasn't ready with that other one, but a left hander would be the thing if they wouldn't have knowed it already because there is more things involved than could come up on the road, even after we been home for a long time."
—**Casey Stengel**

"I think today that a few remarks I might make, we go back to the relationship in this great nation with the people who was the foundation of America, the people they've paid such a price that we may enjoy the blessings of enjoyments that we have, has been spoken this morning."
—**Evan Mecham,
former Arizona governor**

"In the great wealth, the great firmament of your nation's generosities this particular choice may perhaps be found by future generations as a trifle eccentric, but the mere fact of it...the prodigal, pure, human kindness of it...must be seen as a beautiful star in that firmament which shines upon me at this moment, dazzling me a little, but filling me with warmth of the extraordinary elation, the euphoria that happens to so many of us at the first breath of the majestic glow of a new tomorrow."

—Laurence Olivier, on receiving an honorary Oscar (1979)

THE SAGE
OF MONTICELLO

*It only stands to reason that Thomas Jefferson, author
of the Declaration of Independence, would have
some thought-provoking things to say.*

"Advertisements contain the only truths to be found in a newspaper."

"It does me no injury for my neighbor to say there are twenty gods, or no God. It neither picks my pocket, nor breaks my leg."

"It is error alone which needs the support of government. Truth can stand by itself."

"An honest man can feel no pleasure in the exercise of power over his fellow citizens."

"When a man assumes a public trust, he should consider himself as public property."

"The natural progress of things is for liberty to yield and government to gain ground."

"I predict future happiness for Americans if they can prevent the government from wasting the labors of the people under the pretense of taking care of them."

"The price of liberty is eternal vigilance."

TAKING POT SHOTS AT THE PRESIDENT

One of the best parts of politics is watching presidents and their political opponents snipe at each other.

"The moral character of Jefferson was repulsive. Continually puling about liberty, equality, and the degrading curse of slavery, he brought his own children to the hammer, and made money of their debaucheries."

—**Alexander Hamilton**

"Putting Bush and Quayle in charge of the economy is like making General Sherman the fire marshal of Atlanta."

—**Bill Clinton**

"[Bill] Clinton is a two-faced bumpkin from Arkansas."

—**George H. W. Bush**

"Why, this fellow [Ike] doesn't know any more about politics than a pig knows about Sunday."

—**Harry S Truman**

"Being attacked on character by Clinton is like being called ugly by a frog."

—**George H. W. Bush**

"Nixon is a no-good lying bastard. He can lie out of both sides of his mouth at the same time, and even if he caught himself telling the truth, he'd lie just to keep his hand in."

—**Harry S Truman**

"[President] McKinley has no more backbone than a chocolate éclair."

—**Theodore Roosevelt**

"Bill Clinton's foreign policy experience is pretty much confined to having had breakfast at the International House of Pancakes."

—**Pat Buchanan**

"People have said that my language was bad, but Jesus! You should have heard LBJ."

—**Richard Nixon**

After George W. Bush fell off his mountain bike:
"Did the training wheels fall off?"

—**John Kerry**

"THERE'S NO PLACE LIKE HOME"

These classic movie lines have become more than a part of our language—they've become a part of the fabric of our society. See if you can match the quote with the film.

1. "It's alive!!"

2. "What we've got here is a failure to communicate."

3. "You talkin' to me? You talkin' to me?"

4. "Rosebud..."

5. "I'll get you, my pretty, and your little dog, too!"

6. "Frankly, my dear, I don't give a damn."

7. "I'll make him an offer he can't refuse."

8. "I'm *walking* here!"

9. "Stella!"

10. "I think this is the beginning of a beautiful friendship."

a. *Gone with the Wind*

b. *Citizen Kane*

c. *Frankenstein*

d. *Cool Hand Luke*

e. *Midnight Cowboy*

f. *Taxi Driver*

g. *The Godfather*

h. *The Wizard of Oz*

i. *Casablanca*

j. *A Streetcar Named Desire*

Answers

1. c; 2. d; 3. f; 4. b; 5. h; 6. a; 7. g; 8. e; 9. j; 10. i

"Silence is golden when you can't think of a good answer." —Muhammad Ali

WHAT IS ART?

Bathroom Reader Rule of Thumb: If it doesn't have dogs playing poker, it isn't art. But everyone's entitled to their own opinion.

"Creativity is allowing yourself to make mistakes. Art is knowing which ones to keep."
—Scott Adams

"Artists everywhere steal mercilessly all the time and I think this is healthy."
—Peter Gabriel

"Art is sufficiently broad that if you want to lie on the floor and wriggle like a snake, that's art."
—Paul McCartney

"[My grandfather] collects cigarette butts, glues them together, and makes pictures of naked ladies, then sprays the whole thing silver. His stuff was taking trash and making it art. I guess I try to do that, too."
—Beck

"Irresponsibility is part of the pleasure of all art; it is the part the schools cannot recognize."
—James Joyce

"Without art, the crudeness of reality would make the world unbearable."
—George Bernard Shaw

"Art is too serious to be taken seriously."
—Ad Reinhardt

"What garlic is to a salad, insanity is to art."
—Augustus Homer Saint-Gaudens

"Art is a lie that makes us realize the truth."
—Pablo Picasso

"Art, like morality, consists of drawing the line somewhere."
—G. K. Chesterson

"My new goal in life is to take a whole lot of jargonese out of the visual arts and make it more accessible to the people who are not touring academically and cannot plow through the reams of fairly elitist extrapolation of what is the heart and soul of minimalism."
—David Bowie

"Art is spirituality in drag."
—Jennifer Unlimited

"Trust the art, not the artist."
—Bruce Springsteen

BET YER BOTTOM DALI

Surprisingly clear thoughts from a master of surrealism, Salvador Dali.

"Those who do not want to imitate anything produce nothing."

"At the age of six, I wanted to be a cook. At seven, I wanted to be Napoleon. And my ambition has been growing steadily ever since."

"Each morning when I awake, I experience again a supreme pleasure—that of being Salvador Dali."

"Have no fear of perfection—you'll never reach it."

"The only thing that the world will not have enough of is exaggeration."

"Mistakes are almost always of a sacred nature. Never try to correct them. On the contrary: rationalize them, understand them thoroughly. After that, it will be possible for you to sublimate them."

"Take me, I am the drug; take me, I am hallucinogenic."

"The difference between false memories and true ones is the same as for jewels: it is always the false ones that look the most real, the most brilliant."

"Painting is an infinitely minute part of my personality."

ON THE AIR

*It's always entertaining to hear someone
make a major goof on live television.*

"Most cars on our roads have only one occupant, usually
the driver."
—Carol Malia, BBC anchorwoman

"Who is the 'loneliest monk?'"
**—MTV News reporter Tabitha Soren after her inter-
view with Bill Clinton in which Clinton said his dream
was to play sax with jazz musician Thelonious Monk**

"Rolls-Royce announced today that it is recalling all
Rolls-Royce cars made after 1966 because of faulty nuts
behind the steering wheel."
—Walter Cronkite

"A squid, as you know, of course, has ten testicles."
—Graham Kerr, *The Galloping Gourmet*

Christine Jorgenson (a famous transsexual): "Sex is not
determined by genitals alone."
Dick Cavett: "I don't think I quite grasp that…I'm sorry,
that's an awful thing to say."
—*The Dick Cavett Show*

"You will enjoy a Jock Full of Nuts Special at lunchtime."
**—Comedian Morey Amsterdam trying to say 'Chock
Full of Nuts,' one of the sponsors of his TV show**

Joey Bishop (talk show host): "Would you like to be a
regular on this show?"
Senator Barry Goldwater: "No, thank you. I'd much
rather watch you in bed with my wife."

The average American consumes approximately 11.7 pounds of chocolate each year.

THE ANIMAL KINGDOM

*Come along as we explore the animal world with these insights
from the strangest animal of them all, the human animal.*

"I ask people why they have deer heads on their walls. They always say, 'Because it's such a beautiful animal.' There you go! I think my mother's attractive, but I have photographs of her."
—**Ellen Degeneres**

"Dumb animals we call them, while they bark and neigh and moo. They talk as much as we do—to them we seem dumb, too."
—**Rebecca McCann**

"A mule's attention span is equal to roughly twice the length of the board you hit him with."
—**Hank Williams, Jr.**

"No animal should ever jump up on the dining-room furniture unless absolutely certain that he can hold his own in the conversation."
—**Fran Lebowitz**

"Does God get stoned? I think so. Look at the platypus."
—**Robin Williams**

"I have been studying the traits and dispositions of the 'lower animals' (so called) and contrasting them with the traits and dispositions of man. I find the result humiliating to me."
—**Mark Twain**

"A worm has some things going for it. For instance—it can't fall down."
—**Milton Berle**

"Odd things, animals. All dogs look up at you. All cats look down at you. Only a pig looks at you as an equal."
—**Winston Churchill**

"Weaseling out of things is good. It's what separates us from the other animals… except the weasel."
—**Homer Simpson**

"You know, I saw the movie *Crouching Tiger, Hidden Dragon*, and I didn't see any tigers or dragons. Then I realized, it's because they're crouching and hidden."
—**Steve Martin**

The first fish to travel to space: a South American guppy in 1976.

YOU LIKE ME! YOU REALLY LIKE ME!

Most award ceremony acceptance speeches are forgettable, but occasionally one stands out.

LARRY DAVID

Award: A Golden Globe in 2003 for *Curb Your Enthusiasm*

Excerpt: "This is a sad day for the Golden Globes. This is, however, a good day for Larry David. I suspect the wife will be a little forthcoming tonight. Thank you Foreign Press for what should be a rewarding evening."

JACK LEMMON

Award: A Golden Globe in 2000 for *Inherit the Wind*

Excerpt: "In the spirit of Ving Rhames, I'm going to give this award to Jack Lemmon."

Background: Ving Rhames won a Golden Globe in 1998 for Best Actor in a TV movie, but many there that night thought that the award should have gone to Jack Lemmon—including Rhames. So he called Lemmon up to the stage and all but gave him the award. Two years later, Lemmon finally won a Golden Globe of his own.

JACKIE CHAN

Award: A star on the Hollywood Walk of Fame in 2002

Excerpt: "To show my appreciation, I will make better films."

MARTIN SHORT

Award: An honorary degree from McMaster University in 2001

Excerpt: "Receiving this honor is without question one of the greatest moments of my life, second only to that magical evening, backstage in Shelley Winters' dressing room, where I first became a man."

"Not all readers become leaders. But all leaders must be readers." —Harry Truman

MALE CHAUVINIST PIGS

These quotes speak for themselves.

"I don't like to cook. I think it's a woman's place to do the cooking. I'll go this far: I'll light the barbecue for my wife if she wants to fix steaks. When it gets right down to it, I can probably fix them better than she does, but I'd rather have her do it."
—Glen Campbell

"The women, nameless beauties in every town, were as easy as a three-chord progression."
—George Jones

"I'm a really big fan of (Barbara Walters). She's a sexy woman. Got great tits, and she's a really good-looking old broad."
—Geraldo Rivera

"I always get along fine with my women, as soon as they recognize that I am God."
—John Derek

"I like the women's movement—from behind."
—Rush Limbaugh

"Women's intuition is the result of millions of years of not thinking."
—Rupert Hughes

"Charity is taking an ugly girl to lunch."
—Warren Beatty

"A woman will lie about anything, just to stay in practice."
—Philip Marlowe

"If I'm not interested in a woman, I'm straight-forward. Right after sex, I usually say, 'I can't do this any more. Thanks for coming over.'"
—Vince Vaughn

"Women are nothing but machines for producing children."
—Napolean Bonaparte

"The only thing that really bugs me about television sports coverage is those damn women they have down on the sidelines who don't know what the hell they're talking about. A woman has no business being down there trying to make some comment about a football game."
—Andy Rooney

"Women are like elephants to me: nice to look at, but I wouldn't want to own one."
—W. C. Fields

THE DOUBLE STANDARD

Why do men have to put the toilet seat down after using the toilet, if women don't have to put it back up when they're done?

"I get so much bad press for being overtly sexual. When someone like Prince or Elvis or Jagger does the same things, they are being honest, sexual human beings. But when I do it: 'Oh, please, Madonna, you're setting the woman's movement back a million years.'"

—Madonna

"If I was a petite, brunette, ethnic lawyer, then my behavior would be totally acceptable. But we Barbie dolls are not supposed to behave the way I do."

—Sharon Stone

"The fact is, a man can be difficult and people applaud him…a woman can try to get it right and she's a pain in the ass."

—Faye Dunaway

"'Slut' used to mean a slovenly woman. Now it means a woman who will go to bed with everyone. This is considered a bad thing in a woman, although perfectly fabulous in a man. 'Bitch' means a woman who will go to bed with everyone but you."

—Cynthia Heimel

"You know what the word 'difficult' means? It means I'm a woman and can't be controlled."

—Kim Bassinger

*　　*　　*

"On the one hand, we'll never experience childbirth. On the other hand, we can open all our own jars."

—Bruce Willis

WAR IS HELL

Some thoughts on mankind's most dangerous game.

"When the tyrant has disposed of foreign enemies by conquest or treaty, and there is nothing more to fear from them, then he is always stirring up some war or other, in order that the people may require a leader."
—**Plato**

"You can't say civilization doesn't advance—for in every war they kill you in a new way."
—**Will Rogers**

"Freedom's untidy."
—**Sec. of Defense Donald Rumsfeld,** *on looting in Baghdad following U.S. invasion, 2003*

"Wars have never hurt anybody except the people who die."
—**Salvador Dali**

"Religious ideas are inflammatory. There are very few wars over the theory of relativity."
—**Quentin Crisp**

"If women ruled the world and we all got massages, there'd be no war."
—**Carrie Snow**

"As long as war is looked upon as wicked, it will always have its fascination. When it is looked upon as vulgar, it will cease to be popular."
—**Oscar Wilde**

"Human war has been the most successful of our cultural traditions."
—**Robert Ardrey**

"Death. Destruction. Disease. Horror. That's what war is all about. That's what makes it a thing to be avoided."
—**Captain Kirk,** *Star Trek*

"You can no more win a war than you can win an earthquake."
—**Jeannette Rankin**

"Truth is the first casualty of war."
—**P. J. O'Rourke**

"The object of war is not to die for your country, but to make the other bastard die for his."
—**Gen. George Patton**

"So long as there are men there will be wars."
—**Albert Einstein**

"The universe is change; life is understanding." —**Marcus Aurelius**

EPITAPHS

*Here's another page of real
tombstone inscriptions.*

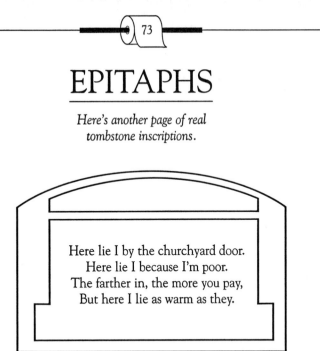

Here lie I by the churchyard door.
Here lie I because I'm poor.
The farther in, the more you pay,
But here I lie as warm as they.

*Here lies John Bunn,
Who was killed by a gun.
His name wasn't Bunn,
but his real name was Wood,
But Wood wouldn't rhyme with gun,
So I thought Bunn should.*

Here lies Jane Smith,
Wife of Thomas
Smith,
Marble Cutter
This monument was
erected by her
husband as a tribute
to her memory
and a specimen
of his work.
Monuments of this
style are
Two hundred and
fifty dollars

"Stranger! Approach
this spot with gravity!
Dr. John Brown is
filling his last cavity!"

GOOD FOR WHAT ALES YOU!

Mmmmm…beer.

Woody: "What's going on Mr. Peterson?"
Norm: "A flashing sign in my gut that says, 'Insert beer here.'"
—*Cheers*

"Beer, it's the best damn drink in the world."
—Jack Nicholson

"A quart of ale is a dish for a king."
—William Shakespeare

"Offstage, I'm Ozzie Nelson. I'm gentle. I walk around eating cookies and milk—well, cookies and beer."
—Alice Cooper

"Milk is for babies. When you grow up you have to drink beer."
—Arnold Schwarzenegger

"I'm drunk on love…and beer."
—Homer Simpson

"Prohibition makes you want to cry into your beer and denies you the beer to cry into."
—Don Marquis

"Make sure that the beer—four pints a week—goes to the troops under fire before any of the parties in the rear get a drop."
—Winston Churchill to his Secretary of War, 1944

"Bread, meat, vegetables and beer."
—Sophocles' philosophy of a moderate diet

"Fermentation may have been a greater discovery than fire."
—David Rains Wallace

"You can't be a real country unless you have a beer and an airline—it helps if you have some kind of a football team, or some nuclear weapons, but at the very least you need a beer."
—Frank Zappa

"Beer is proof that God loves us and wants us to be happy."
—Benjamin Franklin

"I would give all my fame for a pot of ale and safety."
—William Shakespeare, *King Henry V*

"The best way to cheer yourself up: Cheer everybody else up." —Mark Twain

"The human brain can only operate as fast as the slowest brain cells. Excessive intake of alcohol, as we know, kills brain cells. But naturally, it attacks the slowest and weakest brain cells first. In this way, regular consumption of beer eliminates the weaker brain cells, making the brain a faster and more efficient machine. That's why you always feel smarter after a few beers."

—Cliff Claven, *Cheers*

DEEP THOUGHTS

Some of these are as deep as the ocean—others are more like the kiddie pool. Are you deep enough to tell the difference?

"I'm not OK, you're not OK, and that's OK."
—**William Sloane Coffin**

"A problem well stated is a problem half solved."
—**Charles Franklin Kettering**

"Copy from one, it's plagiarism; copy from two, it's research."
—**Wilson Mizner**

"There are few nudities so objectionable as the naked truth."
—**Agnes Repplier**

"Everybody sets out to do something, and everybody does something, but no one does what he sets out to do."
—**George Moore**

"We started off trying to set up a small anarchist community, but people wouldn't obey the rules."
—**Alan Bennett**

"It is easier to live through someone else than to become complete yourself."
—**Betty Friedan**

"If you can keep your head when all about you are losing theirs, it's just possible you haven't grasped the situation."
—**Jean Kerr**

"There are times not to flirt. When you're sick. When you're with children. When you're on the witness stand."
—**Joyce Jillson**

"Men are born with two eyes, but with one tongue, in order that they should see twice as much as they say."
—**Charles Caleb Colton**

"In times like these, it helps to recall that there have always been times like these."
—**Paul Harvey**

"Everything that irritates us about others can lead us to an understanding of ourselves."
—**Carl Jung**

"Discovery consists of seeing what everybody has seen and thinking what nobody has thought."
—**Albert von Szent-Gyorgyi**

SURE-FIRE SAFIRE

Conservative columnist, speechwriter, pundit, and English-language expert, William Safire is a true American treasure.

"Is sloppiness in speech caused by ignorance or apathy? I don't know and I don't care."

"The right to do something does not mean that doing it is right."

"Better to be a jerk that knees than a knee that jerks."

"Remember to never split an infinitive. The passive voice should never be used. Do not put statements in the negative form. Proofread carefully to see if you words out. And don't start a sentence with a conjugation."

"I want my questions answered by an alert and exerienced politician, prepared to be grilled and quoted—not my hand held by an old smoothie."

"The most fun in breaking a rule is in knowing what rule you're breaking."

"Decide on some imperfect Somebody and you will win, because the truest truism in politics is: you can't beat Somebody with Nobody."

"If America cannot win a war in a week, it begins negotiating with itself."

"The first ladyship is the only federal office in which the holder can neither be fired nor impeached."

"The perfect Christmas gift for a sportscaster, as all fans of sports clichés know, is a scoreless tie."

"Last, but not least, avoid clichés like the plague."

"I am as frustrated with society as a pyromaniac in a petrified forest." —A. Whitney Brown

THE BOYS OF SUMMER

If we did a book of quotes without one page on baseball, we'd be throwing you a curveball.

"Baseball has the great advantage over cricket of being sooner ended."
—George Bernard Shaw

"The most-honored ancestors of your matriarch besmirched the season of the orange blossom."
—Nick Bakay, *describing what baseball trash talk sounds like in Japan*

"The biggest honor is what happens on the field. Everything else that happens later in life is anticlimactic."
—Sandy Koufax

"It helps if the hitter thinks you're a little crazy."
—Nolan Ryan

"The pitcher's got only a ball. I've got a bat. So the percentage in weapons is in my favor and I let the fellow with the ball do the fretting."
—Hank Aaron

"Baseball's my life, but it isn't the end of life."
—Tim Wakefield

"Baseball was the big thing with me. I can remember, clear as a bell, sitting on my father's lap in our living room and listening to a 1947 Yankees game on the radio: boy, I loved the Yankees. My father once took me to a Dodgers game at Ebbets Field—in 1949—and I was so ashamed of being there that I wore a Lone Ranger mask so nobody would recognize me."
—Paul Simon

"I wasn't in a slump; I just wasn't getting any hits."
—Dave Henderson

"Baseball is the belly-button of our society. Bring back natural grass and nickel beer. Straighten out baseball, and you straighten out the rest of the world."
—Bill Lee

TOMMY COOPER

From the 1950s until his death in 1984, Tommy Cooper was one of England's best-known magician/comedians. Here are some of his best jokes. (If some of these look familiar, now you know where they came from.)

"The insurance man told me that the accident policy covered falling off the roof but not hitting the ground."

"Apparently, one in five people in the world are Chinese. And there are five people in my family, so it must be one of them. It's either my mum or my dad, or my older brother Colin, or my younger brother Ho-Cha-Chu. But I think it's Colin."

"Two cannibals eating a clown. One says to the other 'Does this taste funny to you?'"

"I was cleaning the attic the other day with the wife. Filthy, dirty, covered with cobwebs… but she's good with the kids."

"I'm on a whiskey diet. I've lost three days already."

"I slept like a log last night. I woke up in a fireplace."

"I went to buy some camouflage trousers the other day but I couldn't find any."

"Police arrested two kids yesterday. One was drinking battery acid, the other was eating fireworks. They charged one and let the other one off."

"A blind bloke walks into a shop with a guide dog. He picks the dog up and starts swinging it around his head. Alarmed, a clerk calls out: 'Can I help, sir?' 'No, thanks,' says the blind bloke. 'Just looking around.'"

"A guy walks into the psychiatrist wearing only Saran wrap for shorts. The shrink says, 'Well, I can clearly see you're nuts.'"

"I inherited a painting and a violin which turned out to be a Rembrandt and a Stradivarius. Unfortunately, Rembrandt made lousy violins and Stradivarius was a terrible painter."

"Most dentists' chairs go up and down, right? The one I was in went back and forwards. I thought, 'This is unusual.' Then the dentist said, 'Cooper, get out of the filing cabinet.'"

THE ENLIGHTENED ONE

According to legend, Siddhartha Gautama (563–483 B.C.) achieved nirvana while meditating beneath a Bodhi tree in India and became the Buddha, or "enlightened one." He spent many years wandering throughout Asia, living simply and sharing his wisdom.

"Believe nothing, no matter where you read it, or who said it, unless it agrees with your own reason and your own common sense."

"Do not overrate what you have received, nor envy others. He who envies others does not obtain peace of mind."

"The tongue, like a sharp knife, kills without drawing blood."

"It is better to travel well than to arrive."

"You yourself, as much as anybody in the entire universe, deserve your love and affection."

"Holding on to anger is like grasping a hot coal with the intent of throwing it at someone else; you are the one who gets burned."

"All that we are is the result of what we have thought. If a man speaks or acts with an evil thought, pain follows him. If a man speaks or acts

with a pure thought, happiness follows him, like a shadow that never leaves him."

"Every human being is the author of his own health."

"What we think, we become."

"However many holy words you read, however many you speak, what good will they do you if you do not act on them?"

"He is able who thinks he is able."

"I do not believe in a fate that falls on men however they act; but I do believe in a fate that falls on them unless they act."

"The world is like a dream and the treasures of the world an alluring mirage. Like the apparent distances in a picture, things have no reality in themselves—they are like heat haze."

"Your work is to discover your world and then with all your heart give yourself to it."

"Childhood is the kingdom where nobody dies." —Edna St. Vincent Millay

MONEY TALKS

"Money talks, they say. All it ever said to me was 'goodbye.'"
—Cary Grant, None But the Lonely Heart

"Jerry died broke. We only have a few hundred thousand dollars in the bank."
—Deborah Koons Garcia

"A billion here, a billion there—sooner or later it adds up to real money."
—Sen. Everett Dirksen

"When it is a question of money, everybody is of the same religion."
—Voltaire

"It is spiritual snobbery that makes people think they can be happy without money."
—Albert Camus

"Our parents were very strict. They didn't want us to grow up spoiled and rich. If we left our tennis rackets out in the rain, we were punished."
—Nancy Ellis,
George H. W. Bush's sister

"It is good to have money and the things it can buy, but it's good, too, to check once in a while to make sure you haven't lost the things it can't buy."
—George Lorimer

"The lack of money is the root of all evil."
—Mark Twain

"All money nowadays seems to be produced with a natural homing instinct for the Treasury."
—Prince Philip

"The only reason to have money is to tell any S.O.B. in the world to go to hell."
—Humphrey Bogart

"Real happiness is when you marry a girl for love and find out later she has money."
—Bob Monkhouse

"My biggest sexual fantasy is we're making love and I realize I'm out of debt."
—Beth Lapides

"Poor is a state of mind. Broke is a state of wallet. You can fix being broke; it's not so easy to fix being poor."
—Ric Edelman

"Part of the loot went for gambling and part for women. The rest I spent foolishly."
—George Raft,
on how he spent $10 million

"Nobody believes the official spokesman, but everybody trusts an unidentified source." —Ron Nesen

WRITERS ON WRITING

Who else would you expect a clever comment from, if not a great writer?

"Everywhere I go I'm asked if I think universities stifle writers. My opinion is that they don't stifle enough of them."
—**Flannery O'Connor**

"If a young writer can refrain from writing, he shouldn't hesitate to do so."
—**Andre Gide**

"To write a novel may be pure pleasure. To live a novel presents certain difficulties. As for reading a novel, I do my best to get out of it."
—**Karl Kraus**

"People say that life is the thing, but I prefer reading."
—**Logan Pearsall Smith**

"It would be an advantage to the literary world if most writers stopped writing entirely."
—**Fran Lebowitz**

"The best time for planning a book is when you're doing the dishes."
—**Agatha Christie**

"There are no dull subjects. There are only dull writers."
—**H. L. Mencken**

"If I didn't have writing, I'd be running down the street hurling grenades in people's faces."
—**Paul Fussel**

"I can write better than anybody who can write faster, and I can write faster than anybody who can write better."
—**A. J. Liebling**

"All writers are vain, selfish, lazy, and at the very bottom, their motives are a mystery."
—**George Orwell**

"You can't wait for inspiration. You have to go after it with a club."
—**Jack London**

"Literature is mostly about having sex and not much about having children. Life is the other way around."
—**David Lodge**

"What an author likes to write most is his signature on the back of a check."
—**Brendan Francis**

"I don't read books. I write them."
—**Henry Kissinger**

NOVEL THINKING

Deep insights from the pages of the world's greatest novels.

"Death and taxes and childbirth! There's never any convenient time for any of them!"
—**Scarlett O'Hara,**
Gone With the Wind, by Margaret Mitchell

"I have no data yet. It is a capital mistake to theorize before one has data. Insensibly one begins to twist facts to suit theories instead of theories to suit facts."
—**Sherlock Holmes, A Scandal in Bohemia,**
by Arthur Conan Doyle

"Sometimes in my sleep I'd feel a body next to me, like an amputee feels a phantom limb."
—**American Splendor, by Harvey Pekar**

"When I really worry about something, I don't just fool around. I even have to go to the bathroom when I worry about something. Only, I don't go. I'm too worried to go. I don't want to interrupt my worrying to go."
—**Holden Caufield, Catcher in the Rye,**
by J. D. Salinger

"He had heard people speak contemptuously of money: he wondered if they had ever tried to do without it."
—**Of Human Bondage, by W. Somerset Maugham**

"Once men turned their thinking over to machines in the hope that this would set them free. But that only permitted other men with machines to enslave them."
—**Dune, by Frank Herbert**

"If you drink from a bottle marked 'poison', it is almost certain to disagree with you, sooner or later."
—**Alice's Adventures in Wonderland,**
by Lewis Carroll

UNCLE JOHN'S QUOTATIONARY

Here's Part 2 of our quotation dictionary.
(Part 1 begins on page 44.)

CABBAGE: a familiar kitchen-garden vegetable about as large and wise as a man's head. (Ambrose Bierce)

CANADIAN: someone who knows how to make love in a canoe. (Pierre Berton)

CAPITAL PUNISHMENT: killing people who kill people to prove that killing people is wrong. (Sister Helen Prejean)

CAMEL: a horse designed by committee. (Alec Issigonis)

CAMOUFLAGE: a game we all like to play where our secrets are as surely revealed by what we want to seem to be as by what we want to conceal. (Russell Lynes)

CAT: a pygmy lion who loves mice, hates dogs, and patronizes human beings. (Oliver Herford)

CELEBRITY: one who is known by many people he is glad he doesn't know. (H. L. Mencken)

CENSOR: a man who thinks he knows more than you ought to. (Laurence J. Peter)

CENSORSHIP: an excuse to talk about sex. (Fran Leibowitz)

CHASTITY: the most unnatural of the sexual perversions. (Aldous Huxley)

CHEESE: milk that you chew. (Chandler, *Friends*)

CHESS: a game life is too short for. (Henry James Byron)

CHILDREN: natural Zen masters whose world is brand new in each and every moment. (John Bradshaw)

CHURCH: a place in which gentlemen who have never been to heaven brag about it to persons who will never get there. (H. L. Mencken)

CITY: a place where you're least likely to get a bite from a wild sheep. (Brenadan Behan)

CIVILIZATION: a race between education and catastrophe. (H. G. Wells)

CLASSIC: something that everybody wants to have read and nobody wants to read. (Mark Twain)

COCKTAIL PARTY: a gathering held to enable forty people to talk about themselves at the same time. The man who remains after the liquor is gone is the host. (Fred Allen)

COMEDY: a funny way of being serious. (Peter Ustinov)

COMMITTEE: a group of men who keep minutes and waste hours. (Milton Berle)

COMMON SENSE: genius dressed up in working clothes. (Ralph Waldo Emerson)

COMPASSION: a luxury of the affluent. (Tony Randall)

CONCEIT: God's gift to little men. (Bruce Barton)

CONCENTRATION: the ability to think about absolutely nothing when it is absolutely necessary. (Ray Knight)

CONCLUSION: what you reach when you get tired of thinking. (Martin Fischer)

CONSCIENCE: a mother-in-law whose visit never ends. (H. L. Mencken)

CONSCIOUSNESS: that annoying time between naps. (Anonymous)

CONSENSUS: what many people say in chorus but do not believe as individuals. (Abba Eban)

CONSERVATIVE: a liberal who got mugged the night before. (Frank Rizzo)

COSMOS (THE): the smallest hole a man can hide his head in. (G. K. Chesterson)

COURAGE: the fear of being thought a coward. (Horace Smith)

CREATIVITY: piercing the mundane to find the marvelous. (Bill Moyers)

CRITIC: a legless man who teaches running. (Channing Pollock)

CULT: not enough people to make a minority. (Robert Altman)

CURVE: the loveliest distance between two points. (Mae West)

CYNIC: one who never sees a good quality in a man and never fails to see a bad one. He is the human owl, vigilant in darkness and blind to light, mousing for vermin, and never seeing noble game. The cynic puts all human actions into two classes—openly bad and secretly bad. (Henry Ward Beecher)

CYNICISM: the intellectual cripple's substitute for intelligence. (Russell Lynes)

DANCING: the vertical expression of horizontal

desire. (George Bernard Shaw)

DEADLINE: negative inspiration—but better than no inspiration at all. (Rita Mae Brown)

DEATH: the cure for all diseases. (Thomas Browne)

DEFINITION: a sack of flour compressed into a thimble. (Remy de Gourmont)

DEMOCRACY: the bludgeoning of the people, by the people, for the people. (Oscar Wilde)

DESTINY: a tyrant's authority for crime and a fool's excuse for failure. (Ambrose Bierce)

DIET: a plan, generally hopeless, for reducing your weight, which tests your will power but does little for your waistline. (Herbert B. Prochnow)

DILEMMA: a politician trying to save both of his faces at once. (John A. Lincoln)

DIPLOMACY: the art of saying 'nice doggie' until you can find a rock. (Will Rogers)

DIVORCE: America's great contribution to marriage. (Edward Fawcett)

DOCTORS: people who prescribe medicines of which they know little, to cure diseases of which they know less, in human beings of whom they know nothing. (Voltaire)

DOG: the god of frolic. (Henry Ward Beecher)

DOOR: what a dog is perpetually on the wrong side of. (Ogden Nash)

DOUBLETHINK: the power of holding two contradictory beliefs in one's mind simultaneously, and accepting both of them. (George Orwell)

DRAMA: life with the dull bits left out. (Alfred Hitchcock)

DRUGS: a bet with the mind. (Jim Morrison)

DRUNKENNESS: temporary suicide. (Bertrand Russell)

For more, see page 131.

*　　*　　*

"What do you get on Mother's Day if you have kids? You know what. A card with flowers that are made out of pink toilet paper— a lot of of pink toilet paper. You get breakfast in bed. Then you get up and fix everybody else their breakfast. And then you go to the bathroom and you are out of toilet paper."

—Liz Scott

"I want to be all used up when I die." —George Bernard Shaw

BILL MAHER

*ABC canned him for his controversial opinions,
but he resurfaced on HBO. Here's the kind
of commentary that got him fired.*

"America is the only country in the world that's still in the business of making bombs that can end the world and TV shows that make it seem like a good idea."

"Should we require a seven-day waiting period to have a child, and if so would it be called the Brady Bunch Bill?"

"The Dalai Lama visited the White House and told the president that he could teach him to find a higher state of consciousness. Then after talking to Bush for a few minutes, he said, 'You know what? Let's just grab lunch.'"

"I think capital punishment works great. Every killer you kill never kills again."

"Whenever the people are for gay marriage or medical marijuana or assisted suicide, suddenly the 'will of the people' goes out the window."

"Bush says, 'Gore's book needs a lot of explaining.' Of course, he says that about every book."

"We have a Bill of Rights. What we need is a Bill of Responsibilities."

POLITICALLY CORRECT SPEAK

It's not what you say, it's how you say it that counts.

"I didn't steal this. It was 'differently acquired.'"
—**Sara Cytron**

"It's about time that people forget that image of strip clubs as seedy places—today's strip clubs are 'capital-intensive female empowerment zones.'"
—**Demi Moore**

"I used to have a dog. And he was a good dog. But these days, he'd be a 'Canine American.'"
—**A. Whitney Brown**

"Death: what politically correct doctors call a 'negative patient outcome.'"
—**John Koshi**

"We protest you calling us little kids. We prefer to be called 'vertically-impaired pre-adults.'"
—**Yakko,** *Animaniacs*

"Oh, 'meltdown.' It's one of those annoying buzzwords. We prefer to call it an 'unrequested fission surplus.'"
—**Montgomery Burns,**
The Simpsons

"Why is it there are so many more horses' asses than there are horses?" —G. Gordon Liddy

FRACTURED PHRASES

More variations on a phrase.

"These impossible women! How they do get around us! The poet was right: 'Can't live with them, or without them.'"
—Aristophanes

"Women...can't live with 'em...pass the beer nuts."
—**Norm Peterson,** *Cheers*

"Women...you can't live with them, and you can't get them to dress up in a skimpy little Nazi costume and beat you with a warm squash or something..."
—Emo Philips

"Men! Can't live with 'em, can't sell 'em for parts."
—**Janine,** *The Real Ghostbusters*

"Women...can't live with 'em...the end."
—**Al Bundy,** *Married...with Children*

"Heav'n hath no rage like love to hatred turn'd, Nor Hell a fury, like a woman scorn'd."
—William Congreve

"Hell hath no fury like a bureaucrat scorned."
—**Milton Friedman**

"Hell hath no fury like a hustler with a literary agent."
—**Frank Sinatra**

"War hath no fury like a non-combatant."
—**C. E. Montaigne**

"Hell hath no fury like a woman scorned for Sega."
—**Brodie Bruce,** *Mallrats*

If life gives you lemons... make lemonade.

"If life gives you lemons, make some sort of fruity juice."
—**Conan O'Brien**

THE MAN UPSTAIRS

Does God exist? We don't know, but we're not taking any chances—that's why we gave him a two-page spread.

"I'm still an atheist, thank God."
—Luis Buñuel

"And God said, 'The only people I like are atheists, because they play hard to get.'"
—Lotus Weinstock

"I contend that we are both atheists. I just believe in one fewer God than you do. When you understand why you dismiss all the other possible Gods, you will understand why I dismiss yours."
—Sir Stephen Henry Roberts

"Not only is there no God, but try finding a plumber on Sunday."

—Woody Allen

"What if God's a woman? Not only am I going to hell, I'll never know why."
—Adam Ferrara

"I think the whole concept of monotheism is a gift from the gods."
—Emo Philips

"God seems to have left the receiver off the hook and time is running out."
—Arthur Koestler

"Black holes are where God divided by zero."
—Steven Wright

"Men reach their sexual peak at eighteen. Women reach theirs at thirty-five. Do you get the feeling that God is playing a practical joke?"
—Rita Rudner

Archie Bunker: "All the pictures I ever seen, God is white."
George Jefferson: "Maybe you were looking at the negatives."
—*All in the Family*

"I think man has ruined God."
—Bono

No rain, no rainbows —Native American saying

"There is nothing written in the Bible—Old or New Testament—that says, 'If you believe in Me, you ain't going to have no troubles.'"
—Ray Charles

"When we talk to God, we're praying. When God talks to us, we're schizophrenic."
—Lily Tomlin

"God is an experience that doesn't require belief."
—Russell Targ

"Forgive, O Lord, my little jokes on thee,
And I'll forgive Thy great big one on me."
—Robert Frost

"I do not feel obliged to believe that the same God who has endowed us with sense, reason, and intellect has intended us to forgo their use."
—Galileo Galilei

"God, the Ten Commandments, and moral teachings are out of the public schools of America. Easter has disappeared, and now we have Earth Day so we can all worship dirt."
—Pat Buchanan

"If there is a supreme being, he's crazy."
—Marlene Dietrich

*   *   *

"I know God will not give me anything I can't handle. I just wish that He didn't trust me so much."
—Mother Teresa

SIGMUND FREUD

He's been called the father of modern psychology; he's also been called the man who's ruined modern psychology. Either way, Sigmund Freud (1856–1938) was a revolutionary.

"The first human being who hurled an insult instead of a stone was the founder of civilization."

"No one who conjures up the most evil of those half-tamed demons that inhabit the human beast, and seeks to wrestle with them, can expect to come through the struggle unscathed."

"Obviously, one must hold oneself responsible for the evil impulses of one's dreams. In what other way can one deal with them?"

"Dogs love their friends and bite their enemies, quite unlike people, who always have to mix love and hate."

"The very emphasis of the commandment thou shalt not kill makes it certain that we are descended from an endlessly long chain of generations of murderers, whose love of murder was in their blood as it is perhaps also in ours."

"Anatomy is destiny."

"A man should not strive to eliminate his complexes but to get into accord with them: they are legitimately what directs his conduct in the world."

"When inspiration does not come to me, I go halfway to meet it."

"From error to error, one discovers the entire truth."

"How bold one gets when one is sure of being loved!"

"What a distressing contrast there is between the radiant intelligence of the child and the feeble mentality of the average adult."

"Neurotics complain of their illness, but they make the most of it, and when it comes to taking it away from them they will defend it like a lioness her young."

"What we call happiness in the strictest sense comes from the (preferably sudden) satisfaction of needs which have been dammed up to a high degree."

Sigmund Freud suffered from constipation.

TIP OF THE SLONGUE

Sometimes Freud works in mysterious ways.

"I would like to spank director Spike Jonze."
**—Meryl Streep, misreading a faxed accept-
ance speech at the 2003 BAFTA Awards**

"We lead in exporting jobs."
**—Dan Quayle, addressing
the Evansville, Indiana, Chamber of
Commerce. He meant to say "products."**

"The United States has much to offer the third
world war."
**—Ronald Reagan,
he meant "Third World"**

"She's a wonderful, wonderful person, and
we're looking forward to a happy and wonderful night—uh, life."
—Ted Kennedy

"I don't want to run the risk of ruining what is
a lovely recession."
**—George H. W. Bush in a
1992 campaign speech in Ridgewood,
New Jersey. He meant to say "reception."**

"I have had great financial sex."
—Ross Perot, meaning to say "success"

BIRDS DO IT, BEES DO IT

Do what? Go ask your mother!

"What do I know about sex? I'm a married man."
—**Tom Clancy**

"I believe that sex is one of the most beautiful, natural, wholesome things that money can buy."
—**Steve Martin**

"Sex is God's joke on human beings."
—**Bette Davis**

"Sex is a bad thing because it rumples the clothes."
—**Jacqueline Kennedy Onassis**

"I have to be physically attracted to someone. But I can't just be with someone just because it's great sex—because orgasms don't last long enough."
—**Courteney Cox**

"Of the delights of this world, man cares most for sexual intercourse. He will go to any length for it—risk fortune, character, reputation, life itself."
—**Mark Twain**

"Madame, you have between your legs an instrument capable of giving pleasure to thousands, and all you have to do is scratch it."
—**Thomas Beecham, to a cellist**

"A couple in a sexual experience is happy for that moment. Then very soon trouble begins."
—**The Dalai Lama**

"We think about sex obsessively except during the act, when our minds begin to wander."
—**Howard Nemerov**

"Women need a reason to have sex. Men just need a place."
—**Billy Crystal**

"Erotic is when you do something sensitive and imaginative with a feather. Kinky is when you use the whole chicken."
—**Elmore Leonard**

"There are many things better than sex, but there's nothing quite like it."
—**W. C. Fields**

"Sex gets people killed, put in jail, beaten up, bankrupted, and disgraced, to say nothing of ruined—personally, politically. Looking for sex can lead to misfortune, and if you get lucky and find it, it can leave you maimed, infected, or dead. Other than that, it's swell."

—Edna Buchanan

LOVE STINKS

Or does it? Here's what some people think.

"There's no love in the world that can't be killed if you beat it to death long enough."
—**Tammy Wynette**

"Love should be simple, but it's not. Hate should be hard, but it's easy."
—**Tanya Tucker**

"God is love, but get it in writing."
—**Gypsy Rose Lee**

"Love: the delusion that one woman differs from another."
—**H. L. Mencken**

"Many a man in love with a dimple makes the mistake of marrying the whole girl."
—**Stephen Leacock**

"It is possible to love a human being if you don't know them too well."
—**Charles Bukowski**

"The only true love is love at first sight; second sight dispels it."
—**Israel Zangwill**

"When you're in love, it's the most glorious two-and-a-half days of your life."
—**Richard Lewis**

"We owe to the Middle Ages the two worst inventions of humanity—gunpowder and romantic love."
—**André Maurois**

"Love is a snowmobile racing across the tundra, and then suddenly it flips over, pinning you underneath. At night, the ice weasels come."
—**Matt Groening**

"The American idea of love is ridiculous. It's a fantasy, a fairytale. It's based on goals that cannot be achieved and fantasies that don't exist."
—**Frank Zappa**

"Love is the word used to label the sexual excitement of the young, the habituation of the middle-aged, and the mutual dependence of the old."
—**John Ciardi**

"There is so much pressure from day one to be with someone forever—and I'm not sure that it really is in our nature to be with something for the rest of our lives."
—**Brad Pitt**

"One is very crazy when in love." —**Sigmund Freud**

DUMB JOCKS

Athletes have a reputation for saying dumb things. They deserve it.

"I dunno. I never smoked any Astroturf."
—**Tug McGraw, asked whether he preferred grass or Astroturf**

"Raise the urinals."
—**Darrel Chaney, on how management could keep the Braves on their toes**

"The only reason I don't like playing in the World Series is I can't watch myself play."
—**Reggie Jackson**

"I am the most loyal player money can buy."
—**Don Sutton, pitcher for the Los Angeles Dodgers, Houston Astros, Milwaukee Brewers, Oakland Athletics and California Angels**

"Always root for the winner. That way you won't be disappointed."
—**Tug McGraw**

"They shouldn't throw at me. I'm the father of five or six kids."
—**Baseball player Tito Fuentes, after getting hit by a pitch**

"Better make it six; I can't eat eight."
—**Pitcher Dan Osinski, when a waitress asked if he wanted his pizza cut into six or eight slices**

"Me and George and Billy are two of a kind."
—**Baseball player Mickey Rivers, on his relationship with George Steinbrenner and Billy Martin**

"The game was closer than the score indicated."
—**Baseball player Dizzy Dean, after a 1-0 game**

"There is one word in America that says it all, and that word is, 'You never know.'"
—**Pitcher Joaquin Andujar**

"I lost it in the sun!"
—**Billy Loes, Brooklyn Dodgers Pitcher, after fumbling a grounder**

"I want all the kids to do what I do, to look up to me. I want all the kids to copulate me."
—**Chicago Cubs outfielder Andre Dawson, on being a role model**

"Everyone has his burden. What counts is how you carry it." —Merle Miller

MAN'S BEST FRIEND

The headquarters of the Bathroom Readers' Institute has always had a canine hanging around. This page is dedicated to our favorite four-legged friend, Porter the Wonder Dog.

"The dog represents all that is best in man."
—**Etienne Charlet**

"A dog is not almost human, and I know of no greater insult to the canine race than to describe it as such."
—**John Holmes**

"A dog is the only thing on Earth that will love you more than you love yourself."
—**Josh Billings**

"To be sure, the dog is loyal. But why, on that account, should we take him as an example? He is loyal to men, not other dogs."
—**Karl Kraus**

"If I have any beliefs about immortality, it is that certain dogs I have known will go to heaven, and very few persons."
—**James Thurber**

"Dogs laugh, but they laugh with their tails. What puts man in a higher state of evolution is that he has got his laugh on the right end."
—**Max Eastman**

"I wonder what goes through his mind when he sees us peeing in his water bowl."
—**Penny Ward Moser**

"Cats are the ultimate narcissists. You can tell because of all the time they spend on personal grooming. A dog's idea of personal grooming is to roll in a dead fish."
—**James Gorman**

"Man is a dog's ideal of what God should be."
—**Holbrook Jackson**

"Getting a dog is like getting married. It teaches you to be less self-centered; to accept sudden, surprising outbursts of affection; and not to be upset by a few scratches on your car."
—**Will Stanton**

"It's a dog-eat-dog world, and I'm wearing Milk Bone shorts."
—**Norm,** *Cheers*

"I can train any dog in five minutes. It's training the owner that takes longer."
—**Barbara Woodhouse**

"Love is a net where hearts are caught like fish." —Muhammad Ali

THIS LAND IS OUR LAND

Where else but in this great country can a man make
a living by making books with toilets on the cover?
Here is a smattering of opinions—good and
bad—about the United States of America.

"America is like a large, friendly dog in a very small room. Every time it wags its tail, it knocks over a chair."
—**Arnold Toynbee**

"Americans are broad-minded people. They'll accept the fact that a person can be an alcoholic, a dope fiend, a wife beater, and even a newspaperman, but if a man doesn't drive there's something wrong with him."
—**Art Buchwald**

"America is the only nation in history which miraculously has gone directly from barbarism to degeneration without the usual interval of civilization."
—**Georges Clemenceau**

"An asylum for the sane would be empty in America."
—**George Bernard Shaw**

"Americans spend $300 billion very year on games of chance, and that doesn't even include weddings and elections."
—**Argus Hamilton**

"No one flower can ever symbolize this nation. America is a bouquet."
—**William Safire**

"I've never been able to look upon America as young and vital, but rather as prematurely old, as a fruit which rotted before it had a chance to ripen. The word which gives the key to the national vice is waste."
—**Henry Miller**

Alex Reiger: Louie, when you walk into that hearing room, you're going to be under oath. You know what that means?

Louie DePalma: Yeah. It means they gotta believe you. I love this country.
—*Taxi*

"America is a mistake, a giant mistake!"
—**Sigmund Freud**

"America is a place where Jewish merchants sell Zen love beads to agnostics for Christmas."
—**John Burton Brimer**

SNL NEWS

The Weekend Update "news" segment of Saturday Night Live is our favorite part of the show.

"Citing the high cost of the series and low ratings, syndicator Pearson Television has cancelled *Baywatch*. Now viewers who love big fake boobs will just have to watch *VIP*, *Jerry Springer*, *Jenny Jones*, *Search Party*, *Extra*, *MTV Spring Break*, *MTV Making the Video*, *Wild on E!*, *Howard Stern*, *Silk Stalkings*, *G-String Divas*, *The Man Show*, *Unhappily Ever After*, *Blind Date*, *Bowflex* Infomercials, *Cleopatra 2525*, the XFL, the NFL, *Sabado Gigante*, *Temptation Island*, *Charmed*, wrestling, Cinemax, Showtime, or commercials."

—**Tina Fey**

"Fashion designer Giorgio Armani confessed last week to bribing Italian tax officials. He was sentenced to six months of wearing brown shoes with a blue suit."

—**Norm MacDonald**

"The Country Music Awards was marred when it was learned that not one of the nominees was really drunk, jilted, or unemployed."

—**Kevin Nealon**

"In Maryland, Bell Atlantic plans to offer a service that will allow customers to learn the address of any listed telephone number in the state. Critics say the service will be an invasion of privacy, while proponents of the plan say that it will help them invade people's privacy."

—**Norm MacDonald**

"Koko, a gorilla who understands sign language, answered questions on America Online. When asked if she liked bananas, Koko replied, 'Hey, that's real funny. It's too bad you're not here so I could rip your arms off.' "

—**Colin Quinn**

"In protest to France's opposition to a U.S. war on Iraq, the U.S. congress' cafeteria has changed French Fries and French Toast to Freedom Fries and Freedom Toast. Afterwards, the congressmen were so pleased with themselves, they all started Freedom Kissing each other."

—**Tina Fey**

"Edmar Fretok, a Brazilian weight-training instructor, broke a world record by doing 111,000 sit-ups in 24 hours. Fretok also set the 24-hour record for most accidental farts."

—Jimmy Fallon

"Queen Elizabeth II visited Russia this week, becoming the first English monarch to set foot in the Soviet Union. The visit, which will last for two weeks, is expected to have absolutely no effect on anything whatsoever."

—Norm MacDonald

"*Sesame Street Workshop* announced that they have laid off 60 workers. News of the firings was brought to the employees by the letters F and U."

—Tina Fey

*　*　*

STAR STRUCK

"I never worked with him, but I had a brief crush on Clark Gable. One day, I happened to mention it to my dentist in his office. I was fairly new to Los Angeles, but a few dentists served most of the stars. This one was also Gable's dentist, and he asked what I particularly liked about Gable. I said, 'His bright smile.' He said, 'Would you like to see that bright smile today?'

"My heart was pounding. I thought Gable must be the next patient, after me. I could hardly wait for the session to end, and then the dentist led me to the adjoining room, and there, under glass, was a pair of Gable's very white dentures…"

—Bette Davis

TAKIN' CARE OF BUSINESS

*A few thoughts from Elvis Presley,
the King of rock 'n' roll.*

"Rhythm is something you either have or don't have, but when you have it, you have it all over."

"The colored people been singing it and playing it just the way I'm doing now, man, for more years than I know. Nobody paid it no mind until I goosed it up."

"I'm afraid of intellectuals— they bring dissention and envy and jealousy."

"I get lonesome sometimes. Sometimes I get lonesome in the middle of a crowd."

Elvis proposed to to Ginger Alden while he was sitting on the toilet.

DON'T!

Don't even think of skipping this page.

"Don't give your advice before you are called upon."
—**Desiderius Erasmus**

"Don't accept rides from strange men, and remember that all men are strange."
—**Robin Morgan**

"If you can't do it with feeling, don't."
—**Patsy Cline**

"Don't judge each day by the harvest you reap, but by the seeds you plant."
—**Robert Louis Stevenson**

"Don't bother about being modern. Unfortunately, it is the one thing that, whatever you do, you cannot avoid."
—**Salvador Dali**

"Don't take a butcher's advice on how to cook meat. If he knew, he'd be a chef."
—**Andy Rooney**

"Don't compare yourself with someone else's version of happy or thin. Accepting yourself burns the most calories."
—**Caroline Rhea**

"Don't ever slam the door; you might want to go back."
—**Don Herold**

"Don't give any sh*t, and put up with very little."
—**Hank Williams, Jr.**

"Don't take life too seriously. You'll never get out of it alive."
—**Elbert Hubbard**

"Don't be afraid to trust your own common sense."
—**Benjamin Spock**

"Don't get mad. Don't get even. Just get elected, then get even."
—**James Carville**

"Don't compromise yourself. You are all you've got."
—**Janis Joplin**

"Don't do drugs, because if you do drugs, you'll go to prison, and drugs are really expensive in prison."
—**John Hardwick**

"The first and great commandment is: don't let them scare you."
—**Elmer Davis**

MEN OF SCIENCE

College tip: The more you keep your science professors blabbing, the less time you'll have to study science.

"When I am working on a problem, I never think about beauty. I think only of how to solve the problem. But when I have finished, if the solution is not beautiful, I know it is wrong."
—**R. Buckminster Fuller**

"Religion hinges upon faith, politics hinges upon who can tell the most convincing lies or maybe just shout the loudest, but science hinges upon whether its conclusions resemble what actually happens."
—**Ian Stewart**

"A goodly number of scientists are not only narrow-minded and dull, but also just stupid."
—**James D. Watson**

"Science has proof without any certainty. Creationists have certainty without any proof."
—**Ashley Montague**

Clarke's Law: "When a distinguished elder scientist states something is impossible, he is almost always wrong."
—**Arthur C. Clarke**

"Not only is the universe stranger than we think, it is stranger than we CAN think."
—**Werner Heisenberg**

"Science is but a perversion of itself unless it has as its ultimate goal the betterment of humanity."
—**Nikola Tesla**

"The goal of science is to build better mousetraps. The goal of nature is to build better mice."
—**Anonymous**

"In making theories, always keep a window open so you can throw one out if necessary."
—**Bela Schick**

"The visible world is the invisible organization of energy."
—**Heinz Pagels**

"If quantum mechanics hasn't profoundly shocked you, you haven't understood it yet."
—**Niels Bohr**

"Science is not a sacred cow. Science is a horse. Don't worship it. Feed it."
—**Abba Eban**

WHEN CELEBRITIES ATTACK

Celebrities are often at their unintentionally funniest when they're attacking other celebrities.

"You have your own ideas of what's country: I think Hank Williams is country. Garth Brooks may not be, you know? Ha ha ha. Nothing derogatory."
—**Willie Nelson**

"Clark Gable's ears make him look like a taxicab with both doors open."
—**Howard Hughes**

"Having Sean Penn as a marriage counselor is like taking sailing lessons from the captain of the *Titanic*."
—**Debra Winger,**
after husband Timothy
Hutton confided in Penn

"Katharine Hepburn runs the gamut of emotions from A to B."
—**Dorothy Parker**

"Plato was a bore."
—**Friedrich Nietzsche**

"John Barrymore was conspicuously unclean and smelled highly on occasions."
—**David Niven**

"The Beatles are not merely awful; they are so unbelievably horrible, so appallingly unmusical, so dogmatically insensitive to the magic of the art, that they qualify as crowned heads of anti-music."
—**William F. Buckley**

"Elizabeth Taylor is so fat, she puts mayonnaise on an aspirin."
—**Joan Rivers**

"Led Zeppelin is just a bunch of stupid idiots who wrote cool riffs."
—**Chris Cornell,**
of Soundgarden

"Rosie Perez? I don't think I could spend eight or ten weeks on a movie with her. Her voice would drive me back to heroin."
—**Charlie Sheen**

"Bette [Davis] and I are good friends. There's nothing I wouldn't say to her face—both of them."
—**Tallulah Bankhead**

Masai warriors considered it an act of kindness to spit at each other.

DUMB PREDICTIONS

Uncle John predicts you'll laugh at least once when
you read this page (and you'll eat some cheese).

ENTERTAINMENT

Prediction: "They've got their own groups. What are we going to give them that they don't already have?"
—**Paul McCartney, shortly before the Beatles arrived in the United States**

Prediction: "A flash in the pan."
—*Billboard* **magazine's 1983 review of Madonna**

Prediction: "I hear Carolina's going to start a freshman, and I know you can't win a national championship with a freshman."
—**Al McGuire, basketball analyst, shortly before freshman Michael Jordan led the North Carolina Tarheels to an NCAA championship in 1981**

POLITICS

Prediction: "Hitler is a queer fellow who will never become chancellor; the best he can hope for is to head the Postal Department."
—**Field Marshal Paul von Hindenburg, president of Germany, 1931**

WAR

Prediction: "No matter what happens, the U.S. Navy is not going to be caught napping."
—**Frank Knox, secretary of the Navy, December 4, 1941**

TECHNOLOGY

Prediction: "Knife and pain are two words that in surgery must forever be associated."
—**Alfred Velpeau, French surgeon, commenting about anesthesia, 1839**

EXPLORATION

Prediction: "I must confess that my imagination, in spite even of spurring, refuses to see any sort of submarine doing anything except suffocating its crew and floundering at sea."
—**H. G. Wells**

Prediction: "Man will not fly for 50 years."
—**Wilbur Wright, 1901**

Prediction: "Space travel is utter bilge."
—**Richard van der riet Wooller, Space advisor to the British government, 1956**

"To see what is right and not do it is want of courage." —Confucius

FEELING LUCKY?

*We couldn't decide whether to include this
page or not, so we flipped a coin. (You lost.)*

"The only sure thing about luck is that it will change."
—**Wilson Mizner**

"It's choice—not chance—that determines your destiny."
—**Jean Nidetch**

"Success is simply a matter of luck. Ask any failure."
—**Earl Wilson**

"Chance is always powerful. Let your hook be always cast in the pool where you least expect it. There will be a fish."
—**Ovid**

"It's a funny thing: the more I practice, the luckier I get."
—**Arnold Palmer**

"A black cat crossing your path signifies that the animal is going somewhere."
—**Groucho Marx**

WE ARE FAMILY

Everybody's got strong feelings about their family. These folks certainly do.

"If you have an enormous nose, I suppose you can have an operation to make it smaller, but you can't operate away an undesirable family member."
—John Simon

"Having a family is like having a bowling alley installed in your brain."
—Martin Mull

"Big sisters are the crabgrass on the lawn of life."
—Linus Van Pelt, *Peanuts*

"I grew up to have my father's looks, my father's speech patterns, my father's posture, my father's walk, my father's opinions—and my mother's contempt for my father."
—Jules Feiffer

"I come from a typical American family. You know, me, my mother, her third husband, his daughter from a second marriage, my step-sister, her illegitimate son."
—Carol Henry

"When I was growing up, there were two things that were unpopular in my family. One was me, and the other was my guitar."
—Bruce Springsteen

"The family—that dear octopus from whose tentacles we never quite escape nor, in our innermost hearts, ever quite wish to."
—Dodie Smith

THE LATE SHOW WITH...

*David Letterman, the funniest former
Indianapolis weatherman on television.*

"Listen to this. This will make you feel old. Corn Flakes is 100 years old today. I was thinking about this—the only other 100-year-old flake I know is Shirley MacLaine."

After open heart surgery:
"Ladies and gentlemen, after what I've been through, I am happy just to be wearing clothes that open in front."

"A professor at Johns Hopkins has come forth with an intriguing thought about a perennial question: he says that if an infinite number of monkeys sat typing at an infinite number of typewriters, the smell in the room would be unbearable."

"Tourists, have some fun with New York's hard-boiled cabbies. When you get to your destination, say to your driver, 'Pay? I was hitchhiking.'"

"Every year when it's Chinese New Year in New York, there are fireworks going off all hours. New York mothers calm their frightened children by telling them it's just gunfire."

"There's no business like show business, but there are several businesses like accounting."

"On my gravestone, I want it to say, 'I told you I was sick.'" —Tom Waits

CUPPA JOE

If you like the Bathroom Readers, *you can thank coffee—
because without it, we'd never get a book to press.*

"I believe humans get a lot done, not because we're smart, but because we have thumbs so we can make coffee."
—**Flash Rosenberg**

"Behind every successful woman…is a substantial amount of coffee."
—**Stephanie Piro**

"I've taken up meditation. I like to have an espresso first to make it more challenging."
—**Betsy Salkind**

"Coffee has two virtues: it is wet and warm."
—**Dutch proverb**

"When I wake up in the morning, I just can't get started until I've had that first, piping hot pot of coffee. Oh, I've tried other enemas…"
—**Emo Philips**

"I have measured out my life with coffee spoons."
—**T. S. Eliot**

"Decaffeinated coffee is kind of like kissing your sister."
—**Bob Irwin**

"Coffee leads men to trifle away their time, scald their chops, and spend their money, all for a little base, black, thick, nasty, bitter, stinking, nauseous puddle water."
—**The Women's Petition Against Coffee, 1674**

"The best maxim I know in this life is, to drink your coffee when you can, and when you cannot, to be easy without it."
—**Jonathan Swift**

"Black coffee must be strong and very hot; if strong coffee does not agree with you, do not drink black coffee. And if you do not drink black coffee, do not drink any coffee at all."
—**Andre Simon**

"Coffee should be as black as hell, strong as death, and sweet as love."
—**Christopher Fry**

After being warned that coffee is a slow poison:
"It must be slow, for I have been drinking it for sixty-five years and I am not yet dead."
—**Voltaire**

> "The voodoo priest and all his powders were as nothing compared to espresso, cappuccino, and mocha, which are stronger than all the religions of the world combined, and perhaps stronger than the human soul itself."
>
> **—Mark Helprin**

CELEBRITY BLOWHARDS

Blah, blah, blah, blah. Ain't I great?
Blah, blah, blah. Ain't I great?

"I've got a talent to act. No matter what any newspaper says about me, I am one of the most sensitive human beings on Earth, and I know it."
—**Jean-Claude Van Damme**

"I considered myself and still consider myself the hippest man on the planet."
—**Barry Manilow**

"A select group of my class-mates thought I was more interesting than anything in the classroom."
—**Bruce Willis**

"I am a great mayor; I am an upstanding Christian man; I am an intelligent man; I am a deeply educated man; I am a humble man.
—**Marion Barry**

"The guy I was reading with got lost because he was so busy watching me."
—**Samuel L. Jackson,**
describing his audition
for *Pulp Fiction*

"I consider Madonna a good friend, and she sure knows how to work that publicity machine. Of course, I don't have breasts. If I did, I'd be in the number one spot over Madonna."
—**Spike Lee**

"I know I am God because when I pray to him I find I'm talking to myself."
—**Peter Barnes**

"When asked whether or not he believed in God:
"We've never been intimate—but maybe we do have a few things in common."
—**Noel Coward**

"When I'm doing well, I like to think I'm doing God's work."
—**Faye Dunaway**

"I don't know what my calling is, but I want to be here for a bigger reason. I strive to be like the greatest people who have ever lived. Like Jesus."
—**Will Smith**

"After thirty, a body has a mind of its own." —Bette Midler

DOWNERS

These people need a hug.

"I am the kind of woman I would run from."
—**Lady Nancy Astor**

"I try to fill the emptiness deep inside me with Cheetos, but I am still depressed. Only now my fingers are stained orange. I am blue. And I am orange."
—**Karen Salmansohn**

"I was sent to bed at 7:30 until I was 10 and thought that it was normal. I finally asked my mother why she made me go to bed so early and she said, 'By 7:30, I couldn't listen to you anymore.'"
—**Fran Lebowitz**

"I knew I was an unwanted baby when I saw that my bath toys were a toaster and a radio."
—**Joan Rivers**

"I've been trying to find ways to overcome my inferiority complex. I considered therapy, till I saw the listings in the yellow pages: 'Abusive Relationships,' 'Eating Disorders,' 'Drug Addiction.' I only have low self-esteem. Even my problems aren't good enough."
—**Anita Wise**

"I'm a particularly loathsome guest and I eat like a vulture. Unfortunately, the resemblance doesn't end there."
—**Groucho Marx**

"I was so ugly when I was born, the doctor slapped my mother."
—**Rodney Dangerfield**

"I look like a duck."
—**Michelle Pfeiffer**

*　　*　　*

"I'm so damned unlucky that if I died and got reincarnated, I'd probably come back as myself."
—**Freddy Fender**

"None of us ever voted for Roosevelt or Truman." —epitaph on a family plot in Elgin, Minnesota

HOMER RULES

*If you have to ask, "Homer who?",
you're not watching enough TV.*

"My job is my identity. If I'm not a safety whats-a-ma-jigger, I'm nothing!"

Homer: "For you, a baby's all fun and games—for me it's all diaper changes and midnight feedings."
Lisa: "Doesn't Mom do that stuff?"
Homer: "Yeah, but I have to hear about it."

"All right, brain. You don't like me and I don't like you, but let's just do this and I can get back to killing you with beer."

"You never know when an old calendar might come in handy! Sure, it's not 1985 right now, but who knows what tomorrow will bring?"

"Donuts. Is there anything they can't do?"

"America's health care system is second only to Japan... Canada, Sweden, Great Britain...well, all of Europe. But you can thank your lucky stars we don't live in Paraguay!"

"To be loved, you have to be nice to others EVERYDAY! To be hated, you don't have to do squat."

"What is a wedding? Webster's Dictionary defines a wedding as 'The process of removing weeds from one's garden.'"

"I saw this movie about a bus that had to SPEED around a city, keeping its SPEED over fifty, and if its SPEED dropped, it would explode! I think it was called *The Bus That Couldn't Slow Down.*"

"Marge! Look at all this great stuff I found at the Marina. It was just sitting in some guy's boat!"

"I hope I didn't brain my damage."

"Dear Lord, the gods have been good to me. As an offering, I present these milk and cookies. If you wish me to eat them instead, please give me no sign whatsoever....Thy will be done."

GOOD vs. EVIL

Who will win?

"All that is necessary for evil to triumph is for good men to do nothing."
—**Edmund Burke**

"The only good is knowledge and the only evil is ignorance."
—**Socrates**

"Goodness without wisdom invariably accomplishes evil."
—**Robert Heinlein**

"It is a man's own mind, not his enemy or foe, that lures him to evil ways."
—**Buddha**

"I've found that evil usually triumphs, unless good is very, very careful."
—**Dr. McCoy,**
Star Trek

"I refuse to accept the view that mankind is so tragically bound to the starless midnight of racism and war that the bright daybreak of peace and brotherhood can never become reality. I believe that unarmed truth and unconditional love will have the final word in reality. That is why right, temporarily defeated, is stronger than evil triumphant."
—**Martin Luther King, Jr.**

"Evil will always triumph, because good is dumb." —Dark Helmet, *Spaceballs*

TALKIN' 'BOUT COUNTRY MUSIC

You don't have to have lost your job, your girl, or your dog to appreciate country music…but it helps.

"I spent the early part of my life looking at the north end of a southbound mule, and it didn't take long to figure out that a guitar was a lot lighter than a plow."
—Glen Campbell

"Country is soul music for white people."
—Paul Shaffer

"I couldn't go pop with a mouthful of firecrackers."
—Waylon Jennings

"I still love those (drinking) songs. There's a lot of feeling in those types of songs. It's almost like a cheating song."
—George Jones

"There are a lot of good-looking women in country music right now, and I like that."
—Johnny Cash

"I love the sound of co-dependence wafting over the prairie."
—Carol Steinel

"It's a lonely business, bein' ballsy."
—Tanya Tucker

"If you want to try something unusual, try passin' out in front of five thousand people."
—Loretta Lynn

"To me, the word 'rules' was just something to rhyme with fools."
—Merle Haggard

"All my songs are about sex. Nashville likes to pretend it doesn't exist. They should loosen up. Everyone's doing it. Aren't they?"
—Mindy McCready

"If you talk bad about country music, it's like saying bad things about my momma. Them's fightin' words."
—Dolly Parton

"It's mysterious and dark and sort of biblical, and it's really the story of our country. It's our heritage."
—Beck

MUHAMMAD ALI

They don't call him "The Greatest" for nothing.

"Service to others is the rent you pay for your room here on Earth."

"It's just a job. Grass grows, birds fly, waves pound the sand. I beat people up."

"It's lack of faith that makes people afraid of meeting challenges, and I believe in myself."

"The man who has no imagination has no wings."

Calling his Parkinson's Disease a blessing:
"I always liked to chase the girls. Parkinson's stops all that. Now I might have a chance to go to heaven."

"Champions aren't made in gyms. Champions are made from something they have deep inside them: a desire, a dream, a vision. They have to have last-minute stamina, they have to be a little faster, they have to have the skill and the will. But the will must be stronger than the skill."

"The only difference between a madman and me is that I'm not mad."

"War on nations change maps. War on poverty maps change."

"Only a man who knows what it is like to be defeated can reach down to the bottom of his soul and come up with the extra ounce of power it takes to win when the match is even."

"I know I got it made while the masses of black people are catchin' hell, but as long as they ain't free, I ain't free."

"I am America. I am the part you won't recognize. But get used to me. Black, confident, cocky; my name, not yours; my religion, not yours; my goals, my own; get used to me."

"I hated every minute of training, but I said, 'Don't quit. Suffer now and live the rest of your life as a champion.'"

Marilyn Monroe was 1947 Miss California Artichoke Queen.

THAT'S DEATH

You're dying to read this page, aren't you?

"The trouble with quotes about death is that 99.99 percent of them are made by people who are still alive."
—**Joshua Bruns**

"After a year of therapy, my psychiatrist said to me, 'Maybe life isn't for everyone.'"
—**Larry Brown**

"No matter how big you get, the size of your funeral depends on the weather."
—**Roger Miller**

"Once you're dead, you're beloved. You know, 'the late, great,' and 'what he did for our music.' But until then, it's always 'troublemakin' son of a bitch."
—**Waylon Jennings**

"Millions long for immortality who do not know what to do with themselves on a rainy Sunday afternoon."
—**Susan Ertz**

"Dying is the most embarrassing thing that can ever happen to you, because someone else has got to take care of all your details."
—**Andy Warhol**

"Those who welcome death have only tried it from the ears up."
—**Wilson Mizner**

"I took a job as a grave digger because I thought it'd help me overcome my fear of death. When I started, the other guys in the cemetery initiated me by putting me in a coffin and closing the lid. That sacred the sh*t out of me—but I've had no fear of death since. It cured me."
—**Rod Stewart**

"There's something about death that is comforting, the thought that you could die tomorrow frees you to appreciate your life now."
—**Angelina Jolie**

"One death is a tragedy; a million deaths is a statistic."
—**Joseph Stalin**

"We are afraid to live, but scared to die."
—**Inderpal Bahra**

"Death is an intellectual matter, but dying is pure pain."
—**John Steinbeck**

A French executioner was once fired because he pawned his guillotine.

"Many an ancient lord's last words have been, 'You can't kill me because I've got magic aaargh.'"
—**Terry Pratchett**

"Of all escape mechanisms, death is the most efficient."
—**Henry Ward Beecher**

"Death is nothing to us, since when we are, death has not come, and when death has come, we are not."
—**Epicurus**

"Death will be a great relief. No more interviews."
—**Katharine Hepburn**

"Life levels all men. Death reveals the eminent."
—**George Bernard Shaw**

"Death is more universal than life; everyone dies but not everyone lives."
—**A. Sachs**

"Death twitches my ear. 'Live,' he says, 'I am coming.'"
—**Virgil**

*   *   *

"I'm looking forward to the most fascinating experience of my life, which is dying. You've got to approach your dying the way you live your life—with curiosity, with hope, with fascination, and with courage."

—**Timothy Leary**

"Blessed are the young, for they shall inherit the national debt." —Herbert Hoover

RIGHT ON THE MARK

Question: What author is generally considered the first truly American novelist? Answer: Samuel Langhorne Clemens, a.k.a. Mark Twain.

"Wrinkles should merely indicate where smiles have been."

"Change is the handmaiden Nature requires to do her miracles with."

"I have too much respect for the truth to drag it out on every trifling occasion."

"Adam was the only man who, when he said a good thing, knew that nobody said it before him."

"I was sorry to have my name mentioned as one of the great authors, because they have a sad habit of dying off. Chaucer is dead, Spenser is dead, so is Milton, so is Shakespeare, and I'm not feeling so well myself."

"I have been complimented myself a great many times, and they always embarrass me— I always feel that they have not said enough."

"All you need in this life is ignorance and confidence; then success is sure."

"Time cools, time clarifies; no mood can be maintained quite unaltered through the course of hours."

"I can teach anybody how to get what they want out of life. The problem is that I can't find anybody who can tell me what they want."

"There is a charm about the forbidden that makes it unspeakably desirable."

One of David Bowie's eyes changed color after being stabbed with a compass in school.

YOU LIKE ME! YOU REALLY LIKE ME!

We asked Julie Andrews how it felt to be mentioned on this page. She said it was a thrill just to be nominated.

JULIE ANDREWS
Award: A Best Actress Oscar in 1964 for *Mary Poppins*
Excerpt: "I'd like to thank all those who made this possible—especially Jack L. Warner."

Background: The year before, Andrews had enjoyed great success starring in the Broadway version of *My Fair Lady*, but when Warner Bros. turned it into a film, they chose Audrey Hepburn for the lead. That meant that when the role of Mary Poppins was announced soon after, Andrews was free to take it.

LOUISE FLETCHER
Award: Best Supporting Actress Oscar for 1975's *One Flew Over the Cuckoo's Nest*
Excerpt: "I want to thank Jack Nicholson for making being in a mental institution like being in a mental institution."

YOGI BERRA
Award: The inauguration of "Yogi Berra Day" in St. Louis in 1947
Excerpt: "I want to thank all the people who made this night necessary."

PRINCE
Award: He was named Minnesota Musician of the Year in 1982.
Excerpt: "When do they give the award for Best Ass?"

NICK FALDO
Award: He won the 1992 British Open
Excerpt: "I would like to thank the press from the heart of my bottom."

SUPPOSEDLY SAID

*Because quoting what other people say is often like playing
a game of "telephone," what ends up in our collective
memory often isn't exactly what the speaker said.*

Who said it: Sally Field
She supposedly said: "You like me. You really like me!"
after receiving the Oscar for her role in 1983's *Places in
the Heart.*
Actually: Comedians making fun of Sally Field have said this a
lot, but what she said was, "I can't deny the fact that you like me.
Right now, you like me."

Who said it: Captain Kirk
He supposedly said: "Beam me up, Scotty."
Actually: Kirk said almost everything except the above phrase:
"Scotty, beam me up," "Beam us up, Scotty," and "One to beam
up, Scotty," but never once, "Beam me up, Scotty."

Who said it: Mae West
She supposedly said: "Is that a gun in your pocket, or are you just
glad to see me?"
Actually: She did say the line, but not in the film that it is most
often attributed to, 1933's *She Done Him Wrong.* The apocryphal
line became so associated with West, though, that she did utter it
in her final film, 1978's *Sextette.*

Who said it: The Voice in the 1989 film *Field of Dreams*
He supposedly said: "If you build it, they will come."
Actually: The Voice said, "If you build it, *he* will come."

Who said it: Sam Goldwyn
He supposedly said: "An oral contract isn't worth the paper it's
written on."
Actually: This clever comment was first said in 1912 by an Irish
attorney named J. C. Percy.

Monica Lewinsky's classmates voted her "Most Likely to Get Her Name in Lights."

Who said it: Queen Elizabeth I, on her death bed
She supposedly said: "All my possessions for a moment of time."
Actually: According to *www.elizabethi.org* (yes, even a queen dead for 400 years has a Web site), "The accounts of her death by witnesses do not mention these words. In all probability, Queen Elizabeth had lost the power of speech sometime before her death, and no one knows what her last words were."

Who said it: Lily Tomlin
She supposedly said: "Even if you win the rat race, you're still a rat."
Actually: Tomlin has said this, but it was first attributed to the Reverend William Sloane Coffin at Yale University.

*   *   *

OOPS!

At a 2002 Democratic fund raiser, Barbra Streisand said to the crowd, "You know, really good artists have a way of being relevant in their time, but great artists are relevant at any time. So in the words of William Shakespeare: 'Beware the leader who bangs the drums of war in order to whip the citizenry into a patriotic fervor, for patriotism is indeed a double-edged sword. It both emboldens the blood, just as it narrows the mind. And when the drums of war have reached a fever pitch and the blood boils with hate and the mind has closed, the leader will have no need in seizing the rights of the citizenry. How do I know? For this is what I have done. And I am Caesar.' "

One problem: the Bard never wrote those words. The quote came from a 2001 Web site dedicated to Shakespeare. It turned out that the site was a hoax. Streisand, after being told of the gaffe, tried to save face. "It doesn't detract from the fact that it is powerful and true and beautifully written. Whoever wrote it is damn talented. I hope he's writing his own play."

ON SHAKESPEARE

Everyone's got an opinion on the
Bard—even aliens from outer space.

"With the exception of Homer, there is no eminent writer, not even Sir Walter Scott, whom I can despise so entirely as I despise Shakespeare, when I measure my mind against his."
—George Bernard Shaw

"You can't appreciate Shakespeare until you've read him in the original Klingon."
—General Chang, *Star Trek VI*

"The remarkable thing about Shakespeare is that he really is very good—in spite of all the people who say he is very good."
—Robert Graves

"I mean, Hamlet is a great story. It's got some great things in it. I mean, there's something like eight violent deaths."
—Mel Gibson

"Hamlet has been played by 5,000 actors—no wonder he is crazy." —H. L. Mencken

MURPHY'S OTHER LAWS

Murphy's Law, named for Capt. Edward A. Murphy, Jr., an engineer for the U.S. Air Force in the 1940s, states that "If anything can go wrong, it will." Here are a few more "laws" just like it.

"What we anticipate seldom occurs; what we least expected generally happens."
—**Benjamin Disraeli**

"The longer one saves something before throwing it away, the sooner it will be needed after it is thrown away."
—**James J. Caufield**

"A shortcut is the longest distance between two points."
—**Charles Issawi**

"If it works, they'll stop making it."
—**Jane Otten**

"At the bank, post office, or supermarket, there is one universal law which you ignore at your own peril: the shortest line moves the slowest."
—**Bill Vaughan**

"Misquotations are the only quotations that are never misquoted."
—**Hesketh Pearson**

"Whenever A annoys or injures B on the pretense of saving or improving X, A is a scoundrel."
—**H. L. Mencken**

"The books that everybody admires are those that nobody reads."
—**Anatole France**

Jerry Springer worked on Robert Kennedy's presidential campaign staff.

FREE ADVICE

A page of people telling you what they think you should do.

"I have a simple philosophy: fill what's empty. Empty what's full. And scratch where it itches."
—**Alice Roosevelt Longworth**

"When things are bad and getting worse, keep a cookie in your purse."
—**Naomi Judd**

"Become who you are."
—**Friedrich Nietzsche**

"Stay busy, get plenty of exercise, and don't drink too much. Then again, don't drink too little."
—**Herman "Jackrabbit" Smith-Johannsen**

"When placed in command, take charge."
—**Norman Schwarzkopf**

"Desire, ask, believe, receive."
—**Stella Terrill Mann**

"The words 'I am...' are potent words; be careful what you hitch them to. The thing you're claiming has a way of reaching back and claiming you."
—**A. L. Kitselman**

"Expose yourself to your deepest fear; after that, fear has no power, and you are free."
—**Jim Morrison**

"If something is wrong, fix it if you can. But train yourself not to worry. Worry never fixes anything."
—**Mary Hemingway**

"Beware of advice, even this."
—**Carl Sandburg**

"I want to share something with you: three little sentences that'll get you through with life. 1. Cover for me. 2. Oh, good idea, boss. 3. It was like this when I got here."
—**Homer Simpson**

"Be sure to wear a good cologne, a nice aftershave lotion, and a strong underarm deodorant. And it might be a good idea to wear some clothes, too."
—**George Burns**

"It is useless to hold a person to anything he says while he's in love, drunk, or running for office."
—**Shirley MacLaine**

"I promise every German girl a husband." —**Adolph Hitler**

REEL FUNNY

Colonel Mustard doesn't have a clue.

Colonel Mustard: Wadsworth, am I right in thinking there is nobody else in this house?

Wadsworth the Butler: Ummm, no.

Colonel Mustard: Then there is someone else in this house?

Wadsworth: No, sorry. I said no meaning yes.

Colonel Mustard: No meaning yes? Look, I want a straight answer. Is there someone else, or isn't there? Yes or no?

Wadsworth: Ummm, no.

Colonel Mustard: No there is, or no there isn't?

Wadsworth: Yes.

—Martin Mull and Tim Curry, *Clue* (1985)

EPITAPHS

*Uncle John's not dead, but he's already
written his epitaph: "Don't forget to flush."*

Against you I will
fling myself,
unvanquished and
unyielding,
O Death!
—**Virginia Woolf**

kata ton daimona eay toy
—**Jim Morrison**
{True to his own spirit.}

In loving memory
from the Family
—**Benjamin "Bugsy" Siegel**

Quoth the
Raven,
"Nevermore."
Edgar Allan Poe

Erected in the
memory of
John Phillips—
Accidentally shot
As a mark of affection
by his brother.

"Mankind is tired of liberty." —**Benito Mussolini**

WHAT'S UP, DOC?

"My doctor told me to watch my drinking. So now, I drink in front of a mirror." —Rodney Dangerfield

"We have not lost faith, but we have transferred it from God to the medical profession."
—**George Bernard Shaw**

"The wish for healing has always been half of health."
—**Lucius Annaeus Seneca**

"The first duties of the physician is to educate the masses not to take medicine."
—**William Osler**

"My kid is a born doctor. Nobody can read anything he writes."
—**Henry Youngman**

"He is the best physician who is the most ingenious inspirer of hope."
—**Samuel Taylor Coleridge**

"The art of medicine consists in amusing the patient while nature cures the disease."
—**Voltaire**

"Whenever a doctor cannot do good, he must be kept from doing harm."
—**Hippocrates**

"*The New England Journal of Medicine* reports that 9 out of 10 doctors agree that 1 out of 10 doctors is an idiot."
—**Jay Leno**

"Doctors are just the same as lawyers; the only difference is that lawyers merely rob you, whereas doctors rob and kill you, too."
—**Anton Chekhov**

"All them surgeons—they're highway robbers. Why do you think they wear masks when they work on you?"
—**Archie Bunker,** *All in the Family*

"Cured yesterday of my disease, I died last night of my physician."
—**Matthew Prior**

"The best doctors in the world are Doctor Diet, Doctor Quiet, and Doctor Merryman."
—**Jonathan Swift**

"Time is generally the best doctor."
—**Ovid**

TEE TIME

Mark Twain described the game of golf as "a good walk spoiled." But that doesn't matter to these folks.

"When I play my best golf, I feel as if I'm in a fog, standing back watching the Earth in orbit with a club in my hands."
—**Mickey Wright**

"That's when you know you're weird."
—**John Ellis, saying that he enjoyed golf so much, he even requested *Golf Digest* for bedtime stories when he was three years old**

"I play in the low 80s. Any hotter than that, I won't play."
—**Joe E. Louis**

"A hole in one is amazing when you think of the different universes this white mass of molecules has to pass through on its way to the hole."
—**Mac O'Grady**

"You can talk to a fade but a hook won't listen."
—**Lee Trevino**

"To be truthful, I think golfers are overpaid. It's unreal, and I have trouble dealing with the guilt sometimes."
—**Colin Montgomerie**

"No matter what happens, never give up a hole.... In tossing in your cards after a bad beginning you also undermine your whole game, because to quit between tee and green is more habit-forming than drinking a highball before breakfast."
—**Sam Snead**

"Don't be in such a hurry. That little white ball isn't going to run away from you."
—**Patty Berg**

"There's an old saying, 'It's a poor craftsman who blames his tools.' It's usually the player who misses those three-footers, not the putter."
—**Kathy Whitworth**

"Through years of experience I have found that air offers less resistance than dirt."
—**Jack Nicklaus on why he tees his ball high**

"If I had cleared the trees and drove the green, it would've been a great shot."
—**Sam Snead**

UNCLE JOHN'S QUOTATIONARY

Here's Part 3 of our quotation dictionary.
(Part 2 begins on page 84.)

EARNESTNESS: enthusiasm tempered by reason. (Blaise Pascal)

EARTH: the lunatic asylum of the solar system. (Samuel Parks Cadman)

ECONOMIST: an expert who will know tomorrow why the thing he predicted yesterday didn't happen today. (Laurence J. Peter)

ECSTASY: a drug so strong it makes white people think they can dance. (Lenny Henry)

EDITOR: a person employed by a newspaper whose business it is to separate the wheat from the chaff, and to see that the chaff is printed. (Elbert Hubbard)

EFFICIENCY: intelligent laziness. (David Dunham)

EGOTISM: the anesthetic that dulls the pain of stupidity. (Frank Leahy)

ELOQUENCE: the ability to describe Kim Basinger without using one's hands. (Michael Harkness)

ENVIRONMENT: everything that isn't me. (Albert Einstein)

EPITAPH: a belated advertisement for a line that has been discontinued. (Irvin S. Cobb)

EQUAL OPPORTUNITY: everyone will have a fair chance at being incompetent. (Laurence J. Peter)

ETIQUETTE: knowing how to yawn with your mouth closed. (Herbert Prochnow)

EVIL: good perverted. (Henry Wadsworth Longfellow)

EXAGGERATION: a truth that has lost its temper. (Kahlil Gibran)

EXCELLENCE: when a man asks of himself more than others do. (Jose Ortega y Gasset)

EXISTENCE: just a brief crack of light between two eternities of darkness. (Vladimir Nabokov)

EXPERIENCE: a comb life gives you after you lose your hair. (Judith Stern)

EXPERT: a man who has

stopped thinking—he knows!
(Frank Lloyd Wright)

FAITH: not wanting to know what is true. (Friedrich Nietzsche)

FAME: a perversion of the natural human instinct for attention. (Al Pacino)

FAN CLUB: a group of people who tell an actor he is not alone in the way he feels about himself. (Jack Carson)

FANATIC: one who can't change his mind and won't change the subject. (Winston Churchill)

FIDELITY: putting all your eggs in one bastard. (Dorothy Parker)

FILM: the world seen from inside. (Don Delillo)

FINANCE: the art of passing currency from hand to hand until it finally disappears. (Robert Sarnoff)

FLASHLIGHT: a case for holding dead batteries. (Anonymous)

FLATTERER: one who says things to your face that he wouldn't dare say behind your back. (George Millington)

FLORIDA: God's waiting room. (Glenn le Grice)

FOOL: anybody who feels at ease in the world today. (Robert Maynard Hutchins)

FORK: an instrument used chiefly for the purpose of putting dead animals into the mouth. (Ambrose Bierce)

FREE SOCIETY: a place where it's safe to be unpopular. (Adlai Stevenson)

FREEDOM: another word for nothing left to lose. (Kris Kristofferson)

FREUDIAN SLIP: when you say one thing, but you're really thinking about a mother. (Cliff Claven, *Cheers*)

FUTURE: that period of time in which our affairs prosper, our friends are true, and our happiness is assured. (Ambrose Bierce)

For more, see page 162.

*   *   *

"There have only been two geniuses in the world. Willie Mays and Willie Shakespeare."

—**Tallulah Bankhead**

"**They can't get you for what you didn't say.**" —Calvin Coolidge

ODE TO PLUMBERS

In Uncle John's world, plumbers rank right up there with presidents and kings—higher, actually—because without plumbers, we'd have no place to read.

"An excellent plumber is infinitely more admirable than an incompetent philosopher. The society that scorns excellence in plumbing just because plumbing is a humble activity, and tolerates shoddiness in philosophy because it is an exalted activity, will have neither good plumbing nor good philosophy. Neither its pipes nor its philosophy will hold water."

—**John William Gardner**

"Everyone likes to think that in the past everything was so quaint, so charming. It's a fairy tale. Life sucked then, too—it just sucked without indoor plumbing!"

—**Scott Patterson,**
Gilmore Girls

"Anybody who has any doubt about the ingenuity or the resourcefulness of a plumber never got a bill from one."

—**George Meany**

"In Cleveland there is legislation moving forward to ban people from wearing pants that fit too low. However, there is lots of opposition from the plumbers' union."

—**Conan O'Brien**

"A plumber never bites his nails."

—**American proverb**

"If I had my life to live over again, I'd be a plumber."

—**Albert Einstein**

*   *   *

"Love: a burnt match skating in the urinal."

—**Hart Crane**

"There is no question that our health has improved spectacularly in the past century. One thing seems certain: it did not happen because of medicine, or medical science, or even the presence of doctors. Much of the credit should go to the plumbers and engineers of the western world. The contamination of drinking water by human feces was at one time the greatest cause of human disease and death for us, but when the plumbers and sanitary engineers had done their work in the construction of our cities, these diseases began to vanish."

**—Lewis Thomas,
medical researcher**

PUN-ISHMENT

Puns appeal to children—that's why they make you groan. Get it? Groan, grown? Oh, forget it.

"You can't make a *Hamlet* without breaking a few egos."
—William Goldman, screenwriter

"If I had a good quote, I'd be wearing it."
—Bob Dylan, when asked for a 'good quote' by a French journalist on a cold night

"My cousin Seymour the dentist married a manicurist, and they're not getting along. They keep fighting tooth and nail."
—Joan Rivers

"Carpe per diem: seize the check."
—Robin Williams

"A critic is one who goes along for deride."
—L. L. Levinson

"I went to a cross-dressing store: 'Susan Be Anthony.'"
—Zach Galifianakis

"Seven days without laughter make one weak."
—Joel Goodman

"A metallurgist is someone who can look at a platinum blonde and tell whether she's virgin material or a common ore."
—Brian Johnson

"The days of the digital watch are numbered."
—Tom Stoppard

"I don't trust him. We're friends." —Bertolt Brecht

> "No one will ever win the battle of the sexes; there's too much fraternizing with the enemy."
> —Henry Kissinger

Jerry Seinfeld turned down $5 million per episode to continue *Seinfeld* past 1998.

BATTLE OF THE SEXES: ROUND 2

Ladies and gentlemen! Can't we all just get along?

"Woman was God's second mistake."
—**Friedrich Nietzsche**

"I love the male body. It's better designed than the male mind."
—**Andrea Newman**

"Women are the most powerful magnet in the universe. And all men are cheap metal. And we all know where north is."
—**Larry Miller**

"The main difference between men and women is that men are lunatics and women are idiots."
—**Rebecca West**

"Fooling a man ain't all that hard. Finding one that ain't a fool is a lot harder."
—**Gladiola Montana**

"Woman begins by resisting a man's advances and ends by blocking his retreat."
—**Oscar Wilde**

"Women are absolutely equal. They just can't lift as much."
—**David Lee Roth**

"The more I see of men, the more I like dogs."
—**Madame Roland, French revolutionary**

"I hate women because they always know where things are."
—**James Thurber**

"A woman's mind is cleaner than a man's; she changes it more often."
—**Oliver Herford**

"Men are such a combination of good and evil."
—**Jacqueline Kennedy Onassis**

"Women should have labels on their foreheads saying, 'Government Health Warning: women can seriously damage your brains, genitals, bank account, confidence, razor blades, and good standing among your friends.' "
—**Jeffrey Bernard**

"Men and women. Women and men. It will never work."
—**Erica Jong**

"Some of my best friends are MX missiles." —Ronald Reagan

IT'S LIKE...A SIMILE

A simile is a figure of speech in which two dissimilar elements are compared using the words "like" or "as."

"Writing about music is like dancing about architecture."
—Elvis Costello

"Dressing a pool player in a tuxedo is like putting whipped cream on a hot dog."
—Minnesota Fats

"Wearing swimsuits is a sport like ketchup is a vegetable."
—Rita Rudner

"Trying to get the presidency to work is like trying to sew buttons on a custard pie."
—James D. Barber

"Naming a national forest after Ronald Reagan is like naming a day-care center after W. C. Fields."
—Bob Hattoy

"Giving money and power to government is like giving whiskey and car keys to teenage boys."
—P. J. O'Rourke

"Eating responsibly at McDonald's is like going to a strip club for the iced tea."
—Roger Ebert

"Sex at 90 is like playing pool with a rope."
—Camille Paglia

"To explain responsibility to advertising men is like trying to convince an eight-year-old that sexual intercourse is more fun than a chocolate ice cream cone."
—Howard Luck Gossage

"Alimony is like buying oats for a dead horse."
—Arthur 'Bugs' Baer

"Hubert Humphrey talks so fast that listening to him is like trying to read *Playboy* with your wife turning the pages."
—Barry Goldwater

"Trying to sneak a fastball past Hank Aaron is like trying to sneak the sunrise past a rooster."
—Joe Adcock

"Trying to predict the future is like trying to drive down a country road at night with no lights while looking out the back window."
—Peter F. Drucker

OPINIONS ON ELVIS

*Love him or hate him, everybody
has an opinion on the King.*

"He's that fella we see every now and then on television, shakin' and screamin' kinda like somebody's beatin' his dog."
—**Sheriff Andy Taylor,**
The Andy Griffith Show

"It isn't enough to say that Elvis is kind to his parents, sends money home, and is the same unspoiled kid he was before all the commotion began. That still isn't a free ticket to behave like a sex maniac in public."
—**Eddie Condon, jazz guitarist (1956)**

"I'm not putting Elvis down, but he was a sh*t*ss, a yellow belly, and I hated him, the f***er."
—**Jerry Lee Lewis**

"If it hadn't been for Elvis, I'd probably be driving a snowplow in Minneapolis."
—**Prince**

COSMIC THOUGHTS

NASA scientist, astronomer, author, and host of PBS's Cosmos, Carl Sagan introduced a nation of viewers to the wonders of the universe.

"It is the tension between creativity and skepticism that has produced the stunning and unexpected findings of science."

"Our species needs, and deserves, a citizenry with minds wide awake and a basic understanding of how the world works."

"Philosophers and scientists confidently offer up traits said to be uniquely human, and the monkeys and apes casually knock them down—toppling the pretension that humans constitute some sort of biological aristocracy among the beings on Earth."

"I would love to believe that when I die I will live again, that some thinking, feeling, remembering part of me will continue. But as much as I want to believe that, and despite the ancient and worldwide cultural traditions that assert an afterlife, I know of nothing to suggest that it is more than wishful thinking. The world is so exquisite with so much love and moral depth, that there is no reason to deceive ourselves with pretty stories for which there's little good evidence. Far better it seems to me, in our vulnerability, is to look death in the eye and to be grateful every day for the brief but magnificent opportunity that life provides."

"Finding the occasional straw of truth awash in a great ocean of confusion requires intelligence, vigilance, dedication, and courage. But if we don't practice these tough habits of thought, we cannot hope to solve the truly serious problems that face us—and we risk becoming a nation of suckers, up for grabs by the next charlatan who comes along."

"Science is a way of thinking much more than it is a body of knowledge."

"Except for children (who don't know enough not to ask the important questions), few of us spend time wondering why nature is the way it is."

"My philosophy is: Don't think." —Charles Manson

BEAM ME UP, SCOTTY

The original Star Trek *only ran for three years, and its ratings were never very good, yet it's gone on to become one of the most influential shows of all time.*

Kirk: Well there it is…war. We didn't want it, but we've got it.
Spock: Curious how often you humans manage to obtain that which you do not want.

McCoy: Does your logic find this fascinating, Mr Spock?
Spock: 'Fascinating' is a word I use for the unexpected. In this case, I should think 'interesting' would suffice.

"I have never understood the female capacity to avoid a direct answer to any question."
—Spock

"You Earth people glorified organized violence for forty centuries—but you imprison those who employ it privately."
—Spock

"One of the advantages of being a captain is being able to ask for advice without necessarily having to take it."
—Kirk

Jenna: So, I'm just a new variable in one of your new computational environments.
Data: You are much more than that, Jenna. I have written a program specifically for you—a program within a program. I have devoted a considerable share of my internal resources to its development.
Jenna: That's the nicest thing anyone's ever said to me.

"Could you please continue the petty bickering? I find it most intriguing."
—Data

"Conquest is easy. Control is not."
—Kirk

*   *   *

"I absolutely hated the '60s. The only good thing that came from the '60s was *Star Trek*."
—Frank Sinatra, Jr.

Jay Leno and David Letterman were both writers for the TV show *Good Times*.

SPEAK YOUR MIND

Just because they're famous, does that mean they have something to say? No...but that's often what makes what they do say interesting.

"Take me or leave me. Or as most people do: both."
—Dorothy Parker

"If he were here, I'd ask him if I could lick his eyeballs."
—**Christian Slater, about his idol, Jack Nicholson**

"It was not my class of people. There was not a producer, a press agent, a director, an actor."
—**Zsa Zsa Gabor, on the jury that convicted her of slapping a Beverly Hills police officer who pulled her over**

"Minks are mean little critters. Vicious, horrible little animals who eat their own. They're not beavers. I wouldn't wear beavers. I'd rather have a mink coat made of mean little critters that are killed in a very nice way and treated nicely their short, mean lives so that I could keep warm."
—**Valerie Perrine**

"If you can't say anything good about someone, sit right here by me."
—**Alice Roosevelt Longworth**

"There are three intolerable things in life—cold coffee, lukewarm champagne, and overexcited women."
—**Orson Welles**

"Give me the luxuries of life and I will willingly do without the necessities."
—**Frank Lloyd Wright**

"I believe in looking reality straight in the eye and denying it."
—**Garrison Keillor**

"It's too bad I'm not as wonderful a person as people say I am, because the world could use a few people like that."
—**Alan Alda**

"Why doesn't everybody just leave everybody else the hell alone?"
—**Jimmy Durante**

"I don't believe in astrology; I'm a Sagittarian and we're skeptical."
—**Arthur C. Clarke**

"I love mankind; it's people I can't stand."
—**Charles Schultz**

Gerald Ford worked as a fashion model.

CHARLIE BROWN, INSOMNIAC

Poor, good ol' Charlie Brown. His depression and rotten luck somehow made us feel better about ourselves.

Sometimes I lie awake at night and ask, "Where have I gone wrong?" Then a voice says to me, "This is going to take more than one night."

Sometimes I lie awake at night, and I ask, "Is life a multiple choice test, or is it a true or false test?" Then a voice comes out of the dark and says: "We hate to tell you this, but life is a thousand-word essay."

Sometimes I lie awake at night and I ask, "Why me?" And the voice says, "Nothing personal, your name just happened to come up."

Sometimes I lie awake at night and I ask, "Is it all worth it?" And then a voice says, "Who are you talking to?" And another voice says, "You mean: to whom are you talking?" And I say, "No wonder I lie awake at night."

Never lie in bed at night asking yourself questions you can't answer.

*   *   *

PEANUTS TRIVIA

Why do the kids on the "Peanuts" animated cartoons have that stilted speaking style? The voice actors on *A Charlie Brown Christmas* (1965) were all children, so they learned their lines phonetically, often not understanding their meanings.

JESUS OF NAZARETH

Historians say Jesus died in 33 A.D. and the first of the Gospels was written around 70 A.D. Here are some of the sayings attributed to Him.

"Ask and it will be given to you; seek and you will find; knock and the door will be opened to you."

"You have heard that it was said, 'Eye for eye, and tooth for tooth.' But I tell you, do not resist an evil person. If someone strikes you on the right cheek, turn to him the other also."

"I tell you, my friends, do not be afraid of those who kill the body and after that can do no more. But I will show you whom you should fear: fear him who, after the killing of the body, has power to throw you into hell."

"The good man brings good things out of the good stored up in his heart, and the evil man brings evil things out of the evil stored up in his heart."

"Out of the overflow of his heart his mouth speaks."

"No one lights a lamp and puts it in a place where it will be hidden. He puts it on its stand, so that those who come in may see the light."

"Do not worry about tomorrow, for tomorrow will worry about itself. Each day has enough trouble of its own."

"For everyone who exalts himself will be humbled, and he who humbles himself will be exalted."

"What shall it profit a man if he gains the whole world but loses his soul?"

"It is easier for a camel to pass through the eye of a needle than for a rich man to enter the Kingdom of Heaven."

ABOUT JESUS

"A man who was completely innocent offered himself as a sacrifice for the good of others, including his enemies, and became the ransom of the world. It was a perfect act."

—Mahatma Gandhi

"Christ was a punk rocker." —Billy Idol

DOLLY...OR DALI?

Quiz time. Some of the quotes below were said by Dolly Parton, the famous country singer; others were said by Salvador Dali, the famous Surrealist painter. And just for kicks, we threw one in there from His Holiness the Dalai Lama. Have fun.

1. "The way I see it, if you want the rainbow, you gotta put up with the rain."

2. "I don't do drugs. I am drugs."

3. "Democratic societies are unfit for the publication of such thunderous revelations as I am in the habit of making."

4. "We never actually starved, but sometimes we never had quite enough to eat."

5. "I seated ugliness on my knee, and almost immediately grew tired of it."

6. "When I'm inspired, I get excited because I can't wait to see what I'll come up with next."

7. "When people say less is more, I say more is more. Less is less. I want more."

8. "It is good taste, and good taste alone, that possesses the power to sterilize and is always the first handicap to any creative functioning."

9. "There are some days when I think I'm going to die from an overdose of satisfaction."

10. "Even though a bird can fly, it must land on Earth."

11. "I may be an eagle when I fly, but I'm a sparrow when it comes to feelings."

12. "Intelligence without ambition is a bird without wings."

ANSWERS

1. Dolly Parton; 2. Salvador Dali; 3. Salvador Dali; 4. Dolly Parton; 5. Salvador Dali; 6. Dolly Parton; 7. Dolly Parton; 8. Salvador Dali; 9. Salvador Dali; 10. the Dalai Lama; 11. Dolly Parton; 12. Salvador Dali

"The biggest sin is sitting on your ass." —Florynce Kennedy

WRITERS ON WRITING

It's interesting to see what writers have to say about their craft.

"A bad book is as much of a labor to write as a good one."
—Aldous Huxley

"If you want to get rich from writing, write the sort of thing that's read by persons who move their lips when reading."
—Don Marquis

"The most essential gift for a writer is a built-in, shockproof sh*t-detector. This is the writer's radar and all great writers have it."
—Ernest Hemingway

"At the end of every book, I feel like killing myself. You think you'll never write one again. Until you use up the advance money."
—Erica Jong

"I like being a famous writer. Problem is, every once in a while, you have to write something."
—Ken Kesey

"No man would set a word down on paper if he had the courage to live out what he believed in."
—Henry Miller

"People always ask me about *The Godfather*, about whether it's my favorite book....The more money I make from it, the better a book I think it is."
—Mario Puzo

"Nothing a man writes can please him as profoundly as something he does with his back, shoulders, and hands. For writing is an artificial activity."
—Brooks Atkinson

"If it sounds like writing, I rewrite it."
—Elmore Leonard

"A kid is a guy I never wrote down to. He's interested in what I say if I make it interesting."
—Dr. Seuss

"If there's a book you really want to read, but it hasn't been written yet, you must write it."
—Toni Morrison

"After writing for 15 years, it struck me that I had no talent for writing. I couldn't give it up. By that time I was already famous."
—Mark Twain

SCHOTT IN THE FOOT

*Some sports personalities are famous for their arms
(Roger Clemens or maybe Barry Bonds); others
for their legs (David Beckham). Marge Schott,
former owner of the Cincinnati Reds, is one
of the few who was famous for her mouth.*

"Only fruits wear earrings."
—**Explaining the club ban on
wearing earrings on the field**

"Everybody knows he was
good at the beginning, but he
just went too far."
—**on Adolf Hitler,
in a 1996 interview**

"Well, I don't like it when
they come here, honey, and
stay so long and then outdo
our kids. That's not right."
—**on Asian-Americans**

"I don't know why we need
them. All they do is watch
baseball games."
—**explaining why she didn't
think scouts were important**

"Pets are always there for you.
They never ask for anything.
They never ask for a raise.
They're very special."
—**announcing that her St.
Bernard, Schottzie, had died**

"Why do they care about one
game when they're watching
another?"
—**after fans complained
that one of her cost-
cutting moves resulted in
elimination of updates
on the scoreboard**

"Some of the biggest problems
in this city come from women
wanting to leave the home
and work. Why do these girl
reporters have to come in the
locker room? Why can't they
wait outside? ...I don't really
think baseball is a woman's
place, honey. I really don't. I
really think it should be left
to the boys."
—**on working women**

"What did I win? Did I win
another championship?"
—**after the Reds beat
the Dodgers in the 1995
division series**

"What you don't do can be a destructive force." —Eleanor Roosevelt

THE AMERICAN-INDIAN EXPERIENCE

Here are some observations about the people who inhabited North America for thousands of years before Europeans arrived.

THE INDIAN WAY

"A Native American elder once described his own inner struggles in this manner: inside of me there are two dogs. One of the dogs is mean and evil. The other dog is good. The mean dog fights the good dog all the time. When asked which dog wins, he reflected."
—**George Bernard Shaw**

"Everything on the Earth has a purpose, every disease an herb to cure it, and every person a mission. This is the Indian theory of existence."
—**Mourning Dove, Salish**

"Silence is the absolute balance of body, mind, and spirit."
—**Ohiyesa, Santee Sioux**

TRAIL OF TEARS

"I have heard you intend to settle us on a reservation near the mountains. I don't want to settle. I love to roam over the prairies. There I feel free and happy, but when we settle down, we grow pale and die."
—**Santana, Kiowa Chief**

"Illegal aliens have always been a problem in the United States. Ask any Indian."
—**Robert Orben**

"All we wanted was peace and to be let alone."
—**Chief Crazy Horse**

"They made us many promises, more than I can remember, but they kept one; they promised to take our land, and they did."
—**Red Cloud, Oglala Lakota**

"A heavy guilt rests upon us for what the whites of all nations have done to the colored peoples. When we do good to them, it is not benevolence—it is atonement."
—**Albert Schweitzer**

"If the white man wants to live in peace with the Indian, he can live in peace.... Treat all men alike. Give them all the same law. Give them all an even chance to live and grow."

—Chief Joseph

MOTHER EARTH

"The most common trait of all primitive peoples is a reverence for the life-giving earth, and the Native American shared this elemental ethic: the land was alive to his loving touch, and he, its son, was brother to all creatures."

—Stewart L. Udall

"The American Indian is of the soil, whether it be the region of forests, plains, pueblos, or mesas. He fits into the landscape, for the hand that fashioned the continent also fashioned the man for his surroundings. He once grew as naturally as the wild sunflowers. He belongs just as the buffalo belonged."

—Luther Standing Bear, Oglala Lakota

"Listen to all the teachers in the woods. Watch the trees, the animals and all the living things—you'll learn more from them than books."

—Joe Coyhis

"The Great Spirit is in all things. He is in the air we breathe. But the Earth is our Mother. She nourishes us. That which we put into the ground she returns to us."

—Big Thunder, Wabanaki Algonquin

*   *   *

ASK THE EXPERTS

Q: *What is the difference between "Native American" and "American Indian?"*

A: The term "Native American" came into usage in the 1960s to denote the groups served by the Bureau of Indian Affairs: American Indians and Alaska Natives (Indians, Eskimos, and Aleuts of Alaska). Later, the term also included Native Hawaiians and Pacific Islanders in some federal programs. It, therefore, came into disfavor among some Indian groups. The preferred term is "American Indian." The Eskimos and Aleuts in Alaska are two culturally distinct groups and are sensitive about being included under the "Indian" designation. They prefer "Alaska Native."

—the Bureau of Indian Affairs, U.S. Department of the Interior

I LOVE ROCK 'N' ROLL

Some thoughts on rock from the folks who make it.

"The blues had a baby, and they called it rock 'n' roll."
—**Muddy Waters**

"Energy is all you need in rock 'n' roll. Energy and three chords."
—**Mick Jagger**

"I've always said that hard rock…is simply folk music delivered at high velocity. Shot from guns."
—**David Lee Roth**

"Rock won't eliminate your problems, but it will let you sort of dance all over them."
—**Pete Townshend**

"Drugs and sex go hand in hand when you're a rock 'n' roll musician. Whereas, if I were a violinist, it might be a little different."
—**Slash, Guns N' Roses**

"Rock 'n' roll starts between the legs and goes through the heart, then to the head. As long as it does those three things, it's a great rock song."
—**John Mellencamp**

"It's written in rock 'n' roll that all you need is love. But you also need a great nose."
—**Bono**

"The typical rock fan isn't smart enough to know when he's being dumped on."
—**Frank Zappa**

"People who are looking for art in rock 'n' roll are looking for something that either doesn't or shouldn't exist."
—**Billy Joel**

"It's no longer sex, drugs, and rock 'n' roll. It's crack, masturbation, and Madonna."
—**Scott Weiland, Stone Temple Pilots**

"The Rock 'n' Roll Hall of Fame was a great idea when it started, but I think they ought to close it. I think it's full."
—**Neil Young**

"There'll always be some arrogant little brat who wants to make noise with a guitar. Rock 'n' roll will never die."
—**Dave Edmunds**

"I got fed up with all the sex and sleaze and backhanders of rock 'n' roll, so I went into politics."

—Tony Blair, British prime minister

POLITICIANS

Politicians aren't getting much respect these days—but then, it sounds like they don't deserve much, either.

"I feel very proud, even though they didn't elect me, to be the president of the Argentines."
    —Junta leader General Leopoldo Galtieri

"I've read about foreign policy and studied—I know the number of continents."
    —Gov. George Wallace, presidential candidate, 1968

"I promise you a police car on every sidewalk."
    —Marion Barry, former mayor of Washington, D.C.

"Only one thing would be worse than the status quo, and that would be for the status quo to become the norm."
    —Elizabeth Dole

"There is no housing shortage in Lincoln today—just a rumor that is put about by people who have nowhere to live."
    —G. L. Murfin, mayor of Lincoln, Nebraska

"In order to become the master, the politician poses as the servant."
    —Charles De Gaulle

"If you don't vote for me I'll hold my breath."
    —Shirley Temple Black

"I don't mind how much my ministers talk, as long as they do what I say."
    —Margaret Thatcher

"In New Hampshire, closest Senate race in the country, this race between Dick Swett and Bob Smith is hot and tight as a too-small bathing suit on a too-long car ride back from the beach."
    —Dan Rather

"Wenlund has an obscure, undistinguished record...and he's a poor dresser, too."
    —Ray Hanania, candidate for Illinois state representative, talking about incumbent Larry Wenlund

LOVE...AND MARRIAGE

*More words of wisdom about a social
institution...if you're ready for an institution.*

"When two people are under the influence of the most violent, most insane, most delusive, and most transient of passions, they are required to swear that they will remain in that excited, abnormal, and exhausting condition until death do them part."

—George Bernard Shaw

"Marriage is the only war where you sleep with the enemy."

—Gary Busey

"Keep your eyes wide open before marriage, half shut afterwards."

—Benjamin Franklin

"Marriage is like a cage; one sees the birds outside desperate to get in, and those inside equally desperate to get out."

—Michel de Montaigne

"A great marriage is not when the 'perfect couple' come together. It is when an imperfect couple learns to enjoy their differences."

—Dave Meurer

"There are two dilemmas that rattle the human skull: How do you hang on to someone who won't stay? And how do you get rid of someone who won't go?"

—Danny DeVito,
The War of the Roses

"My advice to you is to get married. If you find a good wife, you'll be happy; if not, you'll become a philosopher."

—Socrates

"Someone once asked me why women don't gamble as much as men do and I gave the commonsensical reply that we don't have as much money. That was a true but incomplete answer. In fact, women's total instinct for gambling is satisfied by marriage."

—Gloria Steinem

"There's only one way to have a happy marriage and as soon as I learn what it is I'll get married again."

—Clint Eastwood

THE NAKED TRUTH

Time to let it all hang out.

"In dreams we see ourselves naked and acting our real characters, even more clearly than we see others awake."
—Henry David Thoreau

"There are 193 species of monkeys and apes. 192 of them are covered with hair. The exception is a naked ape self-named Homo sapiens."
—Desmond Morris

"In the nude, all that is not beautiful is obscene."
—Robert Bresson

"Some day people will grow up and realize that the only thing vile about human bodies is the small minds some people have developed within them."
—Dick Hein

"Clothes make the man. Naked people have little or no influence on society."
—Mark Twain

"Nudists have no fashion sense."
—Peter Kunkel

"Nakedness reveals itself. Nudity is placed on display. The nude is condemned to never being naked. Nudity is a form of dress."
—John Berger

"There's something therapeutic about nudity. Clothing is one of the external things about a character. Take away the Gucci or Levi's and we're all the same."
—Kevin Bacon

"In California, 50 women protested the impending war with Iraq by lying on the ground naked and spelling out the word peace. Right idea, wrong president."
—Jay Leno

"Men's magazines often feature pictures of naked ladies. Women's magazines also often feature pictures of naked ladies. This is because the female body is a beautiful work of art, while the male body is hairy and lumpy and shouldn't be seen by the light of day."
—Richard Roeper

ON THE JOB

Work: It's a living.

"A decorator can make lots of money—provided she wins the lottery."
—**Wendy Morgan**

"I do not like work even when someone else does it."
—**Mark Twain**

"By working faithfully eight hours a day, you may eventually get to be a boss and work twelve hours a day."
—**Robert Frost**

"I find it rather easy to portray a businessman. Being bland, rather cruel, and incompetent comes naturally to me."
—**John Cleese**

"When you go to work, if your name is on the building, you're rich. If your name is on your desk, you're middle-class. If you're name is on your shirt, you're poor."
—**Rich Hall**

"No one on his deathbed ever said, 'I wish I had spent more time on my business.'"
—**Arnold Zack**

"Nothing is really work unless you'd rather be doing something else."
—**J. M. Barrie**

"Anyone can do any amount of work provided it isn't the work he is supposed to be doing at that moment."
—**Robert Benchley**

A STUDY OF HUMOR

What is humor? Why do we laugh? What makes
something funny? Why do noses run and feet smell?

"There's nothing funnier than
the human animal."
—**Walt Disney**

"I've always thought that a big
laugh is a really loud noise
from the soul saying, 'Ain't
that the truth.'"
—**Quincy Jones**

"Humor is just truth, only
faster!"
—**Gilda Radner**

"If you can't laugh at yourself,
then who can you laugh at?"
—**Tiger Woods**

"If you can't laugh at yourself,
make fun of other people."
—**Bobby Slayton**

"The day most wholly lost is
the day on which one does
not laugh."
—**Nocolas-Sebastien**
Chamfort

"There's a thin line between to
laugh with and to laugh at."
—**Richard Pryor**

"Humor is just another
defense against the universe."
—**Mel Brooks**

"And we should consider every
day lost in which we have not
danced at least once. And we
should call every truth false
which was not accompanied by
at least one laugh."
—**Friedrich Nietzsche**

"We must laugh at man to
avoid crying for him."
—**Napoleon Bonaparte**

"Humor is mankind's greatest
blessing."
—**Mark Twain**

"My way of joking is to tell
the truth; it's the funniest joke
in the world."
—**George Bernard Shaw**

Richard Curtis: "What is the
secret to great com—?"
Rowan Atkinson: "Timing."

"Looks fade, but humor is
forever—I'll take Woody
Allen over Warren Beatty
any day."
—**Bette Midler**

"No joke is old if you haven't
heard it before."
—**Milton Berle**

Italic type dates back to 1500.

EVERYONE'S A COMEDIAN

*It's hard to be funny for a living, but
these folks make it look easy.*

"I read this article. It said the typical symptoms of stress are eating too much, smoking too much, impulse buying, and driving too fast. Are they kidding? This is my idea of a great day!"
—**Monica Piper**

"When I'm not in a relationship, I shave one leg. So when I sleep, it feels like I'm with a woman."
—**Garry Shandling**

"Personally, I'm waiting for caller IQ."
—**Sandra Bernhard**

"A computer once beat me at chess, but it was no match for me at kick boxing"
—**Emo Philips**

"I majored in nursing but I had to drop it because I ran out of milk."
—**Judy Tenuta**

"My sister's got asthma. In the middle of an attack she got an obscene phone call. The guy said, 'Did I call you or did you call me?'"
—**John Mendoza**

"Scientists today announced they have discovered a cure for apathy. Unfortunately, no one seems to care."
—**George Carlin**

"I don't think I'm gay. I don't think I'm straight. I'm just slutty. Where's my parade?"
—**Margaret Cho**

SONG BIRDS

Some observations from rock 'n' roll's better half.

"Onstage, I make love to 25,000 people, then I go home alone."
—Janis Joplin

"Some part of me is feeling that maybe I've done something wrong if I'm this popular."
—Suzanne Vega

"The majority of pop stars are complete idiots in every respect."
—Sade

"I've always felt that a lot of my songs deal with spying on myself."
—Carly Simon

"I get fan letters like all the time, and pretty much every letter just talks about, 'Thank you for not being Britney Spears.'"
—Avril Lavigne

"I never hurt nobody but myself and that's nobody's business but my own."
—Billie Holiday

"Non-violence is a flop. The only bigger flop is violence."
—Joan Baez

"The American public really does have a death wish for me. They want me to die. I'm not going to die."
—Courtney Love

"Taking me seriously is a big mistake. I certainly wouldn't."
—Ani DiFranco

"If a song's about something I've experienced or that could have happened to me, it's good. But if it's alien to me, I can't lend anything to it. Because that's what soul's all about."
—Aretha Franklin

*   *   *

"I'm holding on to my babehood. Somebody's got to do it."
—Deborah Harry at 58

CAT CALLS

*They meow insistently, they shed all over the place, they're
finicky eaters, and they never know whether they want
to be inside or outside. But there is nothing more
satisfying than when a cat shows you affection.*

"In the beginning, God created man, but seeing him so feeble, He gave him the cat."
—**Warren Eckstein**

"Cats think about three things: food, sex, and nothing."
—**Adair Lara**

"If animals could speak, the dog would be a blundering outspoken fellow; but the cat would have the rare grace of never saying a word too much."
—**Mark Twain**

"Cats know how to obtain food without labor, shelter without confinement, and love without penalties."
—**W. L. George**

"No matter how much cats fight, there always seem to be plenty of kittens."
—**Abraham Lincoln**

"The cat could very well be man's best friend but would never stoop to admitting it."
—**Doug Larson**

"When I play with my cat, who knows whether she is not amusing herself with me more than I with her."
—**Montaigne**

"If man could be crossed with the cat, it would improve man but deteriorate the cat."
—**Mark Twain**

"The phrase 'domestic cat' is an oxymoron."
—**George Will**

"A dog, I have always said, is prose; a cat is a poem."
—**Jean Burden**

"A cat's got her own opinion of human beings. She don't say much, but you can tell enough to make you anxious not to hear the whole of it."
—**Jerome K. Jerome**

"The trouble with a kitten is
THAT
Eventually it becomes a
CAT."
—**Ogden Nash**

"Logic is in the eye of the logician." —Gloria Steinem

THEM'S DRINKIN' WORDS

Humans have been consuming alcohol since the beginning of civilization. Maybe that's why civilization is so weird.

"There are more old drunks than there are old doctors."
—**Willie Nelson**

"A drink a day keeps the shrink away."
—**Edward Abbey**

"No animal ever invented anything so bad as drunkenness—or so good as drink."
—**Lord Chesterton**

"Once, during Prohibition, I was forced to live for days on nothing but food and water."
—**W. C. Fields**

"The chief reason for drinking is the desire to behave in a certain way, and to be able to blame it on alcohol."
—**Mignon McLaughlin**

"The problem with the world is that everyone is a few drinks behind."
—**Humphrey Bogart**

"If you resolve to give up smoking, drinking, and loving, you don't actually live longer; it just seems longer."
—**Clement Freud**

"Wine is sunlight, held together by water."
—**Galileo**

"I'm Catholic and I can't commit suicide, but I plan to drink myself to death."
—**Jack Kerouac**

"I'm not an alcoholic. I'm a drunkard. The difference is, drunkards don't go to meetings."
—**Jackie Gleason**

"The night I turned 22, I drank a shot for every year. I was so drunk, I'd just walk up to people in the bar and hit them in the balls. My friends drove me home and left me propped up on the couch holding a bucket. I woke up with vomit all over me. The bucket was clean as a whistle."
—**Jon Stewart**

"There is nothing wrong with sobriety in moderation."
—**John Ciardi**

"When I read about the evils of drinking, I gave up reading."
—**Henny Youngman**

"A narcissist is someone better looking than you are." —**Gore Vidal**

"Bars are installing Breathalyzer vending machines telling people whether they've had too much to drink. Apparently, if you're drunk, the machine warns you not to drive, and if you're really drunk, it warns you not to call your ex-girlfriend."
—Conan O'Brien

"Actually, I'm a drinker with writing problems."
—Brendan Behan

"You know what alcoholics call New Year's Eve? Amateur night."
—Elmore Leonard

"Only Irish coffee provides in a single glass all four essential food groups: alcohol, caffeine, sugar, and fat."
—Alex Levine

"I'll quit coffee. It won't be easy drinking my Bailey's straight, but I'll get used to it. It'll still be the best part of waking up."
—Megan Mullally

"You're not drunk if you can lie on the floor without holding on."
—Dean Martin

"To alcohol, the cause and solution to all of life's problems."
—Homer Simpson

"When I first went to the Betty Ford Center I was very surprised they didn't have a bar there....I thought they taught you how to drink like a gentleman."
—Ozzy Osbourne

*   *   *

COMMANDER ALAN SHEPARD (APOLLO 14) ON MOON GOLFING

First Shot: "I thought, with the same clubhead speed, the ball's going to go at least six times as far. There's absolutely no drag, so if you do happen to spin it, it won't slice or hook 'cause there's no atmosphere to make it turn."

Second Shot: "Got more dirt than ball. Here we go again."

UNCLE JOHN'S QUOTATIONARY

Here's Part 4 of our quotation dictionary.
(Part 3 begins on page 131.)

GARDEN: the best place to seek God—you can dig for Him there. (George Bernard Shaw)

GENTLEMAN: one who never inflicts pain. (Cardinal Newman)

GHOST: the outward sign of an inward fear. (Ambrose Bierce)

GIGOLO: a fee-male. (Isaac Goldberg)

GLAMOUR: Standing still and looking stupid. (Hedy Lamarr)

GOD: a comedian playing to an audience too afraid to laugh. (Voltaire)

GOLF: a cow-pasture pool. (O.K. Bovard, American executive)

GOOD LISTENER: a good talker with a sore throat. (Katherine Whitehorn)

GOOD MANNERS: putting up with other people's bad manners. (H. Jackson Brown, Jr.)

GOOD TASTE: the worst vice ever invented. (Dame Edith Sitwell)

GOSSIP: when you hear something you like about someone you don't. (Earl Wilson)

GOVERNMENT: the great fiction, through which everybody endeavors to live at the expense of everybody else. (Frédéric Bastiat)

GRAVE: a place in which the dead are laid to await the coming of the medical student. (Ambrose Bierce)

GUILT: the gift that keeps on giving. (Erma Bombeck)

HABIT: the nursery of errors. (Victor Hugo)

HAPPINESS: your dentist telling you it won't hurt and then catching his hand in the drill. (Johnny Carson)

HATRED: the coward's revenge for being intimidated. (George Bernard Shaw)

HEALTH: what my friends are always drinking to before they fall down. (Phyllis Diller)

HEAVEN: clement weather, no traffic, and no obligations. (Beck)

"What an ugly beast is the ape, and how like us." —Cicero

HELL: having to listen to our grandparents breathe through their noses when they're eating sandwiches. (Jim Carrey)

HEN: an egg's way of making another egg. (Samuel Butler)

HERO: a man who does what he can. (Romain Rolland)

HIPPIE: someone who looks like Tarzan, walks like Jane, and smells like Cheetah. (Ronald Reagan)

HISTORY: a pack of tricks that we play upon the dead. (Voltaire)

HOLLYWOOD: an emotional Detroit. (Lillian Gish)

HOPE: the feeling you have that the feeling you have isn't permanent. (Jean Kerr)

HUMAN BEING: an ingenious assembly of portable plumbing. (Christopher Morley)

HUMANITY: a work in progress. (Tennessee Williams)

For more see, page 202.

* * *

ROBERT DOWNEY, JR. DISCUSSES LIFE IN JAIL:

"After I got in a fight I was down in this discipline module, which is like a hole. Three times a day, you see a pair of hands and some food comes in. It's pretty awful. One day it opens and there was this lieutenant, with some deputy he'd brought to meet me. I hadn't had a shower in five days. I was sleeping in my clothes, my hair was all (messed) up. But that Hollywood big-shot entertainer thing came in, and I thought, 'Well, I'd better come to. I have company.' And this guy came in and said, 'Listen, I know you don't have a lot to read in here. I hope I wouldn't be crossing the line if I brought a script for you. It's about unicorns. It's not what you think, there's a very human element to it.'"

JAMES MADISON

Some thoughts from America's fourth (and shortest) president.

"If men were angels, no government would be necessary."

"A popular government without popular information, or the means of acquiring it, is but a prologue to a farce or a tragedy, or perhaps both. Knowledge will forever govern ignorance, and a people who mean to be their own governors must arm themselves with the power which knowledge gives."

"I believe there are more instances of the abridgement of the freedom of the people by gradual and silent encroachments of those in power than by violent and sudden usurpations."

"I cannot undertake to lay my finger on that article of the Constitution which granted a right to Congress of expending, on objects of benevolence, the money of their constituents."

"The essence of Government is power; and power, lodged as it must be in human hands, will ever be liable to abuse."

"It will be of little avail to the people that the laws are made by men of their own choice if the laws be so voluminous that they cannot be read, or so incoherent that they cannot be understood."

"The Constitution preserves the advantage of being armed which Americans possess over the people of almost every other nation where the governments are afraid to trust the people with arms."

"The means of defense against foreign danger historically have become the instruments of tyranny at home."

"The purpose of separation of church and state is to keep forever from these shores the ceaseless strife that has soaked the soil of Europe with blood for centuries."

"The truth is, all men having power ought to be mistrusted."

"A standing army is one of the greatest mischiefs that can possibly happen."

Both of James Madison's vice presidents died in office.

AGING

Bad news: by the time you finish reading this,
you'll be older. Good news: but wiser.

"My health is good; it's my age that's bad."
—Roy Acuff

"At 88, how do you feel when getting up in the morning? Amazed."
—George Burns

"My husband will never chase another woman. He's too fine, too decent, too old."
—Gracie Allen

"Wisdom doesn't automatically come with old age. Nothing does—except wrinkles. It's true, some wines improve with age. But only if the grapes were good in the first place."
—Abigail Van Buren

"It's a sobering thought: when Mozart was my age, he was dead for two years."
—Tom Lehrer

"There's one advantage to being 102. No peer pressure."
—Dennis Wolfberg

"The secret to longevity is to keep breathing."
—Sophie Tucker

"Age is mind over matter. If you don't mind, it doesn't matter."
—Satchel Paige

"I love being a great grandparent, but what I hate is being the mother of a grandparent."
—Janet Anderson

"It takes a long time to grow young."
—Pablo Picasso

"The hands on my biological clock are giving me the finger."
—Wendy Liebman

"You know you're getting older when the candles cost more than the cake."
—Bob Hope

"If it's too loud, you're too old."
—Ted Nugent

"You are as old as you think you are."
—Muhammad Ali

"The real fountain of youth is to have a dirty mind."
—Jerry Hall

REEL WITTY

A few clever movie lines.

Marge: "Say Lou, did ya hear the one about the guy who couldn't afford personalized plates so he went and changed his name to J3L-2404?"

Lou: "Yah, that's a good one."

—Frances McDormand and Bruce Bohne, *Fargo*

Joel: "Is there any risk of brain damage?"

Howard: "Well, technically speaking, the operation *is* brain damage."

—Jim Carrey and Tom Wilkinson, *Eternal Sunshine of the Spotless Mind*

"Hey Harry, you know we're sitting on four million pounds of fuel, one nuclear weapon, and a thing that has two hundred thousand moving parts...all built by the lowest bidder. Makes you feel good, doesn't it."

—Steve Buscemi, *Armageddon*

"Once we get out of the eighties, the nineties are gonna make the sixties look like the fifties."

—Dennis Hopper, *Flashback*

John Hammond: "All major theme parks have delays. When they opened Disneyland in 1956, nothing worked."

Dr. Ian Malcolm: "Yeah, but John, if the Pirates of the Caribbean breaks down, the pirates don't eat the tourists."

—Richard Attenborough and Jeff Goldblum, *Jurassic Park*

"How can you diagnose someone with an obsessive compulsive disorder and then act like I have some choice about barging in here?"

—Jack Nicholson, *As Good as It Gets*

"I was in the Virgin Islands once. I met a girl. We ate lobster and drank pina coladas. At sunset, we made love like sea otters. That was a pretty good day. Why couldn't I get that day over and over and over?"

—Bill Murray, *Groundhog Day*

"Does the noise in my head bother you?"

—Narrator, *The Gods Must Be Crazy*

ARTISTS RAP

*Rap music came from the streets in the 1970s and has
since changed the face of the music industry. Word up.*

"I hate it when the very folks who should be listening to rap music are attacking it so hard they miss the point. The point is that children and the neighborhoods—the whole country—is drowning in violence."
—**Stevie Wonder**

"Rap is teaching white kids what it means to be black, and that causes a problem for the infrastructure."
—**Chuck D**

"I think if it wasn't for rap, I'd be in jail or something. I think I'd a murdered something."
—**Tragedy**

"When you're listening to an Ice-T album, you're listening to me in the middle of a park yelling out my attitudes, my ideas. But you should never think everything I'm thinking, because then only one of us is thinking."
—**Ice-T**

"Reality is wrong. Dreams are for real."
—**Tupac Shakur**

"Rap is like the polio vaccine. At first no one believed in it. Then once they knew it worked, everyone wanted it."
—**Grandmaster Flash**

"When I die, bury me on my stomach and let the world kiss my ass."
—**L. L. Cool J**

YOU LIKE ME! YOU REALLY LIKE ME!

*Receiving an award is a humbling honor. And most
of the acceptance speeches are forgettable,
but occasionally one stands out.*

MICHAEL JACKSON
Award: Nothing at all
Background: At the 2002 MTV Video Music Awards, Britney Spears came on stage to present Jackson with a birthday cake for his forty-fourth birthday. Spears explained that for her, Jackson was the "artist of the millennium." And Jackson somehow thought that he was receiving an award for that very thing, when all he was supposed to do was come out and get a piece of cake.

Excerpt: "When I was a little boy growing up in Indiana, if someone told me I'd be getting the Artist of the Millennium award, I'd never have believed it."

Follow up: The speech caused such confusion that an MTV spokeswoman had to explain afterwards: "There is no such award as the Artist of the Millennium. I think some wires got crossed."

KIM BASINGER
Award: Best Supporting Actress Oscar for 1997's *L.A. Confidential*
Excerpt: "I just want to thank everyone I've ever met in my entire life."

JACK BENNY
Award: One of the numerous achievement awards he received later in life
Excerpt: "I don't deserve this, but then, I have arthritis, and I don't deserve that either."

Bob Dylan used to use the stage name Elston Gunn.

ADVICE FROM STORMIN' NORMAN

*It makes sense that Norman Schwarzkopf, the guy
who ran Operation Desert Storm in 1990, would
have a few things to say about leadership.*

"The truth of the matter is that you always know the right thing to do. The hard part is doing it."

"Do what is right, not what you think the high headquarters wants or what you think will make you look good."

"You learn far more from negative leadership than from positive leadership. Because you learn how not to do it. And, therefore, you learn how to do it."

"Leadership is a potent combination of strategy and character. But if you must be without one, be without the strategy."

"It doesn't take a hero to order men into battle. It takes a hero to be one of those men who goes into battle."

WAR IS HELL

More thoughts on mankind's most dangerous game.

"So many young people seem to be getting quite pro-military these days. Somebody should tell them they'll get their legs blown off if they go to war."
—Paul McCartney

"A plan I have is 'World Peace through Formal Introductions.' The idea is that everyone in the world would be required to meet everyone else in the world, formally, at least once. You'd have to look the person in the eye, shake hands, repeat their name, and try to remember one outstanding physical characteristic. My theory is, if you knew everyone in the world personally, you'd be less inclined to fight them in a war: 'Who? The Malaysians? Are you kidding? I know those people!'"
—George Carlin

"I have seen the agony of mothers and wives. I hate war."
—Franklin Delano Roosevelt

"Talking jaw to jaw is better than going to war."
—Winston Churchill

"Mankind must put an end to war, or war will put an end to mankind."
—John F. Kennedy

"When the rich make war, it's the poor who die."
—Jean-Paul Sartre

"War is just when it is necessary; arms are permissible when there is no hope except in arms."
—Niccolo Machiavelli

"I was having a political argument with a lady who said, 'If women ran the world, there would be no war.' That's a load of crap, isn't it? Sure, nobody would start a fight for no reason if women ran the world. It would be like, 'Hi, this is England. How come we're being invaded?' 'Oh, I think you know. I saw you looking at France!'"
—Drew Carey

"I believe in compulsory cannibalism. If people were forced to eat what they kill, there would be no more war."
—Abbie Hoffman

"In Italy for thirty years under the Borgias they had warfare, terror, murder, and bloodshed. They produced Michelangelo, Leonardo da Vinci, and the Renaissance. In Switzerland they had brotherly love, 500 years of democracy and peace, and what did that produce? The cuckoo clock."

—Orson Welles,
The Third Man (1949)

CELEBRITIES ON MONEY

They say money can't buy happiness...but hey, it's worth a try.

"The whole idea of people singing about their misery and being paid for it—there's a terrible contradiction. I mean, once you get paid for it, shut up. You have nothing to be miserable about anymore."
—**Gene Simmons**

"Money doesn't mean anything to me except as an affirmation of the music."
—**John Tesh**

"Money doesn't make you happy. I now have $50 million but I was just as happy when I had $48 million."
—**Arnold Schwarzenegger**

"Everything is money, money, money. All I want to do is play basketball, drink Pepsi, and wear Reebok."
—**Shaquille O'Neal**

"Actually, I have no regard for money. Aside from its purchasing power, it's completely useless as far as I'm concerned."
—**Alfred Hitchcock**

"I grew up with the *Pink Panther* movies and remember just laughing and laughing. And the thought of having other people have those 20-year movie memories is what I do it for. And the money."
—**Steve Martin, on why he made *The Pink Panther***

"For a writer, the two most beautiful words in the English language are 'check enclosed.'"
—**Dorothy Parker**

"I don't give a f**k what color you are. The color of money is green."
—**Eazy-E**

"Someday I want to be rich. Some people get so rich they lose all respect for humanity. That's how rich I want to be."
—**Rita Rudner**

"It isn't necessary to be rich and famous to be happy. It's only necessary to be rich."
—**Alan Alda**

"Once in a while my wife complains about my jokes. I just tell her to go cry in a big bag of money."
—**Ray Romano**

Keith Richards sang in the choir at Queen Elizabeth II's coronation.

"It's easy to make
a buck. It's a lot
tougher to make
a difference."
—Tom Brokaw

CAN WE TALK?

*Joan Rivers' sharp tongue and ascerbic wit makes her one
of America's favorite comedians. And one of ours, too.*

"I said to my husband, 'Why don't you call out my name
when we're making love?' He said, 'I don't want to wake you
up.'"

"When I was in labor, the nurses would look at me and say,
'Do you still think blondes have more fun?'"

"You know you're getting old when work is a lot less fun—
and fun is a lot more work."

"My obstetrician was so dumb that when I gave birth, he
forgot to cut the cord. For a year that kid followed me
everywhere. It was like having a dog on a leash."

"I don't change diapers. The kid's wet? Don't worry—he'll
dry!"

"Last night I was on stage performing and a woman in the
front row was nursing a child. Can you imagine nursing a
child in the front row? The kid was fifteen years old! Thank
God it wasn't hers."

"I hate housework. You make the beds, you wash the dishes,
and six months later you have to start all over again."

"You know, once they're dead, death just scrubs celebrities
clean. Everybody says, 'Oh, they were wonderful.' Suddenly,
Grace Kelly didn't drink."

"A man can sleep around, no questions asked—but if a
woman makes 19 or 20 mistakes, she's a tramp."

ME, ME, ME

There's a fine line between having high self-esteem and being an egomaniac. These celebs may have crossed that line. Match the quote with the egomaniac...er...person with high self-esteem.

1. "Yes, if there is such a thing as genius, I am one."

2. "I see myself hot for the next seven years at least."

3. "I've been planted here to be a vessel for acting."

4. "I look fabulous for my age."

5. "Macho guys might feel threatened by me."

6. "I built my body to carry my brain around."

7. "I'm so damn famous, it's sickening."

8. "I was never a child. I was born a rock god."

9. "I'd date me!"

10. "It's such a burden to be right all the time."

11. "I'm everything."

12. "If I only had a little humility, I'd be perfect."

13. "I am just too much."

a. John Lennon

b. Bette Davis

c. Michael Bolton

d. Brad Pitt

e. Leonardo DiCaprio

f. Richard Grieco

g. Zsa Zsa Gabor

h. David Bowie

i. Jane Fonda

j. Madonna

k. Tom Wolfe

l. Ted Turner

m. Sylvester Stallone

Answers

1. a; 2. f; 3. e; 4. i; 5. c; 6. m; 7. g;
8. h; 9. d; 10. k; 11. j; 12. l; 13. b.

Sylvester Stallone grew up in foster homes until he was 5 years old.

MORE ON MARRIAGE

We dedicate our third page on marriage to those
of you who have been married three times.

"My ex-husband is easier to get along with now that he's on heavy medication. I think our marriage would have lasted with a couple more bottles of NyQuil. It's the 'I'm going to sleep now so I won't be a pain in the ass and we can stay married' medicine."

—Daryl Hogue

"Marriage: a souvenir of love."

—Helen Rowland

"Wife: A former sweetheart."

—H. L. Mencken

"My mom had good advice for me about how to stay married for a long time. She said, 'Always remember, honesty is very important. It must be avoided. And the most important thing is, you have to let your husband be himself and you have to pretend he's someone else.'"

—Rita Rudner

"Before we got engaged he never farted. Now it's like a second language."

—Caroline Rhea

"I love being married. I was single for a long time, and I just got so sick of finishing my own sentences."

—Brian Kiley

"Instead of getting married again, I'm going to find a woman I don't like and just give her a house."

—Rod Stewart

ON DEMOCRACY

Winston Churchill once said, "Democracy is the worst form of government…except for all those other forms that have been tried." Here are some folks who agree.

"Democracy is the art and science of running the circus from the monkey cage."
—H. L. Mencken

"Bad officials are elected by good citizens who do not vote."
—George Jean Nathan

"One of the best ways to get yourself a reputation as a dangerous citizen these days is to go about repeating the very phrases which our fathers used in the great struggle for Independence."
—Charles A. Beard

"Democracy: in which you say what you want but do what you're told."
—Gerald Berry

"Democracy was the right of the people to choose their own tyrants."
—James Madison

"Let the people think they govern and they will be governed."
—William Penn, *Some Fruits of Solitude*

"Democracy encourages the majority to decide things about which the majority is blissfully ignorant."
—John Simon

"A democracy is a government in the hands of men of low birth, no property, and vulgar employments."
—Aristotle

"If we would learn what the human race really is at bottom, we need only observe it at election times."
—Mark Twain

"The best argument against democracy is a five-minute conversation with the average voter."
—Winston Churchill

"What's wrong with being a boring kind of guy?" —George H. W. Bush

TELEVISION INSULTS

One thing many TV viewers have in common is they wish they were as quick with the zingers as their favorite characters are.

The Skipper: "I always thought I'd like to be a cowboy."
Mr. Howell: "Somewhere there breathes a horse who's glad you are not."
—*Gilligan's Island*

Florence: "Is there something you don't like about my cooking?"
George: "Yeah—eating it."
—*The Jeffersons*

"In the world of ulcers, Unger, you're what's known as a carrier."
—**Dr. Gordon,**
The Odd Couple

Vanessa: "You've come to your mother-in-law for help. How flattering."
Laura: "Well, this job requires somebody with no conscience, so naturally, I thought of you."
—*All My Children*

Archie: "After twenty-seven years of marriage you would call me dumb?"
Edith: "I'm sorry Archie, I shouldn't have waited so long."
—*All in the Family*

"She's so anally retentive she wouldn't sit down for fear of sucking up the furniture."
—**Patsy,** *Absolutely Fabulous*

Frank: "I tried nice once. Didn't care for it."
Marie: "Is that what happened to smart?"
—*Everybody Loves Raymond*

Frank: "I'm a pretty fair doctor myself. Ask any of my patients."
Hawkeye: "We can't dig people up just for that."
—*M*A*S*H*

Trixie: "Our husbands. Some gentlemen. Only two seats left on the bus, and who takes them?"
Alice: "Ralph."
—*The Honeymooners*

Cliff Claven: "You ever heard of the lone wolf? The lone wolf, c'est moi. A man by himself, needing no one. I touch no one; no one touches me. I am a rock. I am an island."
Carla Tortelli: "You am a boob."
—*Cheers*

"We can't leave the haphazard to chance." —N. F. Simpson

INSTRUMENTAL THINKING

Musicians spend a lot of time thinking about their
instruments (get your mind out of the gutter).

"There is only one thing more beautiful than one guitar—two guitars."

—Frederic Chopin

"The bagpipes sound exactly the same when you have finished learning as when you start."

—Thomas Beecham

"The American view of music from other countries can be really narrow. In Mexico, the accordion is such an essential instrument, and to us it's just a novelty. The same with the sitar in India. But to me, these are really beautiful, substantial instruments. And they're just as musical, just as valid, as the electric guitar and Marshall stacks."

—Beck

"A gentleman knows how to play the accordion, but doesn't."

—Al Cohn, saxophonist

How sensitve is a violin? The type of varnish used will affect its tone.

THE MATERIAL GIRL

Even if you don't think Madonna is a talented singer,
you've got to admit she has a talent for being outrageous.

"I sometimes think I was born to live up to my name. How could I be anything else but what I am, having been named Madonna? I would either have ended up a nun or this."

"Losing my virginity was a career move."

"When I was a little girl, I wished I was black…but if being black is synonymous with having soul, then yes, I feel that I am."

"I live for meetings with men in suits. I love them because I know they had a really boring week. I walk in there with my orange velvet leggings and drop popcorn in my cleavage and then fish it out and eat it. I like that. I know I'm entertaining them, and I know that they know."

"They send uptight, straight men to review me. They hate me. Don't they know I'm a gay man in a woman's body?"

"So I'm not the world's greatest actress."

"If I weren't as talented as I am ambitious, I would be a gross monstrosity."

"I wanted to be a nun. I saw nuns as superstars."

"Straight men need to be emasculated. I'm sorry. They all need to be slapped around. Women have been kept down for far too long. Every straight guy should have a man's tongue in his mouth at least once."

"Sick and perverted always appeal to me."

"Everyone probably thinks that I'm a raving nymphomaniac, that I have an insatiable sexual appetite, when the truth is, I'd rather read a book."

"I won't be happy until I'm as famous as God."

OPINIONS ON MADONNA

Just about everybody has a strong opinion about her.

"Madonna is so hairy, when she lifted up her arm, I thought it was Tina Turner in her armpit."
—**Joan Rivers**

"Madonna was scheduled to testify against her stalker, saying she saw him wherever she went and she was scared of him—which is kind of how I feel about Madonna."
—**Conan O'Brien**

"I'm irritated that the world we live in— and its culture and society—can build and maintain Madonna."
—**Natalie Merchant**

"I *acted* vulgar. Madonna *is* vulgar."
—**Marlene Dietrich**

"That ugly, shapeless, toe-sucking slut Madonna....The difference between Marilyn Monroe and Madonna is the same difference that exists between champagne and cats' piss."
—**Irma Kurtz**

"She has mentioned that I was important to her, and that's very satisfying. However, a check would be better."
—**Deborah Harry on being a role model to Madonna**

YOU AIN'T GOT IT, KID

*In 1987, a certain publishing company told Uncle John that
making books for the bathroom was a stupid idea. Good
thing for us he didn't listen. Same with these folks.*

What They Said: "Try another profession. Any other."
Who Said it: Head of New York's John Murray Anderson Drama School
Rejected! Lucille Ball

What They Said: "You'd better learn secretarial work or else get married."
Who Said it: Director of the Blue Book modeling agency
Rejected! Marilyn Monroe

What They Said: "I'm sorry, but you just don't understand how to use the English language."
Who Said it: Anonymous publisher
Rejected! Rudyard Kipling's 1889 novel, *The Jungle Book*

What They Said: "If you go on the air with that crap, they're going to kill you right in the streets."
Who Said it: Mickey Rooney
Rejected! Producer Norman Lear, who wanted to cast Rooney for his new sitcom *All in the Family*. Rooney declined and Carrol O'Connor got the part.

What They Said: "It is impossible to sell animal stories in the United States."
Who Said it: Anonymous publisher
Rejected! George Orwell's *Animal Farm*

What They Said: "It's pretty thin, son. I don't think people will follow it."
Who Said it: Henry Fonda
Rejected! *Easy Rider*, a movie made by Henry's son Peter

"It is difficult to keep quiet if you have nothing to say." —Malcolm Margolin

FOUNDERS' WISDOM

Quotations from signers of the Declaration of Independence.

They that can give up essential liberty to obtain a little temporary safety deserve neither liberty nor safety.

— **Benjamin Franklin (1706–1790)**

That these united colonies are, and of right ought to be, free and independent states; that they are absolved from all allegiance to the British crown; and that all political connection between them and the State of Great Britain is, and ought to be, totally dissolved.

— **Richard Henry Lee (1732–1794)**

Liberty cannot be preserved without a general knowledge among the people, who have a right...and a desire to know; but besides this, they have a right, an indisputable, unalienable, indefeasible, divine right to that most dreaded and envied kind of knowledge, I mean of the characters and conduct of their rulers.

— **John Adams (1735–1826)**

While Gen'l Howe with a Large Armament is advancing towards N. York, our Congress resolved to Declare the United Colonies free and Independent States. A Declaration for this Purpose, I expect, will this day pass Congress...It is gone so far that we must now be a free independent State, or a Conquered Country.

— **Abraham Clark (1726–1794)**

The strongest reason for the people to retain the right to keep and bear arms is, as a last resort, to protect themselves against tyranny in government.

— **Thomas Jefferson (1743–1826)**

We must all hang together, or assuredly we shall all hang separately.

— **Benjamin Franklin (1706–1790)**

"All I know is that I am not a Marxist." —Karl Marx

WEDDING DAZE

*Thinking of getting married? You might want
to read these quotes before you say "I do."*

"I wanted to look good for my wedding pictures.
You might be looking at those things for for four or
five years."

—Tom Arnold

"A wedding is just like a funeral, except that you
get to smell your own flowers."

—Grace Hansen

"The trouble with wedlock is that there's not
enough wed and too much lock."

—Christopher Morley

"The majority of husbands remind me of an orang-
utan trying to play the violin."

—Honore' de Balzac

"Marriage is not just spiritual communion, it is also
remembering to take out the trash."

—Joyce Brothers

"The surest way to be alone is to get married."

—Gloria Steinem

"Marriage: a ceremony in which rings are put on
the finger of the lady and through the nose of the
gentleman."

—Herbert Spencer

THE GOLDEN STATE

*California's given us Disneyland, earthquakes, Hollywood,
the Gold Rush, hippies, McDonald's…and this quote page.*

"I love Thanksgiving turkey…it's the only time in Los Angeles that you see natural breasts."
—**Arnold Schwarzenegger**

"It's a scientific fact that if you stay in California you lose one point of your IQ every year."
—**Truman Capote**

"Living in California adds 10 years to a man's life. And those extra 10 years I'd like to spend in New York."
—**Harry Ruby**

"'I'm going to be a big star!' In California, we call that sort of statement 'creative visualization.' In the other 49 states, it's called self-delusion."
—**Maureen Brownsey**

"Los Angeles is 72 suburbs in search of a city."
—**James Gleason**

"There are 2 million interesting people in New York—and only 78 in Los Angeles."
—**Neil Simon**

"Los Angeles is the only town in the world where you can wake up in the morning and listen to the birds coughing in the trees."
—**Joe Frisco**

"It's a wonderful place, even though I do criticize it occasionally. I'm all for it. And if they'd lower the taxes and get rid of the smog and clean up the traffic mess, I really believe I'd settle here until the next earthquake."
—**Groucho Marx,**
You Bet Your Life

"There is science, logic, reason; there is thought verified by experience. And then there is California."
—**Edward Abbey**

THE IMPORTANCE OF BEING ERNEST

Ahh, to live the bohemian Hemingway lifestyle: running with the bulls in Pamplona by day and sipping martinis in Paris at night (not the same night). But Ernest Hemingway did more than just play—he was one of the greatest 20th-century American novelists and he won the Nobel Prize for Literature in 1954.

"In order to write about life, first you must live it!"

"I like to listen. I have learned a great deal from listening carefully. Most people never listen."

"Courage is grace under pressure."

"Every man's life ends the same way. It is only the details of how he lived and how he died that distinguish one man from another."

"There is no friend as loyal as a book."

"All my life I've looked at words as though I were seeing them for the first time."

"To be a successful father there's one absolute rule: when you have a kid, don't look at it for the first two years."

"A man can be destroyed but not defeated."

"Fear of death increases in exact proportion to increase in wealth."

"All things truly wicked start from innocence."

"Solitude, as death proves, is our natural state."

"All good books are alike in that they are truer than if they had really happened."

"For a long time now I've tried simply to write the best I can. Sometimes I have good luck and write better than I can."

"I love sleep. My life has the tendency to fall apart when I'm awake, you know?"

"The world is a fine place and worth fighting for and I hate very much to leave it."

Ernest Hemingway's favorite food while writing: peanut butter sandwiches.

EVER HEARD OF JOHN HEYWOOD?

He may not be a household name, but his words have been household phrases for 500 years. In 1562 this English poet published a collection of poems and proverbs—some he wrote, some were popular sayings that he first put down on paper. Here is a sampling of Heywood's words.

"Haste maketh waste."

"Good to be merie and wise."

"Look ere ye leape."

"The fat is in the fire."

"When the sunne shineth, make hay."

"No man ought to looke a given horse in the mouth."

"We both be at our wittes end."

"Two heads are better then one."

"All is well that endes well."

"Better late than never."

"Beggars should be no choosers."

"The rolling stone never gathereth mosse."

"I pray thee let me and my fellow have a haire of the dog that bit us last night."

"To robbe Peter and pay Poule."

"A man may well bring a horse to the water, but he cannot make him drinke without he will."

"Better one byrde in hand than ten in the wood."

"Rome was not built in one day."

"Children learne to creepe ere they can learne to goe." (Learn to crawl before you learn to walk.)

"One good turne asketh another."

"By hooke or crooke."

"But in deede, A friend is never knowne till a man have neede."

"A peny for your thought."

"Many hands make light warke."

Johnny Cash's real name is JR Cash. (It doesn't stand for anything.)

KILLER QUOTES

Let's just say it's a good thing none of these people acted on their instincts (at the time of this writing).

"There are certain people that are marked for death. I have my little list of those that treated me unfairly."
—**Jennifer Lopez**

"The son of a bitch is a ballet dancer...and if I ever get a chance, I'll kill him with my bare hands."
—**W. C. Fields, on Charlie Chaplin**

"The fastest way to a man's heart is through his chest."
—**Roseanne**

"Be wary of strong drink. It can make you shoot at tax collectors...and miss."
—**Robert A. Heinlein**

"I come to play. I come to beat you. I come to kill you."
—**Leo Durocher**

Lady Nancy Astor:
"Winston, if I were your wife, I'd poison your soup."

Winston Churchill:
"Nancy, if I were your husband, I'd drink it."

"I'm not a total pacifist, you know. I've shot at people. I've missed, but I shot at them. I'm sort of glad I missed."
—**David Crosby**

"Nothing wrong with shooting guns as long as the right people get shot."
—**Clint Eastwood**

"Murder is always a mistake. One should never do anything that one cannot talk about after dinner."
—**Oscar Wilde**

EPITAPHS

Uncle John's not dead, but he's already written his epitaph: "Don't forget to flush."

...that nothing's so sacred as honor and nothing's so loyal as love
—**Wyatt Earp**

"The Entertainer"
He did it all
—**Sammy Davis, Jr.**

A master of comedy
His genius in the art of humor
Brought gladness
To the world he loved.
—**Stan Laurel**

A genius of comedy
His talent brought joy and Laughter to all the world.
—**Oliver Hardy**

WORDS OF FRIENDSHIP

Let's face it, without our friends, it would be a lot harder to get through life.

"I am thankful for the mess to clean after a party because it means I have been surrounded by friends."
—Nancie J. Carmody

"Friendship is not something you learn in school. But if you haven't learned the meaning of friendship, you really haven't learned anything."
—Muhammad Ali

"A friend loves you...anyway."
—Anonymous

"Pizza can wait; friendship cannot."
—Gwendolyn Lockwood

"Never refuse any advance of friendship, for if nine out of ten bring you nothing, one alone may repay you."
—Madame de Tencin

"In prosperity our friends know us; in adversity we know our friends."
—John Churton Collins

"Get not your friends by bare compliments, but by giving them tokens of your love."
—Socrates

"A friend is someone you don't have to talk to anymore once the food is on the table."
—Sabrina Matthews

"It seems to me that trying to live without friends is like milking a bear to get cream for your morning coffee. It is a whole lot of trouble, and then not worth much after you get it."
—Zora Neale Hurston

"A friend that ain't in need is a friend indeed."
—Kin Hubbard

"Friendship is far more tragic than love. It lasts longer."
—Oscar Wilde

"A friend will help you move. A best friend will help you move...a body."
—Dave Attell

"The only way to have a friend is to be one."
—Ralph Waldo Emerson

"Without friends no one would choose to live, though he had all other goods."
—Aristotle

"The only thing better than sex is sex with chocolate on top." —Catherine Zeta-Jones

REEL WISE

Deep thoughts from the Silver Screen.

"Sometimes, you get the bear. Sometimes, the bear gets you."
—The Stranger (Sam Elliott), *The Big Lebowski* (1998)

"Everyone who drinks is not a poet. Some of us drink because we're not poets."
—Arthur (Dudley Moore), *Arthur* (1981)

"You don't throw a whole life away just 'cause it's banged up a little."
—Tom (Chris Cooper), *Seabiscuit* (2003)

"Most of us live our lives devoid of cinematic moments." —Nora Ephron

THE ANIMAL KINGDOM

More animal insights from the strangest animal of all, the human animal.

"Of all the wonders of nature, a tree in summer is perhaps the most remarkable; with the possible exception of a moose singing 'Embraceable You' in spats."
—**Woody Allen**

"There is a natural hootchy-kootchy motion to a goldfish."
—**Walt Disney**

"We hope that, when the insects take over the world, they will remember with gratitude how we took them along on all our picnics."
—**Bill Vaughan**

"Lots of people talk to animals....Not very many listen, though....That's the problem."
—**Benjamin Hoff,**
The Tao of Pooh

"To insult someone we call him 'bestial.' For deliberate cruelty and nature, 'human' might be the greater insult."
—**Isaac Asimov**

"Dangerous at both ends and uncomfortable in the middle."
—**Ian Fleming,**
describing the horse

"The kiss originated when the first male reptile licked the first female reptile, implying in a subtle, complimentary way that she was as succulent as the small reptile he had for dinner the night before."
—**F. Scott Fitzgerald**

"Imagine if birds were tickled by feathers. You'd see a flock of birds fly by, laughing hysterically."
—**Steven Wright**

A caterpillar has more muscles than a human.

DITZY DIVAS

*To quote another diva, Granny Clampett of
The Beverly Hillbillies fame, "if brains was
lard, these gals couldn't grease a pan."*

"I am a really big Elvis fan and I think the reason why
we did the whole Elvis thing is because, you know, he's
from Vegas."

**—Britney Spears (Elvis was born in Tupelo,
Mississippi, but lived in Memphis,
Tennessee, much of his adult life)**

"I love Jordan. He was one of the greatest athletes of
our time."

**—Mariah Carey,
on the death of King Hussein, of Jordan**

"These beautiful, tall ballerinas taught me how to do it.
And I remember thinking that I'd found the neatest
thing. I could eat whatever I wanted and not gain
weight, and it really helped me deal with my feelings
and fears. Because eating disorders are as much about
feelings as they are about food."

**—Paula Abdul,
on how she got bulimia**

"I wish men had boobs because I like the feel of them.
It's so funny—when I record, I sing with a hand over
each of them, maybe it's a comfort thing."

—Baby Spice, of the Spice Girls

"So where is the Cannes Film Festival being held this
year?"

—Christina Aguilera

"The immature poet imitates; the mature poet plagiarizes." —T.S. Eliot

DAVE ATTELL TELLS IT ALL

*The star of Comedy Central's Insomniac
is vulgar, irreverant, and very funny.*

"When *Jaws 1* was made, people stopped going to the ocean, and when *Jaws 2, 3,* and *4* were made, people stopped going to the theater."

"You know, when you're little, your dad, you think he's Superman. Then you grow up and realize he's just a guy who wears a cape."

"I keep seeing commercials on how to get your dream job. 'Call now for information on your dream job.' Wow! Finally, a chocolate factory run by blonde women! Count me in!"

"The best way to watch a *Girls Gone Wild* video is backward, because then it looks like the girls have learned their lesson."

"The moon is like the whore of astronomy: everyone's seen it."

"If you need to know directions, ask a man with one leg.... If there's a shortcut, he knows where it is."

ABOUT ADVICE

Grandpa Uncle John always said, "When someone gives you free advice, remember: You get what you pay for."

"A good scare is worth more than good advice."
—Edgar Watson Howe

"If it's free, it's advice; if you pay for it, it's counseling; if you can use either one, it's a miracle." —Jack Adams

"Advice is probably the only free thing which people won't take." —Lothar Kaul

"I owe my success to having listened respectfully to the very best advice, and then going away and doing the exact opposite."
—G. K. Chesterton

"It is more easy to be wise for others than for ourselves."
—François duc de la Rochefoucauld

"When we ask advice, we are usually looking for an accomplice."
—Marquis de LaGrange

"Wise men don't need advice; fools don't take it."
—Benjamin Franklin

"When a man comes to me for advice, I find out the kind of advice he wants, and I give it to him."
—Josh Billings

"The best advice I can give is to ignore advice. Life is too short to be distracted by the opinions of others."
—Russel Edson

"Advice would always be more acceptable if it didn't conflict with our plans."
—American proverb

"The friend who can be silent with us in a moment of despair or confusion, who can stay with us in an hour of grief and bereavement, who can tolerate not knowing, not curing, not healing and face with us the reality of our powerlessness, that is a friend who cares."
—Henri Nouwen

EINSTEIN SPEAKS

It must be nice to always be the smartest guy in the room.

"To punish me for my contempt for authority, fate made me an authority myself."

"A tyranny based on...deception and maintained by terror must inevitably perish from the poison it generates within itself."

"Force always attracts men of low morality."

"Egoism and competition are, alas, stronger forces than public spirit and sense of duty."

"Everything that is really great and inspiring is created by the individual who can labor in freedom."

"The most beautiful thing we can experience is the mysterious. It is the source of all true art and science. He to whom this emotion is a stranger, who no longer pauses to wonder and stand in rapt awe, is as good as dead."

"The problems that exist in the world today cannot be solved by the level of thinking that created them."

"It would be possible to describe everything scientifically, but it would make no sense; it would be without meaning, as if you described a Beethoven symphony as a variation of wave pressure."

"Science without religion is lame, religion without science is blind."

"The gift of fantasy has meant more to me than my talent for absorbing knowledge."

"A hundred times every day I remind myself that my inner and outer life depend upon the labors of other men, living and dead, and that I must exert myself in order to give in the measure I have received."

"He who joyfully marches in rank and file has already earned my contempt. He has been given a large brain by mistake, since for him the spinal cord would suffice."

"There are two ways to live your life. One is as though nothing is a miracle. The other is as though everything is."

OPINIONS ON EINSTEIN

"No, I don't understand my husband's theory of relativity, but I know my husband, and I know he can be trusted."
　　　　—Elsa Einstein

"The genius of Einstein leads to Hiroshima."
　　　　—Pablo Picasso

"Any man whose errors take 10 years to correct is quite a man."
　　　　—J. Robert Oppenheimer

"I'd have given 10 conversations with Einstein for a first meeting with a pretty chorus girl."
　　　　—Albert Camus

RINGLEADERS

*Some pretty sharp insights from guys who make
a living by getting punched in the head.*

"He hit me so hard I thought I saw the Messiah."
—**Shannon Briggs, on taking George Foreman's best shot**

"The worst thing that happened to managers was when boxers learned to read and write."
—**Paul Pender**

"When I was a champ, it really bothered me that there were all these people around who I didn't know but who were trying to control my life. I lost the title and they all disappeared and I got depressed. I drank so much and then I pigged out. After I got out of hospital, for the sake of my health, I took up boxing. Has there ever been an irony like that?"
—**Buster Douglas, on the bad times that drove him back to the ring**

"Goodness doesn't sell. You got to go to jail or kill someone in the ring before you 'deserve' to be champion. People want people in the sports world to have a bad life."
—**Evander Holyfield**

"I was a contender for almost a couple of decades and knocked on the door a few times, but am I satisied? Hell, no. If you've never been champion of the world you can't be satisfied. Once you make it in the pros in football, baseball, or hockey you could be the 1,000th best in those sports and still make a decent living. But if you're the 1,000th best in boxing, forget it."
—**George Chuvalo**

"In the first round, I hit him and he laughed at me. In the second, I hit him and he sneered. In the third round, he knocked me out."
—**Vince Phillips, on a match with WBA welterweight champ Ike Quartey**

"I remember how he threw that famous left hook. It went swooooosh, sounding like a bullet passing by my head. That's when I started thinking about what I had to do. I didn't want to get hit by that left hook, so I knocked him out."
—**George Foreman, on his title win over Joe Frazier**

"When they tell you to grow up, they mean stop growing." —**Tom Robbins**

"I got caught with a lot of good shots [in my career], but they didn't bother me. All they did was make me mad, and then it's time to go to work." —Marvin Hagler

"Boxing has an advantage over politics. In the ring, you know exactly what your opponent's intentions are." —Eder Jofre, now a politician in his native Brazil

"It gives the fighters one less day to pull out." —promoter Harold Weston, explaining why he moved shows from Fridays to Thursdays

*   *   *

MUHAMMAD ALI ON GREATNESS

"I am the greatest, I said that even before I knew I was."

"I figured that if I said it enough, I would convince the world that I really was the greatest."

"It's the repetition of affirmations that leads to belief. And once that belief becomes a deep conviction, things begin to happen."

"I am the greatest."

"It's hard to be humble when you're as great as I am."

DUMB PREDICTIONS

Think you can foretell the future? Go ahead—make all the
predictions you want. (Just don't write them down.)

TECHNOLOGY

Prediction: "Anyone who expects a source of power from the transformation of the atom is talking moonshine."
—Lord Rutherford, Nobel laureate and scientist, 1933

Prediction: "That is the biggest fool thing we've ever done. The bomb will never go off."
—Harry S Truman, shortly after assuming office in 1945, after being briefed on the Manhattan Project

Prediction: "X-rays will prove to be a hoax."
—Lord Kelvin, physicist, 1896

POLITICS

Prediction: "No woman will in my time be prime minister."
—Margaret Thatcher, 1969

ENTERTAINMENT

Prediction: "Television won't be able to hold on to any market it captures after the first six months. People will soon get tired of staring at a plywood box every night."
—Darryl F. Zanuck, head of 20th-Century Fox, 1946

WAR

Prediction: "I cannot conceive of anything more ridiculous, more absurd, and more affrontive to all sober judgement than the cry that we are profiting by the acquisition of New Mexico and California. I hold that they are not worth a dollar."
—U.S. Senator Daniel Webster of Massachusetts, 1848

EXPLORATION

Prediction: "No flying machine will ever fly from New York to Paris."
—Orville Wright, 1908

Prediction: "Airplanes are interesting toys but of no military value."
—Ferdinand Foch, Professor of Strategy, Ecole Superieure de Guerre, 1911

Prediction: "I cannot see any nation or combination of nations producing the money necessary to put up a satellite in outer space."
—Sir Richard Woolley, Astronomer Royal, 1957

"With politicians, artful evasion is always preferable to the outright lie." —Molly Ivins

THE MIDDLE AGES

This page marks the middle of the book, so what could be more appropriate than a page about being middle-aged.

"Middle age is when anything new in the way you feel is most likely a symptom."
—Laurence J. Peter

"Middle age occurs when you are too young to take up golf and too old to rush up to the net."
—Franklin Pierce Adams

"The really frightening thing about middle age is the knowledge you'll grow out of it."
—Doris Day

"Middle age is when you have met so many people that every new person you meet reminds you of someone else and usually is."
—Ogden Nash

"Middle age is the awkward period when Father Time starts catching up with Mother Nature."
—Harold Coffin

"Middle age is the time when a man is always thinking in a week or two he will feel as good as ever."
—Don Marquis

"I wouldn't mind being called middle-aged if only I knew a few more 100-year-old people."
—Dean Martin

"Middle age is when your weightlifting consists merely of standing up."
—Bob Hope

"The clothes of your life start to fit in middle age."
—Sean Penn

"Childhood is the time of life when you make faces in a mirror. Middle age is when the mirror gets even."
—Mickey Mansfield

"Middle age is the time of life when the most fun you have is talking about the most fun you used to have."
—Gene Perret

"Boys will be boys, and so will a lot of middle-aged men."
—Kin Hubbard

"Thirty-five is when you finally get your head together and your body starts falling apart."
—Caryn Leschen

Jack Nicholson spent every day of an entire school year in detention.

UNCLE JOHN'S QUOTATIONARY

Here's Part 5 of our quotation dictionary.
(Part 4 begins on page 162.)

IDEALISM: the noble toga that political gentlemen drape over their will to power. (Aldous Huxley)

IDEALIST: a cynic in the making. (Irving Layton)

IDIOT: a member of a large and powerful tribe whose influence in human affairs has always been dominant and controlling. (Ambrose Bierce)

IGNORANCE: the womb of monsters. (Henry Ward Beecher)

ILLUSION: the first of all pleasures. (Oscar Wilde)

IMAGINATION: the one weapon in the war against reality. (Jules de Gaultier)

"IN CONCLUSION": the phrase that wakes up the audience. (Herbert Prochnov)

INCOME TAX RETURNS: the most imaginative fiction being written today. (Herman Wouk)

INFORMATION: the currency of democracy. (Ralph Nader)

INMATES: ghosts whose dreams have been murdered. (Jill Johnston)

INSANITY: doing the same thing over and over again and expecting different results. (John Dryden)

INSPIRATION: inhaling the memory of an act never experienced. (Ned Rorem)

INSURANCE: a guarantee that no matter how many necessities a person has to forgo all through life, death is something to which he can still look forward. (Fred Allen)

INTELLECTUAL: someone who can listen to Rossini's 'William Tell' Overture without thinking of the Lone Ranger. (Billy Connolly)

INTERPRETATION: the revenge of the intellect upon art. (Susan Sontag)

JEALOUSY: the dragon which slays love under the pretense of keeping it alive. (Havelock Ellis)

"Time is the coin of life. Only you can determine how it will be spent." —Carl Sandburg

JET TRAVEL: what lets us see less and less of more and more faster and faster. (Leopold Fechtner)

JOB: death without the dignity. (Brendan Behan)

JOURNALISTS: restless voyeurs who see the warts on the world—the imperfection in people and places. (Gay Talese)

JUDGE: a law student who marks his own examination papers. (H. L. Mencken)

JURY: Twelve persons chosen to decide who has the better lawyer. (Robert Frost)

JUSTICE: the ligament which holds civilized beings and civilized nations together. (Daniel Webster)

KARATE: a form of martial arts in which people who have had years and years of training can, using only their hands and feet, make some of the worst movies in the history of the world. (Dave Barry)

KILL: to create a vacancy without nominating a successor. (Ambrose Bierce)

KISS: an application for a better position. (Jeff Rovin)

KLEPTOMANIAC: a person who helps himself because he can't help himself. (Henry Morgan)

KNOWLEDGE: power, if you know it about the right person. (Ethel Watts Mumford)

For more, see page 231.

*   *   *

THREE PIECES OF STRANGE ADVICE

"Never drink Diet Coke. Diet Coke is for fat people."
—**Paris Hilton**

"Never use a long word when a diminutive one will do."
—**William Safire**

"When I buy cookies I eat just four and throw the rest away. But first I spray them with Raid so I won't dig them out of the garbage later. Be careful, though, because Raid really doesn't taste that bad."
—**Janette Barber**

A species of ant was named after actor Harrison Ford.

THE PRESIDENTS SPEAK

*One of the most important parts
of a president's job is to talk.*

"I always figured the American public wanted a solemn ass for president, so I went along with them."
—Calvin Coolidge

"If you want to make enemies, try to change something."
—Woodrow Wilson

"Let us never forget that government is ourselves and not an alien power over us. The ultimate rulers of our democracy are not a president and senators and congressmen and government officials, but the voters of this country."
—Franklin D. Roosevelt

"Good thing I was not born a girl because I could never say no."
—Warren G. Harding

"A man who will steal for me will steal from me."
—Theodore Roosevelt

"May we never confuse honest dissent with disloyal subversion."
—Dwight D. Eisenhower

"Labor to keep alive in your breast that little spark of celestial fire called conscience."
—George Washington

"The right of revolution is an inherent one. When people are oppressed by their government, it is a natural right they enjoy to relieve themselves of oppression, if they are strong enough, whether by withdrawal from it, or by overthrowing it and substituting a government more acceptable."
—Ulysses S. Grant

"Reporters are puppets. They simply respond to the pull of the most powerful strings."
—Lyndon B. Johnson

"The man who is swimming against the stream knows the strength of it."
—Woodrow Wilson

"Some reporters said I don't have any vision. I don't see that."
—George H. W. Bush

"The higher the buildings, the lower the morals." —Noel Coward

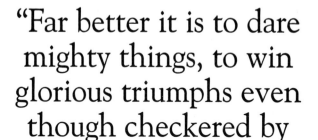

"Far better it is to dare mighty things, to win glorious triumphs even though checkered by failure, than to rank with those poor spirits who neither enjoy nor suffer much because they live in the gray twilight that knows neither victory nor defeat."

—Theodore Roosevelt

Real newspaper headline: "Helicopter Powered By Human Flies"

ROCK TALK

Some rock stars have brilliant minds...
and others have rocks in their heads.

"Our audience is like people who like licorice. Not everybody likes licorice, but people who like licorice really like licorice."
—Jerry Garcia

"I wanted to perform, I wanted to write songs, and I wanted to get lots of chicks."
—James Taylor,
on why he got into music

"Onstage, I've been hit by a grapefruit, beer cans, eggs, spit, money, cigarette butts, mandies, Quaaludes, joints, panties, and a fist."
—Iggy Pop

"The most important thing in the world to me now is being a kind person. I don't think there's anything more hardcore than being loving."
—Flea,
Red Hot Chili Peppers

"I often stand in a stadium full of people and ask myself the same question, 'How the hell did I end up here?'"
—Sting

"I went to hear the Rolling Stones one time in England. They had the music so loud that when I came out, I literally scared myself to death because I couldn't hear. I thought I was losing my hearing. I'm already blind, I can't be no Helen Keller."
—Ray Charles

"I have to laugh when someone asks if we're missing our childhood. When I turn 16, I can flip hamburgers for five bucks an hour, or I can go around the world and perform for thousands of people and make lots of money. What am I missing?"
—Zachary Hanson,
of Hanson

"The worst crime is faking it."
—Kurt Cobain

"Anything Sam Cooke did I would do...apart from getting shot in a hotel room by a hooker."
—Rod Stewart

NEVER THE TWAIN SHALL MEET

Mark Twain is among the most quoted people…ever.
Which makes sense because he had a lot to say. But as
is often the case, a lot of what's attributed to Twain
was either said differently or never said by him at all.

The Quote: "The coldest winter I ever spent was a summer in San Francisco."

Actually: In an 1879 letter, Twain quoted someone else who, when asked if he'd ever seen a colder winter, replied, "Yes, last summer." Twain then added, "I judge he spent his summer in Paris." Because Twain spent so much time in San Francisco, this anonymous observation has become associated with him.

The Quote: "The reports of my death are greatly exaggerated."

Actually: He said, "The report of my death was an exaggeration." In 1897, newspapers reported that Twain's cousin, James Ross Clemens, was near death, and somehow this was corrupted into reports that Twain himself was dying. He cleared it up with the above statement, but revised it later while writing his autobiography, adding the "greatly" to make it sound better.

The Quote "If I had more time I would have written a shorter letter."

Actually: Blaise Pascal wrote this.

The Quote: "Everyone talks about the weather, but nobody does anything about it."

Actually: Charles Dudley Warner was an American novelist and essayist. A contemporary of Twain's, Fuller collaborated with his more famous counterpart on a few novels and coined the phrase above, as well as another famous saying, "Politicians makes strange bedfellows" (which has also been credited to Twain).

The Quote: "I am not an American. I am *the* American."
Actually: Twain was quoting Frank Fuller.

The Quote: "Wagner's music is better than it sounds."
Actually: Twain *wished* he was the first one to say this but admitted later in life that it belongs to another 19th-century humorist named Edgar Wilson Nye.

The Quote: "It is far better to keep one's mouth shut and be thought a fool, than to open one's mouth and erase all doubt."
Actually: Twain was most likely quoting Abraham Lincoln when he said this, but the quote itself is much older than that. It began as a Bible verse. Proverbs 17:28—"Even a fool who keeps silent is considered wise; when he closes his lips, he is deemed intelligent."

The Quote: "It isn't so astonishing the things that I can remember, as the number of things I can remember that aren't so."
Actually: Twain was paraphrasing Josh Billings, who wrote that "I honestly beleave it iz better tew know nothing than two know what ain't so."

The Quote: "There are three kinds of lies: lies, damn lies, and statistics."
Actually: Twain wrote this in his autobiography and correctly attributed it to Benjamin Disraeli, but it has since become associated with the American author and not the English prime minister.

ALSO FALSELY ATTRIBUTED TO TWAIN
• "Quitting smoking is the easiest thing I ever did. I ought to know because I've done it a thousand times."

• "When I was a boy of 14, my father was so ignorant I could hardly stand to have the old man around. But when I got to be 21, I was astonished at how much the old man had learned in 7 years."

• "Whenever I feel the urge to exercise, I lie down until it goes away."

• "There is nothing so annoying as to have two people go right on talking when you're interrupting."

NOVEL THINKING

Deep insights from the pages of the world's greatest novels.

"It's a strange thing, but when you are dreading something, and would give anything to slow down time, it has a disobliging habit of speeding up."
—*Harry Potter and the Goblet of Fire*, by J. K. Rowling

"In my younger and more vulnerable years my father gave me some advice that I've been turning over in my mind ever since. 'Whenever you feel like criticizing anyone,' he told me, 'just remember that all the people in this world haven't had the advantages that you've had.'"
—*The Great Gatsby*, by F. Scott Fitzgerald

"I got a cash flow problem."
"Yeah? What kind of a cash flow problem?"
"I ain't got a cash flow."
"That's a problem."
—*Bloody Mary*, by Gabrielle Kraft

"But we have received a sign, Edith—a mysterious sign. A miracle has happened on this farm...in the middle of the web there were the words 'Some Pig'...we have no ordinary pig."
"Well," said Mrs. Zuckerman, "it seems to me you're a little off. It seems to me we have no ordinary spider."
"Oh, no," said Zuckerman. "It's the pig that's unusual. It says so, right there in the middle of the web."
—*Charlotte's Web*, by E. B. White

"The one who feels no fear is a fool, and the one who lets fear rule him is a coward."
—*Castle Roogna*, by Piers Anthony

"He flung himself from the room, flung himself upon his horse and rode madly off in all directions."
—*Gertrude the Governess*, by Stephen Leacock

Salvador Dali and Walt Disney collaborated on a cartoon called "Destino."

THE DIVINE BOVINE

Here's the most moooving page in this entire book.

"You can only milk a cow so long, then you're left holding the pail."
—**Hank Aaron**

"Cows are amongst the gentlest of breathing creatures; none show more passionate tenderness to their young when deprived of them; and, in short, I am not ashamed to profess a deep love for these quiet creatures."
—**Thomas De Quincey**

"Who was the guy who first looked at a cow and said, 'I think I'll drink whatever comes out of these things when I squeeze 'em!'?"
—**Calvin, *Calvin and Hobbes***

"Sacred cows make the tastiest hamburger."
—**Abbie Hoffman**

"Scientists tell us that the fastest animal on Earth, with a top speed of 120 ft/sec, is a cow that has been dropped out of a helicopter."
—**Dave Barry**

"Cows, as some *Far Side* readers know, are a favorite subject of mine. I've always found them to be the quintessentially absurd animal for situations even more absurd. Even the name 'cow,' to me, is intrinsically funny."
—**Gary Larson**

"I guess cows aren't really into the four food groups, especially when they are two of them."
—**Anthony Clark**

"Facts are like cows. If you look them in the face hard enough they generally run away."
—**Dorothy L. Sayers**

"The cow is of the bovine ilk; One end is moo, the other milk."
—**Ogden Nash**

"There is no politician in India daring enough to attempt to explain to the masses that cows can be eaten."
—**Indira Gandhi**

"Opie, you haven't finished your milk. We can't put it back in the cow, you know."
—**Aunt Bea, *The Andy Griffith Show***

"To err is human, to moo, bovine."
—**Uncle John**

"Some cows actually give more milk when they listen to other music—for example, when they listen to Elvis, like *Love Me Tender*, they increased in milk production. When they listened to La Toya Jackson, they were found to produce sour milk. When they listened to Jerry Garcia, this makes the cow want more grass, apparently. Here's the most startling of all: when they played Michael Jackson, the cows would milk themselves."

—Jay Leno

MORE ON AGING

...Because we're not getting any younger.

"One of the good things about getting older is you find you're more interesting than most of the people you meet."
—Lee Marvin

"You can't stay young forever, but you can be immature for the rest of your life."
—Maxine Wilkie

"There was no respect for youth when I was young, and now that I am old, there is no respect for age. I missed it coming and going."
—J. B. Priestley

"The older I get, the better I used to be."
—Connie Hawkins, pro basketball player

"The age I'm at now, you go from being a young girl to suddenly blossoming into a woman. You ripen, you know? And then you start to rot."
—Liv Tyler

"I am exploring for the first time in my life the amazing wonderland known as senility."
—Timothy Leary

"I look better, feel better, make love better, and I'll tell you something else....I never lied better."
—George Burns

"Nothing is more telling of one's age than who they think is glamorous. So, to me, Cary Grant looks like a movie star, Paul Newman looks like a movie star, Warren Beatty looks like a movie star, but Brad Pitt, to be perfectly honest, looks like a trick."
—Fran Lebowitz

"Age is nothing more than experience, and some of us are more experienced than others."
—Mickey Rooney, on being 77

"You can't be as old as I am without waking up with a surprised look on your face every morning: 'Holy Christ, whaddya know—I'm still around!' It's absolutely amazing that I survived all the booze and smoking and the cars and the career."
—Paul Newman, on being 75

"Pistachio nuts, the red ones, cure any problem." —Paula Danziger

KID STUFF

*If you can read this page all by yourself,
Uncle John's going to give you a cookie.*

"There are three terrible ages of childhood—1 to 10, 10 to 20, and 20 to 30."
—Cleveland Amory

"The secret of dealing successfully with a child is not to be its parent."
—Mel Lazarus

"We are given children to test us and make us more spiritual."
—George F. Will

"The invention of the teenager was a mistake. Once you identify a period of life in which people get to stay out late but don't have to pay taxes—naturally, no one wants to live any other way."
—Judith Martin

"Youth is a wonderful thing. What a crime to waste it on children."
—George Bernard Shaw

"My wife and I just had a baby, and there's nothing relaxed about them. They're like these tense things who scream in order to fall asleep. Just like adults, only more direct."
—Ian Shoales

"The real menace in dealing with a five-year-old is that in no time at all you begin to sound like a five-year-old."
—Jean Kerr

"As a child, I understood how to give; I have forgotten this grace since I became civilized."
—Ohiyesa, Santee Sioux

"Human beings are the only creatures on Earth that allow their children to come back home."
—Bill Cosby

"I love children, especially when they cry, for then someone takes them away."
—Nancy Mitford

"Children are completely egoistic; they feel their needs intensely and strive ruthlessly to satisfy them."
—Sigmund Freud

"Grown men can learn from very little children, for the hearts of the children are pure. Therefore, the Great Spirit may show to them many things which older people miss."
—Black Elk

DUBYA-ISMS

*George W. Bush has declared war on...the
English language! Watch out, English,
you can run, but you can't hide.*

"When I was young and irresponsible, I was young and irresponsible."

"This is still a dangerous world. It's a world of madmen and uncertainty and potential mental losses."

"Redefining the role of the United States from enablers to keep the peace to enablers to keep the peace from peacekeepers is going to be an assignment."

"I've changed my style somewhat, as you know. I'm less—I pontificate less...and I'm more interacting with people."

"The American people's expectations are that we will fail. Our mission is to exceed their expectations."

"Putting subliminable messages into commercials is absurd."

"A hobby I enjoy is mapping the human genome. I hope one day I can clone another Dick Cheney. Then I won't have to do anything."

"We cannot let terrorists and rogue nations hold this nation hostile or hold our allies hostile."

"We want [America] to be a more literate and hopefuller country."

"But the true strength of America is found in the hearts and souls of people like Travis, people who are willing to love their neighbor, just like they would like to love themselves."

"Families is where our nation finds hope, where wings take dream."

"I know how hard it is for you to put food on your family."

"Rarely is the question asked: 'Is our children learning?'"

"Like you, I have been disgraced about what I've seen on TV that took place in prison."

"My job is to, like, think beyond the immediate."

"Recession means that people's incomes, at the employer level, are going down, basically, relative to costs, people are getting laid off."

"In my judgment, when the United States says there will be serious consequences, and if there isn't serious consequences, it creates adverse consequences."

"Now, we talked to Joan Hanover. She and her husband, George, were visiting with us. They are near retirement—retiring—in the process of retiring, meaning they're very smart, active, capable people who are retirement age and are retiring."

"Then you wake up at the high school level and find out that the illiteracy level of our children are appalling."

"I'm also not very analytical. You know I don't spend a lot of time thinking about myself, about why I do things."

"I glance at the headlines just to kind of get a flavor for what's moving. I rarely read the stories and get briefed by people who probably read the news themselves."

"First, let me make it very clear, poor people aren't necessarily killers. Just because you happen to be not rich doesn't mean you're willing to kill."

"I'm the master of low expectations."

*　　*　　*

"Bush isn't stupid. We must be stupid, otherwise he wouldn't talk to us like that."

—Jon Stewart

"HERE'S LOOKIN' AT YOU KID"

Do you remember who said these famous movie lines? Well, do ya, punk?

1. "Look, Daddy! Teacher says every time a bell rings, an angel gets his wings."

2. "I love the smell of napalm in the morning."

3. "Come up and see me some time."

4. "You've got to ask yourself one question: do I feel lucky? Well, do ya, punk?"

5. "I'm as mad as hell, and I'm not going to take this anymore!"

6. "Play it, Sam. Play 'As Time Goes By.'"

7. "I'm sorry, Dave. I'm afraid I can't do that."

a. *Dirty Harry*

b. *2001: A Space Odyssey*

c. *Network*

d. *It's a Wonderful Life*

e. *Goin' to Town*

f. *Apocalypse Now*

g. *Casablanca*

Answers

1. d; 2. f; 3. e; 4. a; 5. c; 6. g; 7. b.

Dirty Harry's badge number is 2211.

OH, PSHAW!

George Bernard Shaw (1856–1950) was born in Dublin, Ireland and moved to London as a young man. He was a theater and music critic, a playwright, and a novelist. He used each of these forums to promote his progressive political agenda and act as a "general consultant to mankind." Here is some of his consulting.

"All great truths begin as blasphemies."

"Few people think more than two or three times a year; I have made an international reputation for myself by thinking once or twice a week."

"Life does not cease to be funny when people die any more that it ceases to be serious when people laugh."

"Most people do not pray; they only beg."

"Forget about likes and dislikes. They are of no consequence. Just do what must be done. This may not be happiness, but it is greatness."

"When a man wants to murder a tiger he calls it sport; when a tiger wants to murder him he calls it ferocity."

"The minority is sometimes right; the majority always wrong."

"There is no satisfaction in hanging a man who does not object to it."

"I'm an atheist and I thank God for it."

"The first condition of progress is the removal of censorship."

"There may be some doubt as to who are the best people to have children, but there is no doubt that parents are the worst."

"It is assumed that the woman must wait motionless until she is wooed. That is how the spider waits for the fly."

"Patriotism is your conviction that this country is superior because you were born in it."

"The reasonable man adapts himself to the conditions that surround him; the unreasonable man adapts surrounding conditions to himself. Progress depends on the unreasonable man."

In high school, Mariah Carey's nickname was "Mirage" because she was absent so often.

THE *TONIGHT* SHOW WITH...

There are "Dave" people, and "Jay" people. This page is for Leno fans.

"The Discovery Channel had a fascinating show on the mating habits of hyenas. They said often times the male hyena will get angry at the female hyena while they are having sex. It doesn't help that the female hyena is laughing at you all the time."

"I don't want to be sexist here, but I think men make better mall Santas. Men have bigger bellies, men are used to sitting for long periods of time, and men have lots of experience making promises they have no intention of keeping."

"Congress voted for tougher laws on corporations. So now when a corporation buys a senator, they need a receipt."

"Bobby Brown is pleading innocent to marijuana possession. He'll swear on the Bible that he hasn't had a hit in 15 years."

"They guy who founded Winchell's Donuts has died. He went peacefully. His eyes just sort of glazed over."

"Nabisco announced recently that it's coming out with new bite-sized Oreos that are easier to eat. How lazy are we getting in this country when people are too exhausted to eat Oreos? Who eats an Oreo and says, 'Let me wrap the rest of this up, I wish they were smaller.'"

"According to *Men's Health* magazine, the average man has had sex in a car 15 times. That's something to keep in mind next time you're looking for a used car."

"If Jay spent as much time studying as he does trying to be a comedian...

IT'S TAX TIME

*Here are a few quotes about taxes. We had a
bunch of really nasty ones, but we're leaving
them out. (We don't want to get audited.)*

"The art of taxation consists of plucking the goose
to obtain the largest possible amount of feathers
with the smallest possible amount of hissing."
—**Jean-Baptiste Colbert**

"The hardest thing in the world is to understand
income tax."
—**Albert Einstein**

"On my income tax form 1040 it says 'Check this
box if you are blind.' I wanted to put a check mark
about three inches away."
—**Tom Lehrer**

"What is the difference between a taxidermist and
a tax collector? The taxidermist takes only your
skin."
—**Mark Twain**

"There's nothing wrong with the younger generation that being taxpayers won't cure."
—**Dan Bennett**

"Only the little people pay taxes."
—**Leona Helmsley**

...he'd be a big star." —Jay Leno's fifth grade report card.

BIG MOUTHS

A classic Far Side *cartoon by Gary Larson depicts God in his kitchen adding all of the ingredients that will become the Earth. One ingredient is a bottle labeled "Jerks," to which God remarks as he's pouring it on: "Just to make it interesting." Here are a few comments from some "interesting" people.*

"It was never my intention to 'market' my son, as some have cynically claimed in the press. Anyone who thinks it was 'marketing' him should know about all the projects we have turned down because they were not the right sort of exposure for him."
—Kathie Lee Gifford

"Of course they have, or I wouldn't be sitting here talking to someone like you."
—Barbara Cartland, *when asked by an interviewer whether she thought class barriers had broken down in England*

"Filipinos want beauty. I have to look beautiful so that the poor Filipinos will have a star to look at from their slums."
—Imelda Marcos

"Once you've seen one ghetto, you've seen them all."
—Vice President Spiro T. Agnew

"As you know, I have a reputation for being difficult, but only with stupid people."
—Val Kilmer

"I don't feel we did wrong in taking this great country away from them. There were great numbers of people who needed new land, and the Indians were selfishly trying to keep it for themselves."
—John Wayne

RITA RUDNER

*Our opinion: Rudner's the funniest
female comedian of her generation.*

"Men would like monogamy better if it sounded less like monotony."

"I got kicked out of ballet class because I pulled a groin muscle. It wasn't mine."

"Men who have pierced ears are better prepared for marriage. They've experienced pain and bought jewelry."

"Marrying a divorced man is ecologically responsible. In a world where there are more women than men, it pays to recycle."

"Men are very confident people. My husband is so confident that when he watches sports on television, he thinks that if he concentrates he can help his team. If the team is in trouble, he coaches the players from our living room, and if they're really in trouble, I have to get off the phone in case they call him."

"When I eventually met Mr. Right I had no idea that his first name was Always."

"These big birthday parties my friends make for their kids: One of my friends had a surprise birthday party for her child. He was one year old. We all snuck around the crib, jumped up, and yelled, 'Surprise!' He's in therapy now."

"My car has this feature that I guess is standard, because it was on my last car, too. It has a rotating gas tank. Whatever side of the pump I pull up to, it's on the other side."

"I hate self-service gas stations so much. I was all dressed up once going to a formal affair, so I was standing there in the middle of the night, in an evening gown, pumping gas. I looked like the gas fairy."

"Halloween was confusing. All my life my parents said, 'Never take candy from strangers.' And then they dressed me up and said, 'Go beg for it.' I didn't know what to do. I'd knock on people's doors and go, 'Trick or treat. No thank you.'"

"Almost everybody is born a genius and buried an idiot." —Charles Bukowski

INTERNATIONAL PROVERBS

Wit and wisdom from around the world.

"The best way to get praise is to die."
—Italy

"We're fools whether we dance or not, so we might as well dance."
—Japan

"Drink nothing without seeing it; sign nothing without reading it."
—Spain

"Hold a true friend with both hands."
—Niger

"Be sure to live your life, because you are a long time dead."
—Scotland

"If you can walk you can dance. If you can talk you can sing."
—Zimbabwe

"Don't give me advice, give me money."
—Spain

"Distrust the advice of the interested."
—Greece

"The advice of a wife is worthless, but woe to the man who does not take it."
—Wales

"Ideas should be clear and chocolate thick."
—Spain

"Fall seven times, stand up eight."
—Japan

"The palest ink is better than the best memory."
—China

"Be honorable yourself if you wish to associate with honorable people."
—Wales

"If only the young knew; if only the old could."
—France

"No chupa, no shtupa—no wedding, no bedding."
—Yiddish

"Let your head be more than a funnel to your stomach."
—Germany

Keanu Reeves onced managed a Toronto pasta shop.

FRACTURED PHRASES

More variations on a phrase.

"When in Rome, do
as the Romans."
—St. Ambrose

"When on Earth, do as
the Earthlings do."
—Mork, *Mork and
Mindy*

"When in the U.S., do as
the French do."
—Michael Greenberg,
MD

"When in Baghdad, do as
Baghdaddies do."
—Patricia Harrington,
The Patsy (1928)

**Rusty Griswald (Jason
Lively):** Who was it that
said when in Rome do as
the Romans do?

**Clark Griswald (Chevy
Chase):** That was Rome,
not Paris. This is Paris and
you're drunk.
—*National Lampoon's
European Vacation*

"It's not whether you
win or lose, it's how
you play the game."

"It's not whether you win
or lose, it's how you place
the blame."
—Oscar Wilde

"Whoever said, 'It's not
whether you win or lose
that counts,' probably lost."
—Martina Navratilova

"It matters not whether you
win or lose; what matters is
whether I win or lose."
—Darrin Weinberg

"It's not how you play the
game, it's whether you win
or lose."
—Davy Jones,
The Monkees

"Son, when you participate
in sporting events, it's not
whether you win or lose—
it's how drunk you get."
—Homer Simpson

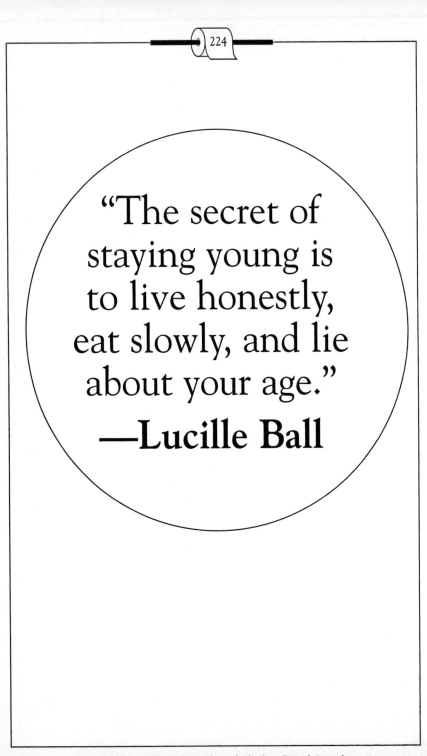

"The secret of staying young is to live honestly, eat slowly, and lie about your age."

—**Lucille Ball**

Tom Hanks is a direct descendant of Abraham Lincoln's uncle.

RODNEY DANGERFIELD

*The guy who "got no respect" was actually one
of the most respected comedians around.*

"I have no self-confidence. When a girl tells me yes,
I tell her to think it over."

"I haven't spoken to my wife in years—I didn't want
to interrupt her."

"My proctologist was laughing. I said, 'What's so
funny?' 'It's an inside joke.'"

"It's great to have gray hair. Ask anyone who's bald."

"If every man was as true to his country as he was to
his wife, we'd be in a lot of trouble."

"Last week I saw my psychiatrist. I told him, 'Doc, I
keep thinking I'm a dog.' He told me to get off his
couch."

"I got a dog, a cocker spaniel. He swallowed a Viagra
pill. Now he's a pointer."

"I wanna tell you, I don't get no respect. When I
was a child, I was kidnapped. They sent my parents a
piece of my finger. My old man said he wanted more
proof."

"My wedding day, that was a beauty. I went to put
the ring on, and she gave me the wrong finger."

WRITERS ON WRITING

More of what writers say about their craft.

"I do most of my work sitting down. That's where I shine."
—**Robert Benchley**

"I write for the same reason I breathe—because if I didn't, I would die."
—**Isaac Asimov**

"Books are never finished—they are merely abandoned."
—**Oscar Wilde**

"Writers get exactly the right amount of fame: just enough to get a good table in a restaurant but not enough so that people are constantly interrupting you while you're eating dinner."
—**Fran Lebowitz**

"Writing has laws of perspective, of light and shade, just as painting does, or music. If you are born knowing them, fine. If not, learn them. Then rearrange the rules to suit yourself."
—**Truman Capote**

"The good writing of any age has always been the product of someone's neurosis, and we'd have mighty dull literature if all the writers that came along were a bunch of happy chuckleheads."
—**William Styron**

"The difference between the right and the nearly right word is the same as that between lightning and the lightning bug."
—**Mark Twain**

"The writer must believe that what he is doing is the most important thing in the world. And he must hold to this illusion even when he knows it is not true."
—**John Steinbeck**

YOU'RE HISTORY!

As the wise Dan Quayle once said, "It's a question of whether we're going to go forward into the future, or past to the back." On this page, we will be going past to the back.

"History would be a wonderful thing—if it were only true." —Leo Tolstoy

"History repeats itself; that's one of the things that's wrong with history." —Clarence Darrow

"History is, in part, a series of madmen deluding people into parting with their children for loathsome and tragic schemes." —Sting

"The course of history shows that as a government grows, liberty decreases." —Thomas Jefferson

"History is simply a piece of paper covered with print; the main thing is still to make history, not to write it." —Otto von Bismarck

"If you can cut the people off from their history, then they can be easily persuaded." —Karl Marx

"A country without a memory is a country of madmen." —George Santayana

"Instead of the Pilgrim Fathers landing on Plymouth Rock, the Plymouth Rock should have landed on the Pilgrim Fathers." —H. L. Mencken

"History is the record of an encounter between character and circumstance." —Donald Creighton

"God alone knows the future, but only an historian can alter the past." —Ambrose Bierce

"Three cheers for war in general." —Benito Mussolini

SNL NEWS

More snippets from "Weekend Update."

"According to newly released documents, tobacco companies gave free cigarettes to celebrities such as Shelley Winters and Jerry Lewis to try to influence the public to smoke. In their defense, the tobacco company executives said, 'No, no, no. We were just trying to kill Shelley Winters and Jerry Lewis.'"

—**Tina Fey**

"In order to feel safer on his private jet, actor John Travolta has purchased a bomb-sniffing dog. Unfortunately for the actor, the dog came six movies too late."

—**Jimmy Fallon**

"Well, this week, after a Los Angeles restaurant refused to seat him, O. J. Simpson demanded and got five hundred dollars in compensation. In addition, the restaurant must now offer separate 'murderer' and 'non-murderer' sections."

—**Norm MacDonald**

"A judge ruled yesterday that reputed mob boss John Gotti can learn the names of the jurors in his upcoming assault trial—but not their businesses or home addresses. Jury foreman John Smith said that he is not worried…but juror Laika Jardel Rapsanick said, 'Yeah, I'm a little worried but, uh…I'm pretty sure he's not guilty.'"

—**Dennis Miller**

"You know, a lot of people come up to me and say, 'Al Franken, why don't you run for president?' Well, I'd like to be president, I think I'd be a great one. Perhaps one of the greatest in our nation's history. But I don't want to submit myself to the intrusive scrutiny characteristic of today's presidential politics. For example, I'd have to give up adultery."

—**Al Franken**

"This week marked the 5,000th performance of the Broadway musical *Cats*. It also marked the 5,000th time a guy turned to his wife and said, 'What the hell is this?'"

—**Norm MacDonald**

"Don't you hate people who say they're not complaining and then complain?" —Edna Ferber

THE PRICE OF FAME

*Comments about life in the spotlight,
from those who know.*

"Any actor who tells you he doesn't want to be famous is full of crap. I've been a waiter, an orderly, a messenger—and I can tell you that being a movie star is much better. No comparison."
—**Jon Lovitz**

"A celebrity is one who works hard all his life to become well-known and then goes through streets wearing dark glasses so no one recognizes him."
—**Fred Allen**

"I stopped believing in Santa Claus at an early age. Mother took me in to see him in a department store and he asked me for my autograph."
—**Shirley Temple Black**

"I buy *The National Enquirer* every week and read it. And love to read it. Until I'm in it. And then I'm furious."
—**Tammy Wynette**

"I'm an actor, not a star. Stars are people who live in Hollywood and have heart-shaped swimming pools."
—**Al Pacino**

"I'm not going to be modest anymore. I'm a movie star, and it's lovely."
—**Anthony Hopkins**

"People get the idea that if you're famous, you've got some exalted sense of humanity. The truth is really just the opposite."
—**Aimee Mann**

"We expect our celebrities to be super human. But think about it—the thing that drives people to become celebrities is this need for overwhelming love. And when many people got the fame they crave, they don't feel they deserve it. And so they screw up."
—**Boy George**

"Fame has its price, and the price is expensive."
—**Glen Campbell**

"I may be a living legend, but that sure don't help when I've got to change a tire."
—**Roy Orbison**

"The legend part is easy. It's the living that's hard."
—**Keith Richards**

MY COUNTRY 'TIS OF THEE

More opinions on America.

"The administration says the American people want tax cuts. Well, duh. The American people also want drive-through nickel beer night. The American people want to lose weight by eating ice cream. he American people love the Home Shopping Network because it's commercial free."
—**Will Durst**

"America is a nation that conceives many odd inventions for getting somewhere but can think of nothing to do when it gets there."
—**Will Rogers**

"Nowhere in the world is superiority more easily attained, or more eagerly admitted. The chief business of the nation, as a nation, is the setting up of heroes, mainly bogus."
—**H. L. Mencken**

"The United States right now is simultaneously the world's most loved, hated, feared, and admired nation. In short, we're Frank Sinatra."
—**Dennis Miller**

"You know how Americans are—when it comes to sex, the men can't keep from lying and the women can't keep from telling the truth."
—**Robin Zander**

"God protects fools, drunks, and the United States of America."
—**Otto von Bismarck**

"Thank God we're living in a country where the sky's the limit, the stores are open late, and you can shop in bed thanks to television."
—**Joan Rivers**

"The thing that impresses me most about America is the way parents obey their children."
—**Duke of Windsor**

"America's greatest strength, and its greatest weakness, is our belief in second chances, our belief that we can always start over, that things can be made better."
—**Anthony Walton**

UNCLE JOHN'S QUOTATIONARY

Here's Part 6 of our quotation dictionary.
(Part 5 begins on page 202.)

LAUGHTER: the shortest distance between two people. (Victor Borge)

LAWS: spider webs through which the big flies pass and the little ones get caught. (Honoré de Balzac)

LAWSUIT: a machine which you go into as a pig and come out as a sausage. (Ambrose Bierce)

LAWYERS: people who prove that talk definitely isn't cheap. (Justine McCarthy)

LAZINESS: nothing more than the habit of resting before you get tired. (Jules Renard)

LEADERSHIP: duty, honor, country, character, and listening from time to time. (George W. Bush)

LESS: more. (Robert Browning)

LIBERALS: people who can understand everything except people who don't understand them. (Lenny Bruce)

LIBERTY: the right to do whatever the laws permit. (Montesquieu)

LIES: the basic building blocks of good manners. (Quentin Crisp)

LIFE: one damned thing after another. (Elbert Hubbard)

LOGIC: If it was so, it might be; and if it were so, it would be; but as it isn't, it ain't. That's logic. (Tweedledee, *Alice Through the Looking Glass*, by Lewis Carroll)

LOVE: an ocean of emotions entirely surrounded by expenses. (Thomas Dewar)

LUCK: being ready. (Brian Eno)

LUNATIC: anyone surrounded by lunatics. (Ezra Pound)

MAJOR LEAGUE BASE-BALL TEAM: a collection of 25 youngish men who have made the Major Leagues and discovered that, in spite of it, life remains distressingly short of ideal. (Roger Kahn)

MAKE-UP: what it takes to look natural. (Calvin Klein)

MANKIND: nature's sole mistake. (W. S. Gilbert)

MANUSCRIPT: something sub-

"Life is change: growth is optional." —Karen Kaiser Clark

mitted in haste and returned at leisure. (Oliver Herford)

MAPLE LEAF GARDENS: the most important religious building in Canada. (William Kilbourn)

MARRIAGE: a souvenir of love. (Helen Rowland)

MASTURBATION: sex with someone you love. (Woody Allen)

MATURITY: be able to stick with a job until it is finished. Be able to bear an injustice without having to get even. Be able to carry money without spending it. Do your duty without being supervised. (Ann Landers)

MEDIA: plural for mediocre. (Rene Saguisag)

MEMORIAL SERVICES: the cocktail parties of the geriatric set. (Ralph Richardson)

MEMORY: the thing you forget with. (Alexander Chase)

MIDDLE AGE: when your age starts showing around the middle.

(Bob Hope)

MILITARY GLORY: the attractive rainbow that rises in showers of blood. (Abraham Lincoln)

THE MIND: a woman's most erogenous zone. (Raquel Welch)

MISTAKES: the portals of discovery. (James Joyce)

MODERN ART: a square lady with three breasts and a guitar up her crotch. (Noel Coward)

MODESTY: the gentle art of enhancing your charm by pretending not to be aware of it. (Oliver Herford)

MONEY: the aphrodisiac which fate brings you to cloak the pain of living. (William Powell)

MONOGAMY: the Western custom of one wife and hardly any mistresses. (Saki)

MORAL INDIGNATION: jealousy with a halo. (H. G. Wells)

MUSIC: order out of chaos, and the world is chaos. (Sting)

For more, see page 292.

For more, see page 292.

*　　*　　*

ON HOUSEWORK

"My second favorite household chore is ironing. My first being hitting my head on the top bunk bed until I faint."

—**Erma Bombeck**

MUSIC TO YOUR EARS

And now for your listening pleasure…a musical interlude.

"All music is folk music. Ain't never heard no horse sing a song!"
—**Louis Armstrong**

"Music is the wine that fills the cup of silence."
—**Robert Fripp**

"Songs are funny things. They can slip across borders. Proliferate in prisons. Penetrate hard shells. I always believed that the right song at the right moment could change history."
—**Pete Seeger**

"It's the music that kept us all intact…kept us from going crazy. You should have two radios in case one gets broken."
—**Lou Reed**

"Music is the timeless experience of constant change."
—**Jerry Garcia**

"A painter paints his picture on canvas. But musicians paint their pictures on silence. We provide the music. You provide the silence."
—**Leopold Stokowski**

"There's really only one song in the whole wide world, and Adam and Eve hummed it to each other, and everything else is a variation on it in one form or another, you know?"
—**Keith Richards**

"Hell is full of musical amateurs."
—**George Bernard Shaw**

"I think for every situation there's a song."
—**Bjork**

"The world is craving spirituality so much right now. If they could sell it at McDonald's, it would be there. But it's not something you can get like that. You only wake up to it, and music is the best alarm."
—**Carlos Santana**

"Music is a means of rapid transportation."
—**John Cage**

"Of all noises, I think music is the least disagreeable."
—**Samuel Johnson**

The bagpipe was originally made from the skin of a dead sheep.

"There's an epidemic in the music industry that needs to be stopped. I'm talking about spending hard-earned money to see your favorite band in concert and they have the nerve not to sing their big hits. Sometimes these old rockers like the Rolling Stones will throw you a medley crumb, five bars of 'Brown Sugar,' to make room for every song off the new album. When the band says, 'Here's something from our new album,' why don't they just say, 'Everyone get up and go to the bathroom.'"

—David Spade

WINNING

What's it like to win? How would we know?
But here are some people who do.

"Victory goes to the player who makes the next-to-last mistake."
—**Savielly Grigorievitch Tartakower, chessmaster**

"We all have great inner power. The power is self-faith. There's really an attitude to winning. You have to see yourself winning before you win. And you have to be hungry. You have to want to conquer."
—**Arnold Schwarzenegger**

"In real life, of course, it is the hare who wins. Every time. Look around you. And in any case it is my contention that Aesop was writing for the tortoise market.... Hares have no time to read. They are too busy winning the game."
—**Anita Brookner**

"Chemistry is B.S. I'll tell you what gives you good chemistry: winning. Losing gives you bad chemistry."
—**Mike Piazza**

Matt Groening played "the creator of *Futurama*" on an episode of *The Simpsons*.

DON'T!

Thinking of skipping this page? Don't!

"Don't discuss yourself, for you are bound to lose: if you belittle yourself, you are believed; if you praise yourself, you are disbelieved."
—**Michel de Montaigne**

"Don't go to sleep. So many people die there."
—**Mark Twain**

"Don't set your own rules when you are someone's guest."
—**Italian proverb**

"Don't try to perform beyond your abilities—but never perform below them."
—**Frank Robinson**

"Don't dig for water under the outhouse."
—**Cowboy proverb**

"Don't tell your friends about your indigestion. 'How are you' is a greeting, not a question."
—**Arthur Guiterman**

"Don't look back. Something might be gaining on you."
—**Satchel Paige**

"Don't worry about the world coming to an end today. It's already tomorrow in Australia."
—**Charles Schulz**

"Don't ever send a man window shopping. He'll come back carrying a window."
—**Diana Jordan and Paul Seaburn, A *Wife's Little Instruction Book***

"Don't approach a goat from the front, a horse from the back, or a fool from any side."
—**Yiddish proverb**

"Don't eat too many almonds; they add weight to the breasts."
—**Colette, French novelist**

"Don't knock the weather; nine-tenths of the people couldn't start a conversation if it didn't change once in a while."
—**Kin Hubbard**

"Don't walk behind me; I may not lead. Don't walk in front of me; I may not follow. Just walk beside me and be my friend."
—**Albert Camus**

THAT'S CRAZY TALK

So the one cow says to the other cow, "Whaddaya think about all this mad cow disease going around?" And the other cow says, "What do I care? I'm a helicopter!"

"I don't buy temporary insanity as a murder defense. Breaking into someone's home and ironing all their clothes is temporary insanity."
—**Sue Kolinsky**

"We do not have to visit a madhouse to find disordered minds; our planet is the mental institution of the universe."
—**Goethe**

"We're all crazy and the only difference between patients and their therapists is the therapists haven't been caught yet."
—**Max Walker**

"When dealing with the insane, the best method is to pretend to be sane."
—**Hermann Hesse**

"Insane people are always sure that they are fine. It is only the sane people who are willing to admit that they are crazy."
—**Nora Ephron**

"Do you know what crazy is? Crazy is majority rules!"
—**Jeffrey Goines**

"When we remember we are all mad, the mysteries disappear and life stands explained."
—**Mark Twain**

"Those who can laugh without cause have either found the true meaning of happiness…or have gone stark raving mad."
—**Norm Papernick**

"Illusions commend themselves to us because they save us pain and allow us to enjoy pleasure instead. We must therefore accept it without complaint when they sometimes collide with a bit of reality against which they are dashed to pieces."
—**Sigmund Freud**

"Those who danced were thought to be quite insane by those who could not hear the music."
—**Angela Monet**

"Honesty is the best policy, but insanity is a better defense. "
—**Steve Landesberg**

"Show me a sane man and I will cure him for you." —**C. G. Jung**

MORE MALE CHAUVINIST PIGS

It's kind of sad that we found enough of these quotes to fill up two pages. We promise this will be the last one (in this book).

Clayton Williams, Republican candidate for governor of Texas: I sure do like your pigtails.

Native American Director of the Inter-Tribal Center: This is a traditional hairstyle and we call them braids.

Williams: Well, I think your pigtails are real cute.

"If combat means living in a ditch, females have biological problems staying in a ditch for thirty days because they get infections and they don't have upper body strength. I mean, some do, but they're relatively rare."

—Newt Gingrich

"As much as when you see a blonde with great t*ts and a great a**, you say to yourself, 'Hey, she must be stupid or must have nothing else to offer,' which maybe is the case many times. But then again, there is the one that is as smart as her breasts look, great as her face looks, beautiful as her whole body looks gorgeous, you know, so people are shocked."

—Arnold Schwarzenegger, in an interview with *Esquire*

"Most of these feminists are
radical, frustrated lesbians, many
of them, and manhaters, and
failures in their relationships with
men, and who have declared war
on the male gender."
—**Jerry Falwell**

"When a woman becomes a
scholar, there is usually something
wrong with her sexual organs."
—**Friedrich Nietzsche**

"Feminism encourages
women to leave their husbands,
kill their children, practice
witchcraft, destroy capitalism,
and become lesbians."
—**Pat Robertson,
speaking at the 1992
GOP convention**

I AM WOMAN. HEAR ME ROAR!

Because life's too short to be a shrinking violet.

"A woman without a man is like a fish without a bicycle."
—**Gloria Steinem**

"Women might start a rumor, but not a war."
—**Marga Gomez**

"A girl can wait for the right man to come along, but in the meantime, that still doesn't mean she can't have a wonderful time with all the wrong ones."
—**Cher**

"God made man and then said, 'I can do better than that,' and made woman."
—**Adela Rogers St. Johns**

"Whatever women must do they must do twice as well as men to be thought half as good. Luckily, this is not too difficult."
—**Carlotte Whitton**

"If they can put one man on the moon why can't they put them all there?"
—**Chocolate Waters**

"As far as I am concerned, being any gender is a drag."
—**Patti Smith**

"We are our own worst enemies a lot of the time…but I still blame men."
—**Janeane Garofalo**

AH, CHOCOLATE

Forrest Gump is famous for saying, "Life is like a box of chocolates."
Here's what some other folks have to say about the "food of the gods."

"It's not that chocolates are a substitute for love. Love is a substitute for chocolate. Chocolate is, let's face it, far more reliable than a man."
—**Miranda Ingram**

"Other things are just food. But chocolate's chocolate."
—**Patrick Skene Catling**

"All I really need is love, but a little chocolate now and then doesn't hurt!"
—**Lucy Van Pelt, Peanuts**

"I never met a chocolate I didn't like."
—**Deanna Troi, Star Trek: The Next Generation**

"Avoid any diet that discourages the use of hot fudge."
—**Don Kardong**

"Don't wreck a sublime chocolate experience by feeling guilty. Chocolate isn't like premarital sex. It will not make you pregnant. And it always feels good."
—**Lora Brody, Growing Up on the Chocolate Diet**

"Biochemically, love is just like eating large amounts of chocolate."
—**John Milton, The Devil's Advocate**

"What you see before you, my friend, is the result of a lifetime of chocolate."
—**Katharine Hepburn**

"Inside some of us is a thin person struggling to get out, but they can usually be sedated with a few pieces of chocolate cake."
—**Anonymous**

"I owe it all to little chocolate donuts."
—**John Belushi**

"Research tells us 14 out of any 10 individuals likes chocolate."
—**Sandra Boynton**

"Researchers have discovered that chocolate produces some of the same reactions in the brain as marijuana. They also discovered other similarities between the two but can't remember what they are."
—**Matt Lauer**

MAMA ALWAYS SAID...

*It is the duty of every family's elders to pass their wisdom
on to the kids...even when the wisdom is suspect.*

"My dad always told me the more you stomp in crap the worse it stinks."
—**Billy Ray Cyrus**

"My mom always said, 'Keep your chin up.' That's how I ran into the door."
—**Daryl Hogue**

"My granddad used to say, 'If everybody liked the same thing, they'd all be after your grandma.'"
—**Gary Muledeer**

"My father said, 'You must never try to make all the money that's in a deal. Let the other fellow make some money too, because if you have a reputation for always making all the money, you won't have many deals.'"
—**J. Paul Getty**

"My mom used to say it doesn't matter how many kids you have...because one kid'll take up 100% of your time, so more kids can't possibly take up more than 100% of your time."
—**Karen Brown**

"And, as my father [Duke] used to tell me growing up, 'Play it beautiful, play it beautiful.' He said, 'I don't care if you don't hit all of the notes. If you don't move a person's heart, it's not music.'"
—**Christopher Parkening,
guitarist**

"Whenever anything went wrong in my life, my mother would say, 'All things happen for the best.' And I'd ask, 'Whose best?' And she'd say, 'Gotta go.'"
—**Rita Rudner**

"My grandfather always said, 'Don't watch your money; watch your health.' So one day while I was watching my health, someone stole my money. It was my grandfather."
—**Jackie Mason**

GONE FISHIN'

Uncle John likes fishing…for compliments.

"My biggest worry is that when I'm dead and gone, my wife will sell my fishing gear for what I said I paid for it."
—**Koos Brandt**

"Lots of people committed crimes during the year who would not have done so if they'd been fishing. The increase of crime is among those deprived of the regenerations that impregnate the mind and character of the fisherman."
—**Herbert Hoover**

"Fishing is the only sport where sitting on your butt under a tree looks like a concentrated activity."
—**Jeff MacNelly**

"There is no greater fan of fly fishing than the worm."
—**Patrick McManus**

"Give a man a fish and you feed him for a day. Teach a man to fish and you get rid of him on weekends."
—**Nancy Gray**

"If people concentrated on the really important things in life, there'd be a shortage of fishing poles."
—**Doug Larson**

"Fly-fishing is the most fun you can have standing up."
—**Arnold Gingrich**

"The best time to go fishing is whenever you can get away."
—**Robert Traver**

"Men and fish are alike. They both get into trouble when they open their mouths."
—**Jimmy Moore**

"I fish, therefore, I lie."
—**Tom Clark**

What do you call a fish who makes you an offer you can't refuse? The codfather.

WHY WEIGHT?

*Enjoy these tasty quotes. They're satisfying food
for thought. (And they won't make you fat.)*

"I was once on a diet for two weeks running. All I lost was two weeks."
—George Foreman

"The alimentary canal is thirty-two feet long. You control only the first three inches of it. Control it well."
—Kin Hubbard

"I bought a talking refrigerator that said 'Oink' every time I opened the door. It made me hungry for pork chops."
—Marie Matt

"When we lose twenty pounds, we may be losing the twenty best pounds we have! We may be losing the pounds that contain our genius, our humanity, our love and honesty."
—Woody Allen

"In the Middle Ages, they had guillotines, stretch racks, whips, and chains. Nowadays, we have a much more effective torture device called the bathroom scale."
—Stephen Phillips

"No diet will remove all the fat from your body because the brain is entirely fat. Without a brain, you might look good, but all you could do is run for public office."
—George Bernard Shaw

"The second day of a diet is always easier than the first. By the second day, you're off it."
—Jackie Gleason

"I went on a diet. Had to go on two diets at the same time because one diet wasn't giving me enough food."
—Barry Marder

"My doctor told me to stop having intimate dinners for four—unless there are three other people."
—Orson Welles

"At the end of every diet, the path curves back to the trough."
—Mason Cooley

"A waist is a terrible thing to mind."
—Jane Caminos

MAKING A DIFFERENCE

Dr. Albert Schweitzer (1875–1965) dedicated his life to serving mankind. He built hospitals in Africa, wrote books on theology and philosophy, and was awarded the Nobel Prize for Peace in 1952.

"A man does not have to be an angel in order to be a saint."

"You must give some time to your fellow men. Even if it's a little thing, do something for others, something for which you get no pay but the privilege of doing it."

"Example is not the main thing in influencing others. It is the only thing."

"Constant kindness can accomplish much. As the sun makes ice melt, kindness causes misunderstanding, mistrust, and hostility to evaporate."

"Do something wonderful. People may imitate it."

"Man is a clever animal who behaves like an imbecile."

"The time must come when inhumanity protected by custom and thoughtlessness will succumb before humanity championed by thought. Let us work that this time may come."

"Wherever a man turns he can find someone who needs him."

"Seek always to do some good, somewhere. For remember, you don't live in a world all your own. Your brothers are here, too."

"Man must cease attributing his problems to his environment, and learn again to exercise his will—his personal responsibility."

"As we acquire more knowledge, things do not become more comprehensible, but more mysterious."

"Whoever is spared personal pain must feel himself called to help in diminishing the pain of others. We must all carry our share of the misery which lies upon the world."

"A man can do only what a man can do. But if he does that each day he can sleep at night and do it again the next day."

Albert Schweitzer was a renowned organist and wrote the definitive book on the life of J. S. Bach.

WORLD'S
SHORTEST QUOTE

*From Muhammad Ali, delivered at a Harvard
University commencement address.*

"Me, we."

PANNING THE CRITICS

*Reading criticism is fun. But it's even more
fun to read when critics' victims return fire.*

"Any fool can criticize, and many of them do."

—Cyril Garbett

"I've got a review that calls me a genius right next to the one that calls me a jerk."

—Barry Manilow

"On any given night, we're still a damn good band. And on some nights, maybe even the best band in the world. So screw the press and their slagging about the 'Geritol Tour.' You a**h**es. Wait until you get our age and see how you run. I've got news for you, we're still a bunch of tough b*st*rds. String us up and we still won't die."

—Keith Richards

"Critics are a dissembling, dishonest, contemptible race of men. Asking a working writer what he thinks about critics is like asking a lamppost what it feels about dogs."

—John Osborne

"Don't pay attention to bad reviews. Today's newspaper is tomorrow's toilet paper."

—Jack Warner

"Don't pay any attention to the critics—don't even ignore them."

—Samuel Goldwyn

"Unless the b*st*rds have the courage to give you unqualified praise, I say ignore them."

—John Steinbeck

"Critics are like eunuchs in a harem:
they know how it's done, they've
seen it done every day, but they're
unable to do it themselves."

—Brendan Behan

"To be 70 years young is far more hopeful than to be 40 years old." —Oliver Wendell Holmes, Jr.

WHAT? MORE DUMB JOCKS?

The BRI has been quoting dumb jocks since 1988. We're amazed (and a little alarmed) at how many great new quotes keep dribbling out every year.

"We all get heavier as we get older because there's a lot more information in our heads."
—**Vlade Divac, L. A. Lakers**

"Ball handling and dribbling are my strongest weaknesses."
—**David Thompson, Denver Nuggets player**

"All I want is for my case to be heard in front of an impractical decision maker."
—**Pete Rose**

"We'll do it right if we capitalize on our mistakes."
—**Mickey Rivers, Texas Rangers outfielder**

"The only problem I have in the outfield is with fly balls."
—**Carmelo Martinez, San Diego Padres outfielder**

"I would like to thank my parents—especially my mother and father."
—**Greg Norman, in his winning speech at the 1983 World Matchplay Championship**

"Either you give me what I demand, or I'll take what you're offering!"
—**Joe Torre, St. Louis Cardinals, during salary negotiations**

"Sure there have been injuries and deaths in boxing—but none of them serious."
—**Alan Minter**

"Ol' Diz knows the king's English. And not only that, I know the queen is English."
—**Dizzy Dean, responding to a letter on air that said he didn't know the king's English**

Alice Cooper owns one of the Os in the "Hollywood" sign.

YOU AIN'T GOT IT, KID

*Sometimes the secret to success is just
not taking "no" for an answer.*

What They Said: "That kid can't play baseball."
Who Said it: Tommy Holmes, minor league manager
Rejected! Henry "Hank" Aaron

What They Said: "We fancy that any real child might be more puzzled than enchanted by this stiff, overwrought story."
Who Said it: Children's Books review
Rejected! Lewis Carroll's *Alice in Wonderland*, 1865

What They Said: "Every woman is frightened of a mouse."
Who Said it: Loius B. Mayer, head of MGM
Rejected! Walt Disney

What They Said: "That's a face you'll never see on a lunchbox."
Who Said it: NBC executive Brandon Tartikoff
Rejected! Michael J. Fox, who was primed to star in *Family Ties*

What They Said: "Mentally slow, unsociable, and adrift forever in his foolish dreams."
Who Said it: Elementary school teacher
Rejected! Albert Einstein

What They Said: "It contains 52 fundamental errors."
Who Said it: Parker Brothers executive
Rejected! A proposed board game called Monopoly

What They Said: "Get rid of the pointed ears guy."
Who Said it: NBC executive to *Star Trek* creator Gene Roddenberry
Rejected! Mr. Spock

Longest Oscar acceptance speech: Greer Garson in 1943 at more than seven minutes.

SIMON SAYS

Simon Cowell made his name in the music business for his ability to recognize the truly talented. But he has since become famous on American Idol for his ability to degrade the truly untalented.

"Jenny, that was extraordinary. Unfortunately, extraordinarily bad."

"You have just invented a new form of torture."

"If you would have been singing like this 2,000 years ago, people would have stoned you."

"If your lifeguard duties were as good as your singing, a lot of people would be drowning."

"My advice would be if you want to pursue a career in the music business, don't."

Simon: I've heard better people singing outside the subway.
Nathaniel: That's fine, but I worked really hard, and...
Simon: So do they!
Nathaniel: Well, that's fine, but did they stand out in the cold and...
Simon: They're standing outside the subway! So yes!

"Don't take this the wrong way, but I prefer you when I close my eyes."

"I'm going to reach out with a hook if you don't shut up."

"I think you invented notes never ever heard before in music."

"You're so terrible, you're not even good enough for Bulgarian Idol!"

"I would rather to listen to fingers going down a blackboard than buy a William Hung album."

Juanita: Why wasn't it good?
Simon: Because you sang it.

"Are you taking singing lessons? Who's your teacher? Do you have a lawyer? Get a lawyer and sue her."

"You sang like you were in a dentist's chair."

"When you entered this competition, did you really believe that you could become an American Idol? [Contestant nods yes.] Well, then, you're deaf. Thank you. Goodbye."

Neil Diamond once considered the stage name "Neil Kaminsky."

"The object of this competition is not to be mean to the losers but to find a winner. The process makes you mean because you get frustrated. Kids turn up unrehearsed, wearing the wrong clothes, singing out of tune, and you can either say, 'Good job,' and patronize them, or tell them the truth, and sometimes the truth is perceived as mean."

"I am poor, misunderstood Simon. I'm really the nice one, and no one gets it."
—**Simon Cowell**

IT CAME FROM OUTER SPACE

What do aliens think of humans? Don't know—
we couldn't find any real aliens to tell us.
So we asked some Hollywood aliens.

"Strange, isn't it? Everything you know, your entire civilization, it all begins right here…in this little pond of goo."
—**Q, Star Trek: The Next Generation**

"I'd like to share a revelation that I've had during my time here. It
came to me when I tried to classify your species. I realized that
you're not actually mammals. Every mammal on this planet
instinctively develops a natural equilibrium with the surrounding
environment, but you humans do not. You move to an area, and
you multiply, and multiply, until every natural resource is con-
sumed. The only way you can survive is to spread to another area.
There is another organism on this planet that follows the same
pattern. A virus. Human beings are a disease, a cancer of this
planet, you are a plague, and we are the cure."
—**Agent Smith, The Matrix**

"I think man is the most interesting insect, don't you?"
—**Marvin the Martian, Bugs Bunny Show**

"I came here to give you these facts. It is no concern of ours how
you run your own planet. But if you threaten to extend your violence, this Earth of yours will be reduced to a burned-out cinder."
—**Klaatu, The Day the Earth Stood Still**

Zete: "Does all of Earth look like this?"
Terl: "Oh, I'm afraid so, sir."
Zete: "Pathetic. All the green and the blue sky. They told me this
planet was ugly, but this has got to be one of the ugliest crap holes
in the entire universe."
—*Battlefield Earth*

"Shall I tell you what I find beautiful about you humans? You are at your very best when things are worst."

—Starman, *Starman*

Leeloo: "Everything you create, you use to destroy."
Korben Dallas: "Yeah, we call it human nature."

—*The Fifth Element*

"I'm frequently appalled by the low regard you Earthmen have for life."

—Mr. Spock, *Star Trek*

"Live as one of them, Kal-El, to discover where your strength and power are needed. And always hold in your heart the pride of your special heritage. They can be a great people, Kal-El. They wish to be. They only lack the light to show the way. For this reason, above all, their capacity for good, I have sent them you, my only son."

—Jor-El, *Superman*

*   *   *

MAN AND SUPERMAN

"Unlike Batman and Spider-Man, Superman stands alone. Superman did not *become* Superman, Superman was *born* Superman. When Superman wakes up in the morning, he is Superman. His alter ego is Clark Kent. His outfit with the big red S is the blanket he was wrapped in as a baby when the Kents found him. Those are his clothes. What Kent wears—the glasses the business suit—that's the costume. That's the costume Superman wears to blend in with us. Clark Kent is how Superman views us. And what are the characteristics of Clark Kent? He's weak, unsure of himself...he's a coward. Clark Kent is Superman's critique on the whole human race."

—David Carradine, *Kill Bill Vol. II*

LEVANT GARDE

*The pianist Oscar Levant made an entire career out of his neurosis:
he was not a happy man. In the late '20s, Levant became known as
much for his razor-sharp wit as for his musical skills. This led to film
roles, usually playing himself, which according to Jon Winokur in*
The Portable Curmudgeon, *was "a chain-smoking, wise-cracking,
tortured genius." Here are some of Levant's wisest cracks.*

"The first thing I do in the morning is brush my teeth and sharpen my tongue."

"I was once thrown out of a mental hospital for depressing the other patients."

"I've given up reading books; it takes my mind off myself."

"There is a thin line between genius and insanity. I have erased this line."

"Underneath this flabby exterior is an enormous lack of character."

"I envy people who drink. At least they have something to blame everything on."

"I am no more humble than my talents require."

"The only difference between Democrats and Republicans is that Democrats allow the poor to be corrupt, too."

"I once said cynically of a politician, 'He'll doublecross that bridge when he comes to it.' "

"I have no trouble with my enemies. But my friends—they're the ones that keep me walking the floors at night."

"Happiness isn't something you experience; it's something you remember."

"I'm a concert pianist. That's a pretentious way of saying I'm unemployed at the moment."

"I'm a self-made man. Who else could help?"

"Roses are red, violets are blue, I'm schizophrenic, and so am I."

"Every time I look at you I get a fierce desire to be lonesome."

"What the world needs is more geniuses with humility; there are so few of us left."

"An invasion of armies can be resisted, but not an idea whose time has come." —Victor Hugo

CELEBRITY TOMBSTONES

More epitaphs of the rich and famous.

Called Back
—**Emily Dickinson**

A star on Earth—
a star in heaven
Karen Carpenter

"That's All Folks!"
—**Mel Blanc**

At Rest
An American Soldier
And Defender of the
Constitution
—**Jefferson Davis**

Sting wrote the Police song "Every Breath You Take" on Noel Coward's piano.

SPORTSCASTERS

Some days it seems like "dumb jocks" aren't just on the field—they're in the booth.

"I'm going to make a prediction: it could go either way."
—**Ron Atkinson**

"From the waist down, Earl Campbell has the biggest legs I've ever seen."
—**John Madden**

"The batsman's Holding, the bowler's Willey."
—**Brian Johnston, reporting a cricket match between Michael Holding and Peter Willey**

"It's a hot night at the Garden, folks, and at ringside I see several ladies in gownless evening straps."
—**Jimmy Powers**

"There've been times when they've had hits from time to time, but they weren't timely hits at the right time."
—**Gary Carter**

"Azinger is wearing an all-black outfit: black jumper, blue trousers, white shoes, and a pink 'tea-cosy' hat."
—**Renton Laidlaw, golf commentator**

"If there's a pile-up there, they'll have to give some of the players artificial insemination."
—**Curt Gowdy**

"Juantorena opens wide his legs and shows his class."
—**Ron Pickering, commenting on a runner at the 1976 Olympics**

"That's a very sad-looking Wattana, but you'd never know it to look at his face."
—**Ted Love**

"You couldn't really find two more completely different personalities than these two men, Tom Watson and Brian Barnes; one is the complete professional golfer, and the other, the complete professional golfer."
—**Peter Alliss**

"That's the fastest time ever run—but it's not as fast as the world record."
—**David Coleman**

"With eight minutes left, the game could be won in the next five or ten minutes."
—**Jimmy Armfield**

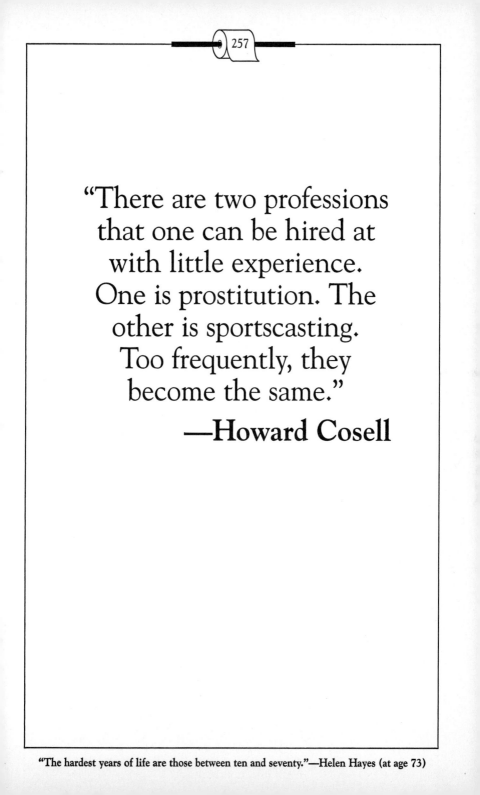

"There are two professions that one can be hired at with little experience. One is prostitution. The other is sportscasting. Too frequently, they become the same."

—Howard Cosell

TAKE THAT, CONSERVATIVES!

Conservatives think they know everything.
Here's what liberals say about conservatives.

"A conservative is a man who just sits and thinks, mostly sits."
—**Woodrow Wilson**

"What is conservatism? Is it not adherence to the old and tried, against the new and untried?" —**Abraham Lincoln**

"A conservative is one who admires radicals centuries after they're dead."
—**Leo C. Rosten**

"Conservatives are not necessarily stupid, but most stupid people are conservative."
—**John Stuart Mill**

"If the Republicans will stop telling lies about us, we will stop telling the truth about them."
—**Adlai Stevenson**

"The effectiveness of the right's echo chamber has been that every time the Democrats dissent, or people protest, they had this megaphone that was able to drown them out, make them seem 'liberal,' taint them with that word."
—**Bill Moyer**

"Republicans now have their own network in Fox, so guys who don't like to answer questions, like Trent Lott, have a place to go to hit softballs." —**James Carville**

"The Republican convention started this past weekend, so don't forget to turn your clocks back 400 years."
—**Jay Leno**

"I believe there's a commonality to all humanity. We all suck."—**Bill Hicks**

TAKE THAT, LIBERALS!

Liberals think they know everything. Here's
what conservatives say about liberals.

"Liberals think you can reform an ax murderer. They don't want to kill anything. They want to change the Listerine labels to 'Rehabilitate the germs that cause bad breath.'"
—Marc Pierce

"A liberal is a man who leaves the room when the fight begins."
—Heywood Broun

"Liberalism thinks nothing of average people. You're incapable, incompetent, you're idiotic, you cannot read. That's what they think."
—Rush Limbaugh

"If God had been a liberal, we wouldn't have had the Ten Commandments—we'd have the Ten Suggestions."
—Malcolm Bradbury

"Liberals claim to want to give a hearing to other views, but then are shocked and offended to discover that there are other views."
—William F. Buckley

"Ultraliberalism today translates into a whimpering isolationism in foreign policy, a mulish obstructionism in domestic policy, and a pusillanimous pussyfooting on the critical issue of law and order."
—Spiro T. Agnew

"At the core of liberalism is the spoiled child—miserable, as all spoiled children are, unsatisfied, demanding, ill-disciplined, despotic, and useless. Liberalism is a philosphy of sniveling brats."
—P. J. O'Rourke

"A liberal is a man too broadminded to take his own side in a quarrel."
—Robert Frost

"We're prepared to place our trust in the people to reshape the government. Liberals place their trust in the government to reshape the people."
—Newt Gingrich

2 + 2 = A QUOTE PAGE

We tried to subtract all the mathematical pages from this book, but we got the wrong answer—there's one left.

"Insofar as the laws of mathematics are certain, they do not refer to reality, and insofar as they refer to reality, they are not certain."
—**Albert Einstein**

"If you are truly serious about preparing your child for the future, don't teach him to subtract—teach him to deduct."
—**Fran Lebowitz**

"317 is a prime, not because we think so, or because our minds are shaped in one way rather than another, but because it *is* so. Mathematical reality is built that way."
—**Godfrey Hardy**

"As long as there is algebra, there will be prayer in school."
—**Larry Miller**

"A school in Connecticut has a 'power nap club.' We called that 'algebra.'"
—**Jay Leno**

"Numbers are the only universal language."
—**Nathaniel West**

"I know that two and two make four—and should be glad to prove it, too, if I could—though I must say if by any sort of process I could convert two and two into five, it would give me much greater pleasure."
—**Lord Byron**

"Stand firm in your refusal to remain conscious during algebra. In real life, I assure you there is no such thing as algebra."
—**Fran Lebowitz**

Professor: If I gave you a dollar and your father gave you a dollar, how much would you have?
Larry: One dollar.
Professor: You don't know your arithmetic.
Larry: You don't know my father.
—***The Three Stooges***

MORE TOILET TALK

*A few more thoughts for the throne
that overflowed from our first page.*

"The flush toilet is
the basis of Western
civilization."

—Alan Coult

"Like when I'm in the bathroom
looking at my toilet paper, I'm
like 'Wow! That's toilet paper?'
I don't know if we appreciate
how much we have."

—Alicia Silverstone

"When a child is locked in the
bathroom with water running
and he says he's doing nothing,
but the dog is barking, call 911."

—Erma Bombeck

"You can say, 'Can I use your
bathroom?' and nobody cares.
But if you ask, 'Can I use the
plop-plop machine?' it always
breaks the conversation."

—Dave Attell

When a society has to resort to the lavatory for its humor, the writing is on the wall." —Alan Bennett

HIS BECKNESS

His real name is Beck Hansen, and his first big hit was "Loser."
You'd never know it by that song title, but he ws one of the
most succesful and influential musicians of the 1990s.

"I think my whole generation's mission is to kill the cliché."

"I don't have enough hair to be a genius. I think you have to have hair going everywhere."

"I think the idea of albums has been demeaned by so many bad albums."

"I got into playing blues when I was 15. I lived that music for years and had no inclination or desire to ever pick up an electric guitar or be a part of any dominant musical cultures at the time."

"I guess most people would have the fear of getting up in front of a large audience of people and making a fool of themselves. I've gotten over that."

"I always try to leave in the mistakes—that's the interesting stuff. If someone walked into the room while you were doing a little falsetto lead and said, 'The burritos are here,' that's the best part. That's the part people will remember."

"Music is less popular than inline skating."

"I think life is somewhat mundane, you know? Especially these days—we don't live these big dramatic lives. There's no linear story, just a collection of moments and mundane pleasures—reading a newspaper, looking at a tree."

"The nature of the universe is fairly whimsical and nonsensical. In the most somber, beatific peacefulness there's complete chaos and maniacal laughter. Music that doesn't reflect that is boring."

"People work all their lives to make a certain amount of money, they sort of put their real life on hold until they get to this certain place, and when they get there, life's over. You've got to live in the moment, because that's all we have."

"I think dreams are based on indigestion."

The so-called Generation X is an easy target. Most of Generation X can't even defend themselves. They don't know how to put the words together to bring out their inner experience. That's a big loss. And then when somebody does come out full of angst—which is something commonly associated with this generation—it's written off simply as whining.

—Beck

NEVER...

Uncle John's credo: never follow the advice of experts.

"Never attribute to malice what can adequately be explained by stupidity."
—**Nick Diamos**

"Never allow your child to call you by your first name. He hasn't known you long enough."
—**Fran Lebowitz**

"Never trouble another for what you can do for yourself."
—**Thomas Jefferson**

"Never eat at a place called Mom's. Never play cards with a man called Doc. Never go to bed with a woman whose troubles are greater than your own."
—**Nelson Algren**

"Never trust a man with short legs. Brains too near their bottoms."
—**Noel Coward**

"Never miss an opportunity to relieve yourself; never miss a chance to sit down and rest your feet."
—**King George V**

"Never purchase beauty products in a hardware store."
—**Miss Piggy**

"Never trust a member of Congress who quotes the Bible, the Internal Revenue Code, or the Rules of the House."
—**Eugene McCarthy**

"Never lend books, for no one ever returns them; the only books I have in my library are books that other people have lent me."
—**Anatole France**

"Never trust a man that speaks well of everybody."
—**John Churton Collins**

"Never refuse to do a kindness unless the act would work great injury to yourself, and never refuse to take a drink—under any circumstances."
—**Mark Twain**

"Never go to bed mad. Stay up and fight."
—**Phyllis Diller**

WHEN CELEBRITIES ATTACK

*Celebrities are often at their unintentionally funniest
when they're attacking other celebrities.*

"Mick Jagger has child-bearing lips."
—Joan Rivers

"You better ask the bitch."
—Keith Richards, when asked if there would be an end to the bitching between he and Mick Jagger

"Sometimes Howard [Cosell] makes me wish I was a dog and he was a fireplug."
—Muhammad Ali

"I'm glad I gave up drugs and alcohol. It would be awful to look like Keith Richards."
—Elton John

"The reason so many people showed up at Louis B. Mayer's funeral was because they wanted to make sure he was dead."
—Sam Goldwyn

"I wanted to be just like Richard Pryor, except for the drug habit, the failed marriages, the temper, and the guns."
—Damon Wayans

"Sam [Donaldson] is a sonata for harp and jackhammer."
—Diane Saywer

"The great thing about Errol [Flynn] was that you knew precisely where you were with him—because he always let you down."
—David Niven

"In real life, [Diane] Keaton believes in God. But she also believes that the radio works because there are tiny people inside it."
—Woody Allen

"Charo is a one-note song played off key."
—Ethel Merman

"Barbara Streisand has as much talent as a butterfly's fart."
—Walter Matthau

"You're confusing the size of your paycheck with the size of your talent."
—Marlon Brando to Val Kilmer

PHILOSOPHY

Time to step off the deep end.

"O Lord, if there is a Lord, save my soul, if I have a soul."
—**Ernest Renan, French philosopher**

"To teach how to live without certainty and yet without being paralysed by hesitation is perhaps the chief thing that philosophy, in our age, can do for those who study it."
—**Bertrand Russell**

"What lies behind us and what lies before us are small matters to what lies within us."
—**Ralph Waldo Emerson**

"Our spiritual life is a constant battle between the part of the soul that loves others and the part of the soul that will gladly eat them up."
—**Robert Bly**

"All are lunatics, but he who can analyze his delusion is called a philosopher."
—**Ambrose Bierce**

90% of all animal species in the history of the Earth are now extinct.

FROM THE MOUTHS OF BABES

*More pearls of wisdom from the
world's most beautiful supermodels.*

"Because modeling is lucrative, I'm able to save
up and be more particular about the acting roles I
take."
—**Kathy Ireland, star of *Alien from L.A.*,
Danger Island, and other bombs**

"When I feel low, I don't buy a pair of shoes, I
change the color of my hair! It puts me in a good
mood."
—**Linda Evangelista**

"Spiritual beings are also sexual. It's an aspect of
being human. I believe posing for *Playboy* was definitely part of my life's path—I was meant to do it,
maybe set an example for other people. To help
other people. It was my fate."
—**Tishara Cousino**

"I don't wake up for less than $10,000 a day."
—**Linda Evangelista**

"My husband was just OK looking. I was in labor
and I said to him, 'What if she's ugly? You're ugly.'"
—**Beverly Johnson**

"Sometimes when I reflect back on all the beer I drink I feel ashamed. Then I look into the glass and think about the workers in the brewery and all of their hopes and dreams. If I didn't drink this beer, they might be out of work and their dreams would be shattered. Then I say to myself, 'It is better that I drink this beer and let their dreams come true than be selfish and worry about my liver.'"

—**Jack Handey**

HAVE ANOTHER BEER!

The only thing better than beer is peanuts and beer.

"I would kill everyone in this room for a drop of sweet beer."
—**Homer Simpson**

"They who drink beer will think beer."
—**Washington Irving**

"Life, alas, is very drear. Up with the glass! Down with the beer!"
—**Louis Untermeyer**

"Beer that is not drunk has missed its vocation."
—**Meyer Breslau**

"I am a firm believer in the people. If given the truth, they can be depended upon to meet any national crisis. The great point is to bring them the real facts, and beer."
—**Abraham Lincoln**

"Beer makes you feel the way you ought to feel without it."
—**Henry Lawson**

"Here's to a long life and a merry one; a quick death and an easy one; a pretty girl and a true one; a cold beer, and another one."
—**Lewis Henry**

"I'm allergic to grass. Hey, it could be worse. I could be allergic to beer."
—**Greg Norman**

"I work until beer o'clock."
—**Steven King**

"Cover a war in a place where you can't drink beer or talk to a woman? Hell no!"
—**Hunter S. Thompson**

"I was at a bar nursing a beer. My nipple was getting quite soggy."
—**Emo Philips**

"The pub knows a lot, almost as much as the churches."
—**Joyce Carey**

"He was a wise man who invented beer."
—**Plato**

"Anheuser-Busch gives two free cases of beer to its employees at all of its parks, like Busch Gardens. That's a comforting thought the next time you're getting ready to get on the roller coaster!"
—**Jay Leno**

"Using words to describe magic is like using a screwdriver to cut roast beef." —**Tom Robbins**

MR. UNIVERSE

Even theoretical physicist Stephen Hawking admits
that his illness makes him "instantly recognizable
as 'that scientist in a wheelchair.'"

"We are just an advanced breed of monkeys on a minor planet of a very average star. But we can understand the universe. That makes us something very special."

"In less than a hundred years, we have found a new way to think of ourselves. From sitting at the center of the universe, we now find ourselves orbiting an average-sized sun, which is just one of millions of stars in our own Milky Way galaxy."

"The whole history of science has been the gradual realization that events do not happen in an arbitrary manner, but that they reflect a certain underlying order, which may or may not be divinely inspired."

"To confine our attention to terrestrial matters would be to limit the human spirit."

"Not only does God play dice... he sometimes throws them where they cannot be seen."

"Common sense is just another name for the prejudices we've been taught all our lives."

"My goal is simple. It is a complete understanding of the universe, why it is as it is and why it exists at all."

"I don't think the human race will survive the next thousand years, unless we spread into space. There are too many accidents that can befall life on a single planet."

Stephen Hawking was born on January 8, 1942 (300 years after the death of Galileo).

"I think computer viruses should count as life. I think it says something about human nature that the only form of life we have created so far is purely destructive. We've created life in our own image."

"One is always a long way from solving a problem until one actually has the answer."

"Why is the universe as we observe it? The answer, of course, is that if it were otherwise, there would not be anyone to ask the question."

"When I gave a lecture in Japan, I was asked not to mention the possible recollapse of the universe, because it might affect the stock market."

"In the long term, I am more worried about biology. Nuclear weapons need large facilities, but genetic engineering can be done in a small lab. The danger is that either by accident or design, we create a virus that destroys us."

"In contrast with our intellect, computers double their performance every 18 months. So the danger is real that they could develop intelligence and take over the world."

"The expansion of the universe spreads everything out, but gravity tries to pull it all back together again. Our destiny depends on which force will win."

*   *   *

A DUMB PREDICTION

"When the Paris Exhibition closes, electric light will close with it and no more will be heard of it."

—**Professor Erasmus Wilson, Oxford University, 1878**

"The gods too are fond of a joke." —Aristotle

BITS & BYTES

*Didn't they say modern technology
would make our lives easier?*

"I'm very frightened of my computer. I got a computer expert to come to my home and weed out all the options. Now I just have On, Off, Save, and Print. If I see another option come up, I'll feel like weeping."
—**Mia Farrow**

"The real danger is not that computers will begin to think like men, but that men will begin to think like computers."
—**Sydney J. Harris**

"You can't fail to get along with a computer; it will never turn upon you, it will never insist on talking about what it wants to or doing what it wants to. It will never find you boring, never forget to call, never ask for a favor."
—**Greg Easterbrook**

"In a few seconds, a computer can make a mistake so great that it would take many men months to equal it."
—**Merle A. Meacham**

"Computers are useless. They only give you answers."
—**Pablo Picasso**

FARTS

Maybe it's a by-product of making the Uncle John's Bathroom Reader for Kids Only *series, but we've been reminded of our own childhoods—you know, when farts were funny. Guess what? They still are!*

"My philosophy of dating is to just fart right away."
—Jenny McCarthy

"That Gerald Ford. He can't fart and chew gum at the same time."
—Lyndon Johnson

"I find it's easier to fart and blame it on someone else when you live in an urban area."
—Madonna

"Being popular is like being in a crowded elevator: you are just a fart away from being hated."
—Braxton Fart Theory

"Cameron Diaz is one of those girls who can burp and fart and still look cute. I'm not one of them."
—Anne Hathaway

"When I was growing up, if we wanted a Jacuzzi, we had to fart in the tub."
—Eddie Murphy, *Trading Places*

OH, JACKIE

Jacqueline Kennedy Onassis was one of the most admired first ladies in American history.

"It takes an awful lot of effort to make everything look effortless."

"If you bungle raising your children, I don't think whatever else you do well matters very much."

"I don't understand it. Jack will spend any amount of money to buy votes, but he balks at investing a thousand dollars in a beautiful painting."

"Every moment one lives is different from the other. The good, the bad, the hardship, the joy, the tragedy, love, and happiness are all interwoven into one single, indescribable whole that is called life."

"I don't think there are any men who are faithful to their wives."

"Whenever I was upset by something in the papers, Jack always told me to be more tolerant, like a horse flicking away flies in the summer."

"You cannot separate the good and the bad, and perhaps there is no need to do so."

"I want minimum information given with maximum politeness."

"The first time you marry for love, the second for money, and the third for companionship."

"The only routine with me is no routine at all."

"There are many little ways to enlarge your child's world. Love of books is the best of all."

"An aim in life is the only fortune worth finding."

"People have too many theories about rearing children. I believe simply in love, security, and discipline."

"Happiness is not where you think you'll find it. I'm determined not to worry. So many people poison every day worrying about the next."

WILL DURST
OR WON'T HE?

*Will Durst is a social commentator par excellence. (We don't know
what that means, either, but we think Durst's a funny guy.)*

"We yell at working mothers for not staying home with their kids, then yell at welfare mothers for not having jobs."

"In America we pride ourselves on our ability to get a pizza to our door faster than an ambulance."

"Don't you think it's a little too ironic the AARP appoints its executive director for life?"

"Jesse Ventura refereed a WCW event and caused an outcry. The wrestlers were afraid the appearance of a politician would cheapen the sport."

"Donald Trump is running, too. I'm all in favor of billionaires running for president instead of politicians. That way, we eliminate the middle men."

"Some critics see Canada's attempt to decriminalize marijuana a lame attempt to encourage more people to sample the local cuisine."

"Bush met with the Dalai Lama. What a pair. One is totally out of touch with how the real world works and is mainly a figurehead and so is the other."

"The Senate is investigating profiteering on oil and gas. The important questions are: 1. Which oil companies are raking in huge profits? and 2. How big of contributors are they?"

"It may not be a pretty tale, but there are indirect positive effects from smokers. Smokers save the government money. We die quick. None of this drawn out lingering crap."

"Colleges are banning alcohol on campus, sending the message to kids, 'If you want to drink, get a car.'"

"That's my best advice. That and you can mix wine with beer and beer with hard liquor but not wine with hard liquor."

QUOTES AND THEIR CONSEQUENCES

*More quotes from public figures that created
a backlash and caused themselves headaches.*

Speaker: George H. W. Bush
Quote: "Just as Poland had a rebellion against totalitarianism, I am rebelling against broccoli, and I refuse to give ground. I do not like broccoli and I haven't liked it since I was a little kid and my mother made me eat it. Now I'm president of the United States and I'm not going to eat any more broccoli."

Consequences: Needless to say, the broccoli industry was upset. Broccoli, it seemed, had become Public Enemy Number One. After it was banned at the White House, some schools dropped it from their menu. At home, many of the nation's children followed suit and boycotted broccoli at the dinner table. Result: broccoli sales fell significantly in 1990.

It wasn't only the broccoli industry that was miffed—nutrition advocates blasted the president for sending a message to kids that vegetables were bad. Bush didn't help his case when he appointed pork rinds as the official snack on Air Force One (where broccoli was also banned).

To protest the president's position, broccoli growers from around the country sent tons of the vegetable to the White House. Bush stayed far away from the cases and ordered them delivered to various food banks and shelters in the Washington, D.C. area. As the 1990s rolled on, broccoli was found to help prevent cancer; it is currently making a comeback.

Speaker: Kevin Garnett
Quote: "This is it. It's for all the marbles. I'm sitting in the house loading up the pump, I'm loading up the Uzis, I've got a couple of M-16s, couple of nines, couple of joints with some silencers on them, couple of grenades, got a missile launcher. I'm ready for war."

Background: One of professional basketball's best players, the star forward of the Minnesota Timberwolves said this the day before a deciding playoff game against the Sacramento Kings. While such a comment might not be noticed in other years, this was said in May of 2004 while U.S. troops were mired in a bloody war in Iraq and Afghanistan.

Consequences: Families with sons and daughters serving in the war were irate. The NBA and Minnesota Timberwolves received a barrage of complaints demanding an apology, which Garnett swiftly gave: "Sincerely, I apologize for my comments earlier," he said. "I'm a young man and I understand when I'm appropriate, and this is totally inappropriate. I was totally thinking about basketball, not reality." No argument there. The flak died down after Garnett's lengthy apology, and Wolves' coach Flip Saunders had to remind his team to concentrate on basketball and not their star player's taunts to the press.

But Kings center Brad Miller, one of Garnett's biggest rivals, wouldn't let it go and added his own brand of ammunition to the mix: "I'm bringing my shotgun, my bow and arrow, my four-wheel drive truck, and four wheelers and run over him." In the end, Miller's shotgun was no match for Garnett's Uzis—the Wolves won.

Speaker: Paul Newman
Quote: "24 hours in a day, 24 beers in a case. Coincidence? I think not."
Consequences: Although this witty remark has often been attributed to the famous actor, salad dressing maker, and racecar driver, Newman never said it. Nevertheless, the quote has taken on a life of its own, especially at Princeton University in New Jersey. Every April 24, some of the rowdier students participate in "Newman's Day." Their goal: to drink one beer an hour for an entire day— while attending all of their classes. When Newman found out that such an event was named in his honor, he did not feel honored. He called on the university to "bring an end to this tradition." Princeton officials responded by saying that it was not a sanctioned event—they've been trying to stop it for years. So Newman and the university joined forces in 2004 to call on students to forgo Newman's Day. Although the event still happened, its numbers were reportedly down from previous years.

Sad Irony: Newman's own son Scott died of a drug overdose at age 28, prompting his father to create the Scott Newman Center in 1980, a nonprofit organization "dedicated to the prevention of substance abuse through education."

Speaker: Hillary Clinton
Quote: "I'm not sitting here like some little woman standing by my man like Tammy Wynette."
Background: "Stand By Your Man," a country music classic recorded in 1968, was Wynette's biggest hit. Its simple lyrics basically say that if a woman truly loves her man, then she'll remain loyal when he goes a little wayward, " 'Cause after all, he's just a man."

During the 1992 presidential campaign, Bill and Hillary Clinton appeared on CBS' *60 Minutes*. Hillary made the comment after being asked about Bill's alleged affair with Gennifer Flowers.

Consequences: The comment did well for establishing Hillary Clinton as a strong, modern woman, but Tammy Wynette was infuriated. She fumed that the statement had "offended every true country music fan and every person who has made it on their own with no one to take them to a White House." It even served as fodder for country music DJs to label the Clintons as "country music-hating liberals." Not good press in an election year.

Clinton apologized profusely, saying that she meant no disrespect, and Wynette accepted. (She could have even thanked Clinton—all of the press put her name back in the headlines and gave new life to a 25-year-old song.) To show there was no bad blood, Wynette later performed "Stand By Your Man" at a Clinton fundraiser. And in the end, Hillary did stand by her man.

*　　*　　*

THE PRICE OF FAME

"People still think of me as a cartoonist, but the only thing I lift a pen or pencil for these days is to sign a contract, a check, or an autograph."

—Walt Disney

DEAD ROCKERS

The irony is so thick you could cut it with a knife…

"It's funny the way most people love the dead. Once you're dead you're made for life."
—Jimi Hendrix

"Well, some people die and some people are survivors. I'm a survivor."
—Janis Joplin

"I don't think there's anything else in life apart from a near-death experience that shows you how extensive the mind is."
—Jerry Garcia

"Some of us can be examples about going ahead and growing, and some of us, unfortunately, don't make it there, and end up being examples because they had to die."
**—Stevie Ray Vaughn,
who died in a helicopter crash
after becoming clean and sober**

"I wouldn't mind dying in a plane crash. It'd be a good way to go. I don't want to die in my sleep, or of old age, or O.D. I want to feel what it's like. I want to taste it, hear it, smell it. Death is only going to happen to you once; I don't want to miss it."
—Jim Morrison

"I'll sleep when I'm dead."
—Warren Zevon

Jimi Hendrix, Janis Joplin, and Jim Morrison were all 27 years old when they died.

THE PRICE OF FAME

Comments about life in the spotlight, from those who know.

"I still feel like I gotta prove something. There are a lot of people hoping I fail. But I like that. I need to be hated."
—**Howard Stern**

"There is only one thing in the world worse than being talked about, and that is not being talked about."
—**Oscar Wilde**

"The thing most people don't understand about show business personalities is that our lives are often just as normal as theirs. And if normal means being screwed up, then yes, I am normal and screwed up."
—**Marvin Gaye**

"If you become a star, you don't change. Everyone else does."
—**Kirk Douglas**

"When I was 19 years old I was the number one star of the world for two years. When I was 40 nobody wanted me."
—**Mickey Rooney**

"Getting fame, fortune, and money is supposed to make people happy. But sometimes, it's just unsettling."
—**Goldie Hawn**

"If you want a place in the sun, you have to expect a few blisters."
—**Loretta Young**

Jim Henson made Kermit the Frog out of his mother's overcoat.

LEGAL BRIEFS

Q: Why don't sharks eat lawyers? A: Professional courtesy. (Okay, we're just kidding—no, really.)

"**Lawyers are** the only persons in whom ignorance of the law is not punished."
—**Charles Lamb**

"**What do they do?** They don't produce anything. All they do is guide you through the labyrinth of the legal system that they created—and they keep changing it just in case you start to catch on."
—**Merle Kessler, aka Ian Shoales**

"**Criminal lawyer.** Or is that redundant?"
—**Will Durst**

"**If I wrote about** honest lawyers, I wouldn't be able to give the books away."
—**John Grisham**

"**Lawyers, I suppose,** were children once."
—**Charles Lamb**

"**A lawyer with** his briefcase can steal more than a thousand men with guns."
—**Mario Puzo**

Mark Twain coined the phrase "gossip column" in 1893.

PLASTIC SURGERY

*The closest Uncle John has come to plastic surgery was
when he cut up Mrs. Uncle John's credit cards.*

"My only original parts are my elbows."
—Phyllis Diller

"Drug kingpin Amado Carillo Fuentes died from nine hours of liposuction and plastic surgery—or, as it's commonly known here in Beverly Hills, natural causes."
—Bill Maher

"I don't need plastic in my body to validate me as a woman."
—Courtney Love

"I wish I had a twin, so I could know what I'd look like without plastic surgery."
—Joan Rivers

"I looked at myself and thought, 'Sh*t, I'm all nose.'"
—Cher, on her nose job

"Why a nose job? Because I was a very small girl attached to a very large nose."
—Jennifer Grey

"I don't plan to grow old gracefully. I plan to have facelifts until my ears meet."
—Rita Rudner

"He's an artist. He's resculpted himself."
—Lisa Marie Presley, on then husband Michael Jackson's plastic surgery

"They can take the fat from your rear and use it to bang out dents in your face. Now that's what I call recycling. It gives a whole new meaning to dancing cheek to cheek."
—Anita Wise

"If you eat right and you exercise and you get breast implants, you can look like me."
—Gena Lee Nolin

"Plastic surgeons are always making mountains out of molehills."
—Dolly Parton

"Isn't that the American dream? To purchase new breasts on credit?"
—Jenny McCarthy

"God has given you one face, and you make yourself another."
—William Shakespeare

"In her seventies, my mother tried to have her breasts lifted. I tried to dissuade her. I said, 'It's ridiculous at your age.' She said, 'If I meet a man, he'll certainly want me to have attractive breasts.' I said, 'I suppose he would.' And she said, 'Everybody's doing it—why can't I?' The doctor told her she could die on the operating table. She said, 'Don't worry about that. If the worst happens, you'll bury me topless.'"

—George Hamilton

A "DAILY" DOSE

The Daily Show's Jon Stewart is an author, comedian, talk show host, and political pundit. And he's very quotable.

"News used to hold itself to a higher plane and slowly it has dissolved into, well, me."

"In 1981 I lost my virginity, only to gain it back again on appeal in 1983."

"My life is a series of Hollywood orgies and Kabala center brunches with the cast of *Friends*. At least that's what my handlers tell me. I'm actually too valuable to live my own life and spend most of my days in a vegetable crisper to remain fake-news-anchor fresh."

"I heard Dennis Kucinich say in a debate, 'When I'm president...' and I just wanted to stop him and say, 'Dude.'"

"I was born with an adult head and a tiny body. Like a 'Peanuts' character."

"You have to remember one thing about the will of the people: it wasn't that long ago that we were swept away by the Macarena."

"We grew up in the good old days before kids had these damn computers and actually played outside."

"The KKK adopted a highway. Joke's on them: it's black."

"The nation of Dubai banned the movie *Charlie's Angels* because it's 'offensive to the religion of Islam.' Apparently, the religion of Islam is offended by anything without a plot."

"As long as I don't end up hosting a skin care commercial with Cher, I'm happy."

"I celebrated Thanksgiving in an old-fashioned way. I invited everyone in my neighborhood to my house, we had an enormous feast, and then I killed them and took their land."

"There are a hell of a lot of jobs that are scarier than live comedy. Like standing in the operating room when a guy's heart stops, and you're the one who has to fix it!"

MAN'S BEST FRIEND

*We are dogged in our determination to
give you another page of dog quotes.*

"The great pleasure of a dog is that you may make a fool of yourself with him and not only will he not scold you, but he will make a fool of himself, too."
—Samuel Butler

"Scratch a dog and you'll find a permanent job."
—Franklin P. Jones

"There is no psychiatrist in the world like a puppy licking your face."
—Ben Williams

"If you pick up a starving dog and make him prosperous, he will not bite you. That is the difference between dog and man."
—Mark Twain

"I don't understand why everyone says dogs are man's best friend. Do you really want a best friend who licks his butt before he kisses you?"
—Vicki Larson

"Even a little dog can piss on a big building."
—Jim Hightower

"A dog teaches a boy fidelity, perseverance, and to turn around three times before lying down."
—Robert Benchley

"If a dog will not come to you after having looked you in the face, you should go home and examine your conscience."
—Woodrow Wilson

"My wife left me and ran off with my best friend. Now I don't have a dog anymore."
—Rodney Dangerfield

"My little dog—a heartbeat at my feet."
—Edith Wharton

"Dogs are not our whole life, but they make our lives whole."
—Roger Caras

"If you're a dog and your owner suggests that you wear a sweater, suggest that he wear a tail."
—Fran Lebowitz

"The cat will mew, and dog will have his day."
—William Shakespeare

"Beware of puppy love; it can lead to a dog's life." —Gladiola Montana

LIFE SUCKS

If you don't have anything nice to say (and you're funny), we'll put it on this page.

"Being born is like being kidnapped. And then sold into slavery."
—**Andy Warhol**

"A man gazing at the stars is proverbially at the mercy of the puddles in the road."
—**Alexander Smith**

"Life is a God-damned, stinking, treacherous game, and nine hundred and ninety-nine men out of a thousand are bastards."
—**Theodore Dreiser**

"There is a theory that if ever anybody discovers exactly what the Universe is for and why it is here, it will instantly disappear and be replaced by something even more bizarre and inexplicable. There is another theory which states that this has already happened."
—**Douglas Adams**

"Life is a sexually transmitted disease—and the mortality rate is 100 percent."
—**R. D. Laing**

"Look at the Golden Rule—it's the first thing I was taught. 'Do unto others as you'd have them do unto you.' If we could all just do that, what a great place this world would be. One crummy little rule, and none of us can follow it."
—**John Mellencamp**

"Life is like playing a violin solo in public and learning the instrument as you go."
—**Edward Bulwer-Lytton**

"Life's a bitch and then they call you one."
—**Mary Frances Connely**

"If you want a picture of the future, imagine a boot stomping on a human face—forever."
—**George Orwell**

"If I could get my membership fee back, I'd resign from the human race."
—**Fred Allen**

"You only live once—but if you work it right, once is enough."
—**Joe E. Lewis**

"Smut" gets its name from a fungus that lives on corn kernels.

CHEER UP, IT COULD BE WORSE

Most people think life sucks, and then you die. Not me. I beg to differ. I think life sucks, then you get cancer, then your dog dies, your wife leaves you, the cancer goes into remission, you get a new dog, you get remarried, you owe ten million dollars in medical bills but you work hard for thirty-five years and you pay it back and then—one day—you have a massive stroke, your whole right side is paralyzed, you have to limp along the streets and speak out of the left side of your mouth and drool but you go into rehabilitation and regain the power to walk and the power to talk and then—one day— you step off a curb at 67th Street, and BANG you get hit by a city bus and then you die. Maybe.

—Denis Leary

THE BEATLES ON ...THE BEATLES

A few thoughts from the fab four.

"We reckoned we could make it because there were four of us. None of us could've made it alone, because Paul wasn't quite strong enough, I didn't have enough girl appeal, George was too quiet, and Ringo was the drummer. But we thought that everyone would be able to dig at least one of us, and that's how it turned out."
—John Lennon

"Somebody said to me, 'But the Beatles were anti-materialistic.' That's a huge myth. John and I literally used to sit down and say, 'Now, let's write a swimming pool.'"
—Paul McCartney

"You have to be a bastard to make it, and that's a fact. And the Beatles are the biggest bastards on earth."
—John Lennon

"As far as I'm concerned, there won't be a Beatles reunion as long as John Lennon remains dead."
—George Harrison

"It was really difficult to know what to do, 'cause you were either going to say, 'Okay, I've been a Beatle, and now I'll go back to the sweet shoppe or do something else with my life.' Or, 'I'll try to continue the music.' But then the thought came, 'Yeah, but you're gonna have to try and top the Beatles,' and that's not an easy act to follow."
—Paul McCartney

"I'd like to end up sort of unforgettable."
—Ringo Starr

"John could be a maneuvering swine, which no one ever realized."
—Paul McCartney

"A hundred years from now, it's Yoko Ono the world's going to remember, not John Lennon and the Beatles."
—Charlotte Moorman, performance artist, 1989

"[The Beatles] were just a band, that's all."
—John Lennon

About the Beatles: "Bad-mannered little sh*ts." —Noel Coward

CARTOON COMEDY

Some thoughts and musings from our two-dimensional friends.

Peter: "Hey Brian, there's a message in my Alpha Bits! It says 'OOOOOO.'"
Brian: "Peter, those are Cheerios."
—*The Family Guy*

"It takes a smart man to know he's stupid."
—**Barney Rubble,**
The Flintstones

"There are no stupid questions, only stupid people."
—**Mr. Garrison,** *South Park*

Squidward: "I have a theory. People talk loud when they want to act smart, right?"
Plankton: "CORRECT!"
—*SpongeBob SquarePants*

Dot: "Do you think this plan will work?"

Yakko: "It better. We don't have any more commercial breaks."
—*Animaniacs*

"I'm not bad. I'm just drawn that way."
—**Jessica Rabbit,** *Who Framed Roger Rabbit?*

"That girl, I say, that girl is like the road between Dallas and Fort Worth—no curves."
—**Foghorn Leghorn**

"Oh boy, the Shatner's really hit the fan now."
—*Space Ghost*

"Don't be a noble fighter, 'cause kindness is righter."
—*Popeye*

Jimmy: "We found the lost tomb!"
Cindy: "Shouldn't we call *National Geographic* or Harvard?"
Libby: "Or Harrison Ford?"
—*The Adventures of Jimmy Neutron: Boy Genius*

"Animation can explain whatever the mind of man can conceive." —Walt Disney

DIRECTORS ON DIRECTING

Lights! Check! Cameras rolling! Check! And...Action!
Cut! That was great. Now, one more time, with feeling.

"Look, I'm not a natural-born director. Now that I'm actually doing it, I wonder why everyone wants to in the first place. You have to think of everything!"

—Diane Keaton

"I have 10 commandments. The first 9 are, 'Thou shalt not bore.' The tenth is, 'Thou shalt have right of final cut.'"

—Billy Wilder

"I know my films upset people. I want to upset people."

—John Waters

"I made some mistakes in drama. I thought drama was when the actor cried. But drama is when the audience cries."

—Frank Capra

"A film director is a ringmaster, a psychiatrist, and a referee."

—Robert Aldrich

"I steal from every movie ever made."

—Quentin Tarantino

ACTING 101

Here we save you thousands of dollars and years of film school.
If you want to learn how to act, just listen to these folks.

"The subtlest acting I've ever seen is by ordinary people trying to show they feel something they don't or trying to hide something. It's something everyone learns at an early age."
—**Marlon Brando**

"Method acting? There are quite a few methods. Mine involves a lot of talent, a glass, and some cracked ice."
—**John Barrymore**

"Before I played Napoleon I called the AMA to get his autopsy. He had several diseases when he died, and learning about them helped me play him. It made him more human to me."
—**Rod Steiger**

"I'm from the let's-pretend school of acting."
—**Harrison Ford**

"I don't act. I react."
—**Jimmy Stewart**

"The secret of acting is sincerity—if you can fake that, you've got it made."
—**George Burns**

" 'What evil lurks in you to play such bad characters?' There is no evil. I just wear tight underwear."
—**Dennis Hopper**

"For an actress to succeed, she must have the face of a Venus, the brains of a Minerva, the grace of Terpsichore, the memory of a Macaulay, the figure of Juno, and the hide of a rhinoceros."
—**Ethel Barrymore**

"There are 100 rules for being a hero. Never blink your eyes when you shoot. If you want to show power or anger convincingly, never move your head when you say your lines. John Wayne never moved his head."
—**Arnold Schwarzenegger**

"The important thing in acting is to be able to laugh and cry. If I have to cry, I think of my sex life. If I have to laugh, I think of my sex life."
—**Glenda Jackson**

"Just learn your lines and don't bump into the furniture."
—**Spencer Tracy**

UNCLE JOHN'S QUOTATIONARY

Here's Part 7 of our quotation dictionary.
(Part 6 begins on page 231.)

NAGGING: the repetition of unpalatable truths. (Edith Summerskill)

NAIL: something you aim at before hitting your thumb with a hammer. (Peter Eldin)

NAME: an uncertain thing that you can't count on. (Bertolt Brecht)

NATION: a society united by its ancestry and by common hatred of its neighbors. (William Inge)

NATIONALISM: an infantile disease; the measles of mankind. (Albert Einstein)

NATURE: a mutable cloud which is always and never the same. (Ralph Waldo Emerson)

NEUROSIS: a secret you don't know you're keeping. (Kenneth Tynan)

NEUROTICS: those who founded our religions and created our masterpieces. (Marcel Proust)

NEW YORK: The nation's thyroid gland. (Christopher Morley)

NEWSPAPER: a device for making the ignorant more ignorant and the crazy crazier. (H. L. Mencken)

NIGHT: a stealthy, evil Raven, Wrapt to the eyes in his black wings. (Thomas Bailey Aldrich)

NONVIOLENCE: avoiding not only external physical violence but also internal violence of spirit. You not only refuse to shoot a man, but you refuse to hate him. (Martin Luther King, Jr.)

NORMAL: just a cycle on the washing machine. (Whoopi Goldberg)

NOSE: the extreme outpost of the face...never so happy as when thrust into the affairs of others, from which some physiologists have drawn the inference that the nose is devoid of the sense of smell. (Ambrose Bierce)

NOSTALGIA: a thing of the past. (Janet Rogers)

OBSCURITY: the refuge of incompetence. (Robert Heinlein)

OPENING NIGHT: the night before the play is ready to open. (George Jean Nathan)

OPERA: when a guy gets stabbed in the back and, instead of bleeding, he sings. (Ed Gardner)

OPTIMISM: the doctrine, or belief, that everything is beautiful, including what is ugly, everything good, especially the bad, and everything right that is wrong....It is hereditary, but fortunately, not contagious. (Ambrose Bierce)

OPTIMIST: someone who tells you to cheer up when things are going his way. (Edward R. Murrow)

ORIGINALITY: undetected plagiarism. (W. R. Inge)

For more, see page 326.

*   *   *

GOING GONZO

Cynical observations from writer Hunter S. Thompson, inventor of "gonzo journalism."

"Journalism is a low trade and a habit worse than heroin, a strange seedy world full of misfits and drunkards and failures. A group photo of the Top Ten journalists in America on any given day would be a monument to human ugliness."

"[Nixon] has the integrity of a hyena and the style of a poison toad."

"I hate to advocate drugs, alcohol, violence, or insanity to anyone, but they've always worked for me."

"The music business is a cruel and shallow money trench, a long plastic hallway where thieves and pimps run free, and good men die like dogs. There's also a negative side."

THE LAST LION

He's best known as one of the great leaders of World War II.
But British Prime Minister Winston Churchill has another
claim to fame—he won a Nobel Prize for Literature in 1953.

"There is nothing more exhilarating than to be shot at without result."

"Mr. Atlee is a very modest man. But then he has much to be modest about."

"Man will occasionally stumble over the truth, but usually manages to pick himself up, walk over or around it, and carry on."

"However beautiful the strategy, you should occasionally look at the results."

"He [Charles de Gaulle] looks like a female llama surprised in her bath."

"By swallowing evil words unsaid, no one has ever harmed his stomach."

"The truth is incontrovertible. Malice may attack it, ignorance may deride it, but in the end, there it is."

"If you're going through hell, keep going."

"Those who can win a war well can rarely make a good peace and those who could make a good peace would never have won the war."

"When I look back on all these worries I remember the story of the old man who said on his deathbed that he had a lot of trouble in his life, most of which had never happened."

"I am prepared to meet my Maker. Whether my Maker is prepared for the ordeal is another matter."

*   *   *

On Churchill:

"He would make a drum out of the skin of his mother the louder to sing his own praises."

—David Lloyd George

LIVE AND LEARN

We've had people write in and tell us that they've learned more from Bathroom Readers *than they ever did in school. Uh-oh.*

"Men are born ignorant, not stupid; they are made stupid by education."
—**Bertrand Russell**

"Education is a state-controlled manufactory of echoes."
—**Norman Douglas**

"I have never let my schooling interfere with my education."
—**Mark Twain**

"If you think education is expensive, try ignorance."
—**Derek Bok**

"Conservatives say teaching sex education in the schools will promote promiscuity. With our education system, if we promote promiscuity like we do math or science, they've got nothing to worry about."
—**Beverly Mickins**

"Education is what survives when what has been learned has been forgotten."
—**B. F. Skinner**

"Good teaching is 1/4 preparation and 3/4 theater."
—**Gail Godwin**

"What does education often do? It makes a straight-cut ditch out of a free, meandering brook."
—**Henry David Thoreau**

"College is something you complete. Life is something you experience."
—**Jon Stewart**

"Natural ability without education has more often raised a man to glory and virtue than education without natural ability."
—**Marcus Aurelius**

"The highest result of education is tolerance."
—**Helen Keller**

"The mediocre teacher tells, the good teacher explains, the superior teacher demonstrates, the great teacher inspires."
—**William Arthur Ward**

"To teach is to learn twice."
—**Joseph Joubert**

"The object of teaching a child is to enable him to get along without his teacher."
—**Elbert Hubbard**

"Humor is a universal language." —**Joel Goodman**

TEE TIME, PART II

More comments on the game of golf.

"A game in which you claim the privileges of age, and retain the playthings of childhood."
—Samuel Johnson

"I'm into golf now. I'm getting pretty good. I can almost hit the ball as far as I can throw the clubs."
—Bob Ettinger

"I played golf. I did not get a hole in one, but I did hit a guy. That's way more satisfying."
—Mitch Hedberg

"Golf is second only to Christianity, and is its greatest ally in the development of the highest standard of American manhood and womanhood."
—Rev. Paul Arnold Peterson

"If you drink, don't drive. Don't even putt."
—Dean Martin

"I love wearing the clothes. The golf course is the only place I can go dressed like a pimp and fit in perfectly. Anywhere else, lime-green pants and alligator shoes, and I got a cop on my ass."
—Samuel L. Jackson

"It took me 17 years to get to 3,000 hits in baseball. I did it in one afternoon on the golf course."
—Hank Aaron

"Golf and sex are the only things you can enjoy without being good at it."
—Jimmy Demaret

"Actually, the Lord answers my prayers everywhere except on the golf course."
—Billy Graham

"You don't know what pressure is until you play for five bucks a hole with only two bucks in your pocket."
—Lee Trevino

"Talking about golf is always boring. (Playing can be interesting, but not the part where you try to hit the little ball; only the part where you drive the cart.)"
—Dave Barry

"Someone once told me that there is more to life than golf. I think it was my ex-wife."
—Bruce Lansky

"I've been studying the game of golf pretty considerably. I guess I understand now how it's played. It's this way. You take a small ball into a big field and try to hit it—the ball, not the field. At the first attempt, you hit the field and not the ball. After that, you probably hit the air or else the boy who is carrying your bag of utensils. When you've gone on long enough, you possibly succeed in obtaining your original object. If the boy's alive, you send him off to look for the ball. If he finds it the same day, you've won the game."

—**Mark Twain**

"Love looks through a telescope; envy, through a microscope." —Josh Billings

SEINFELD

Jerry Seinfeld had such a successful TV show, you might forget that he is also a superb stand-up comedian.

"Why do women dress to emphasize body parts men are already looking at? The short skirts, the push-up bras—do we really need the coaching? I'm sure men are total failures at every aspect of conducting a relationship, but you're going to tell me we need help with the leering and the gawking?"

"Once a relationship is underway, then I would say deafness would come in handy. Then once you're married and have kids, paralysis. 'I'd love to drive you kids to that game, but I've got to sit in that chair and watch football on television.'"

"There's very little advice on sex in men's magazines, because men think, 'I know what I'm doing; just show me somebody naked.'"

On remote controls:
"Men aren't interested in what's on. They're interested in what else is on."

"The idea behind the tuxedo is the woman's point of view that men are all the same, so we might as well dress them that way. That's why a wedding is like the joining together of a beautiful, glowing bride and some guy."

"I once had a leather jacket that got ruined in the rain. Why does moisture ruin leather? Aren't cows outside a lot of the time? When it's raining, do cows go up to the farmhouse, 'Let us in! We're all wearing leather! Open the door! We're going to ruin the whole outfit here!'"

"I was in front of an ambulance the other day, and I noticed that the word 'ambulance' was spelled in reverse print on the hood of the ambulance. And I thought, 'Well, isn't that clever.' I look in the rear-view mirror, I can read the word 'ambulance' behind me. Of course while you're reading, you don't see where you're going, you crash, you need an ambulance. I think they're trying to drum up some business on the way back from lunch."

MIXED METAPHORS

Sometimes people combine two clichés that have nothing to do with each other—or just make up new clichés all together. Well, if the shoe fits, take it to the cleaners.

"I've been up and down so many times that I feel as if I'm in a revolving door."
—**Cher**

"[John McCain] can't have it both ways. He can't take the high horse and then claim the low road."
—**George W. Bush**

"A zebra does not change its spots."
—**Al Gore**

"If you let that sort of thing go on, your bread and butter will be cut right out from under your feet."
—**Ernest Bevin, former British foreign minister**

"It's like an Alcatraz around my neck."
—**Thomas Menino, Boston mayor, on the shortage of parking spaces in his city**

"This isn't a man who is leaving with his head between his legs."
—**Dan Quayle, commenting on Chief of Staff John Susnunu's resignation**

"That's just the tip of the ice cube."
—**Neil Hamilton, BBC**

"Mr. Milosevic has to be careful. The calendar is ticking."
—**Richard Haas, NBC News**

"Well, that was a cliff-dweller."
—**Wes Westrum, baseball coach, about a close game**

"We don't want to skim the cream off the crop here."
—**Gib Lewis, speaker of the Texas House**

"No one wants to say the sky is falling, but in this instance, I am afraid the emperor has no clothes. Despite Herculean efforts by the Council and Council staff, we are still only dealing with the tip of the iceberg."
—**Charles Millard, NYC councilman**

"If you don't like the heat in the dressing room, get out of the kitchen."
—**Terry Venables**

"If you don't know where you are going, you might wind up someplace else." —Yogi Berra

GOOD GRIEF!

Good ol' Charlie Brown. His depression and rotten luck somehow made us feel better about ourselves.

"Nothing takes the taste out of a peanut butter sandwich quite like unrequited love."

"When you have to get up at 7:00, 6:59 is the worst part of the day."

"Rats. Nobody sent me a Christmas card. I know nobody likes me. Why do we have to have a holiday season to emphasize it?"

"Life is like an ice-cream cone, you have to lick it one day at a time."

"Nothing echoes like an empty mailbox."

"In the book of life, the answers aren't in the back."

"I've developed a new philosophy. I only dread one day at a time."

"The secret to life: replace one worry with another."

ACTION JACKSON

*Betcha an Andrew Jackson you don't know
which U.S. president is on the $20 bill.*

"Any man worth his salt will stick up for what he believes right, but it takes a slightly better man to acknowledge instantly and without reservation that he is in error."

"There is no pleasure in having nothing to do; the fun is having lots to do and not doing it."

"Peace, above all things, is to be desired, but blood must sometimes be spilled to obtain it on equable and lasting terms."

"No one need think that the world can be ruled without blood. The civil sword shall and must be red and bloody."

"Never take counsel of your fears."

"It is a damn poor mind indeed which can't think of at least two ways to spell any word."

"Take time to deliberate; but when the time for action arrives, stop thinking and go in."

"Every good citizen makes his country's honor his own, and cherishes it not only as precious but as sacred. He is willing to risk his life in its defense and is conscious that he gains protection while he gives it."

"The brave man, inattentive to his duty, is worth little more to his country than the coward who deserts in the hour of danger."

CELEBRITY BLOWHARDS

Why doesn't Uncle John appear on this page? Because appearing with such people would diminish his stature.

"I was so handsome that women became spellbound when I came into view. In San Francisco, in rainy seasons, I was often mistaken for a cloudless day."
—**Mark Twain, reminiscing about his earlier years**

"I'm a multifaceted, talented, wealthy, internationally famous genius."
—**Jerry Lewis**

"I'm nowhere near as sexy as I come off on camera. Film just loves me."
—**David Caruso**

"I hate tooting my own horn, but after Steven (Spielberg) saw *Yentl*, he said, 'I wish I could tell you how to improve your picture, but I can't. It's the best film I have seen since *Citizen Kane*.'"
—**Barbara Streisand**

"I'm not an egomaniac like a lot of people say. But I am the world's best dancer, that's for sure."
—**Michael Flatley, Lord of the Dance**

"I've given up reading books. I find it takes my mind off myself."
—**Oscar Levant**

"I've outdone anybody you can name—Mozart, Beethoven, Bach, Strauss. Irving Berlin, he wrote 1,001 tunes. I wrote 5,500."
—**James Brown**

"I don't want keep proving myself to the world. I've done that."
—**Cindy Crawford**

"I am obsessed with myself. I've always though about myself. I get on the scale every day. I will look in the mirror—I've never been bored."
—**Dustin Hoffman**

"I am one of the most romantic men you will ever meet."
—**Antonio Banderas**

"My butt fascinates me....I mean, I like it so much that when I dance, I'm always looking back at it."
—**Tori Spelling**

PHYLLIS DILLER

Proof that it's never too late to be funny: Phyllis Diller was 37 when she started her comedy career.

"What I don't like about office Christmas parties is looking for a job the next day."

"You can get a driver's license when you're sixteen years old, which made a lot of sense to me when I was sixteen but now seems insane."

"The only thing that my husband and I have in common is that we were married on the same day."

"I've never made Who's Who but I'm featured in What's That."

"I put on a peekaboo blouse. He peeked and booed."

"I know people who are so clean you can eat off their floors. You can't eat off my table. Fang, my husband, says the only thing domestic about me is that I was born in this country."

"My Playtex Living Bra died—of starvation."

On Mickey Rooney: "His favorite exercise is climbing tall people."

"Sex is identical to comedy in that it involves timing."

"The best contraceptive for old people is nudity."

"That's why I still take the pill. I don't want any more grandchildren."

"Think of me as a sex symbol for the men who don't give a damn."

"I'm at an age where my back goes out more than I do."

"Housework can't kill you, but why take a chance?"

FRACTURED PHRASES

More variations on a phrase.

"Laugh and the world laughs with you; weep and you weep alone."

—Ella Wheeler Wilcox, American poet

"Laugh and the world laughs with you; cry and the world laughs at you."

—Caryn Leschen

"Laugh and the world laughs with you; stub your toe and the world laughs whether you do or not."

—Linda Perret's Humor Files

"Laugh and the world laughs with you; snore and you sleep alone."

—Anthony Burgess

"It's better to give than to receive."

"Remember, it's better to give than to get five across your lip."

—Fred Sanford, *Sanford and Son*

"Money can't buy happiness."

"Money can't buy you happiness, but it does bring you a more pleasant form of misery."

—Spike Milligan

"Money can't buy happiness, but it will certainly get you a better class of memories."

—Ronald Reagan

"Money can't buy happiness, but it can make you awfully comfortable while you're being miserable."

—Clare Boothe Luce

"Money can't buy happiness, but then, happiness can't buy government insured C.D.s."

—Bruce Willis, *Moonlighting*

"People who say money can't buy happiness don't know where to shop."

—Zsa Zsa Gabor

"Money can't buy you happiness. I just helps you look for it in more places."

—Milton Berle

Dwight Eisenhower hated cats so much he ordered that any found on his property be shot.

OH, CANADA!

Some observations on our neighbor to the north.

"Canada could have enjoyed:
English government,
French culture,
And American know-how.
Instead it ended up with:
English know-how,
French government,
And American culture."
—**John Robert Colombo**

"Canadians live with liberal rhetoric, but we conduct our lives as social conservatives."
—**David Crombie**

"What is it with Canadians and rock music? When they're good, they are very, very good. When they're bad, they are Bryan Adams."
—**Charles Shaar Murray**

"I've been to Canada, and I've always gotten the impression that I could take the country over in about two days."
—**Jon Stewart**

"A Canadian is a person who has become a North American without becoming an American."
—**Arthur Phelps**

"I don't even know what street Canada is on."
—**Al Capone**

"Canada is a country so square that even the female impersonators are women."
—*Outrageous!*

"I'm Canadian. It's like American, but without the gun."
—**Dave Foley**

"I learned nothing about Canada in school. Canada was to the north; Mexico was to the south. The dumb kids got it wrong."
—**Larry King**

"Canadians look down on the United States and consider it Hell. They are right to do so."
—**Irving Layton**

"Canadians are generally indistinguishable from Americans and the surest way to tell the two apart is to make this observation to a Canadian."
—**Richard Starnes**

THE BOOB TUBE

You can learn a lot from TV. For instance, you can learn that you might be better off reading a book.

"Television is a medium of entertainment which permits millions of people to listen to the same joke at the same time, and yet remain lonesome."
—T. S. Eliot

"You know something? If you couldn't read, you couldn't look up what was on television."
—Beaver Cleaver, *Leave it to Beaver*

"Television has done so much for psychiatry by spreading information about it, as well as contributing to the need for it."
—Alfred Hitchcock, *Alfred Hitchcock Presents*

"I would say that anything that is indecent and violent in TV is a crime against humanity and they should shoot the head man responsible."
—Ted Turner

"I watch *Cops* regularly just to see if any of my relatives are on it."
—Travis Tritt

"Do you know what our suicide rate would be if we didn't have television? Do you know how much happiness I've brought to people who couldn't get out of the house but could watch Love Boat?"
—Aaron Spelling

"Television has proved that people will look at anything rather than each other."
—Ann Landers

"It's a strange thing, this television. God didn't design anyone to be recognized by two billion people."
—Peter Falk

"The only way to get any feeling from a television set is to touch it when you're wet."
—Larry Gelbart

"An audience doesn't know what it wants; it only knows when it sees it."
—William G. Stewart

"On TV, you can use sex to sell anything except sex."
—Stephanie Black

"Left to their own devices, the three networks would televise live executions. Except Fox—they'd televise live naked executions."

—David Goldberg, TV producer

...requested song at funerals in England.

IF…THEN

If you're a quote whiz, then this quiz is for you. Math the first half of the quote in column A with the second half in column B. Then see if you can guess who said it. (Answers at the end.)

A

1. "If the bedroom were a kitchen…"

2. "If your head is wax…"

3. "If a thing is worth doing…"

4. "If a thing is worth doing…"

5. "If it doesn't fit…"

6. "If we don't succeed…"

7. "If you can't convince" them…"

8. "If you can't be kind…"

9. "If you can't beat them…"

10. "If you choose not to decide…"

11. "If you ever see me getting beaten by the police…"

12. "If you have to be in a soap opera…"

13. "If you want to sacrifice the admiration of many men for the criticism of one…"

B

a) "arrange to have them beaten."

b) "try not to get the worst role."

c) "it is worth doing badly."

d) "you have to take the spoon out of the cup."

e) "we run the risk of failure."

f) "you must acquit."

g) "you still have made a choice."

h) "you're on time."

i) "women would be crockpots and men would be microwaves."

j) "confuse them."

k) "a single rose says : 'I'm cheap!'"

l) "don't walk in the sun."

m) "go ahead, get married."

Dustin Hoffman wore a size 36C bra in *Tootsie*.

A	B
14. "If you want to say it with flowers…"	**n)** "put down the video camera and come help me."
15. "If your eyes hurt after you drink coffee…"	**o)** "it is worth doing slowly—very slowly."
16. "If you're there before it's over…"	**p)** "at least be vague."

ANSWERS

1. i—George Carlin; 2. l—Boy George; 3. c—G. K. Chesterton; 4. o—Norm Crosby; 5. f—Dan Quayle; 6. e—Johnnie L. Cochran, Jr.; 7. j—Harry S Truman; 8. p—James Walker; 9. a—Diana Jordan ; 10. g—Rush; 11. n—Delta Burke; 12. b—Benjamin Franklin; 13. m—Katharine Hepburn; 14. k—Bobcat Goldthwait; 15. d—Gypsy Rose Lee; 16. h—Judith Manners

* * *

P. J. O'ROURKE ON LIFE AND RESPONSIBILITY

"One of the annoying things about believing in free will and individual responsibility is the difficulty of finding somebody to blame your problems on. And when you do find somebody, it's remarkable how often his picture turns up on your driver's license."

"It is a popular delusion that the government wastes vast amounts of money through inefficiency and sloth. Enormous effort and elaborate planning are required to waste this much money."

"If Columbus had had an advisory committee, he'd probably still be at the dock." —Arther Goldberg

MORE FREE ADVICE

A few pages of people telling you what they think you should do.

"Remember there's a big difference between kneeling down and bending over."
—**Frank Zappa**

"Trust your husband, adore your husband, and get as much as you can in your own name."
—**Joan Rivers**

"There's only one corner of the universe you can be certain of improving, and that's your own self."
—**Aldous Huxley**

"Get a sense of humor. If you don't, it'll be incredibly frustrating."
—**Jon Stewart**

"Be suspicious of any doctor who tries to take your temperature with his finger."
—**Dave Letterman**

"Keep cool; it will be all one a hundred years hence."
—**Ralph Waldo Emerson**

"Learn all the rules, every one of them, so that you will know how to break them."
—**Irvin S. Cobb**

"Be careful to choose your enemies well. Friends don't much matter. But the choice of enemies is very important."
—**Oscar Wilde**

"When you are in a hole, stop digging."
—**Denis Healey**

"Go confidently in the direction of your dreams! Live the life you've imagined. As you simplify your life, the law of the universe will be simpler."
—**Henry David Thoreau**

"Begin challenging your own assumptions. Your assumptions are your windows on the world. Scrub them off every once in awhile, or the light won't come in."
—**Alan Alda**

"If opportunity doesn't knock, build a door."
—**Milton Berle**

"Beware the pull on your heartstrings—it's often the pursestrings that are actually being reached for."
—**Barbara Mikkelson**

PAPPY MAVERICK

He was the wisest character in television history that no one ever saw. But thanks to his sons, Brett and Bart Maverick, his pearls of wisdom live on.

"Never cry over spilt milk. It could have been whiskey."

"Never play in a rigged game, unless you rig it yourself."

"If you haven't got something nice to say about a man, it's time to change the subject."

"Most of us, by the time we're up on the rules, are generally too old to play."

"Love's the only thing in life you've got to earn. Everything else you can steal."

"Son, stay clear of weddings, because one of them is liable to be your own."

"Marriage is the only game of chance I know of where both people can lose."

"Man is the only animal you can skin more than once."

"It's fine to turn over a new leaf, but there's always somebody trying to snoop through the old pages."

"If you can't fight 'em, and they won't let you join 'em, best get out of the country."

"A man does what he has to do, if he can't get out of it."

"If at first you don't succeed, try something else."

"Faint heart never filled a flush."

"Hell has no fury like a man who loses with a four of a kind."

"He who plays and runs away lives to run another day."

"Work is fine for killing time, but it's a shaky way to make a living."

"A coward dies a thousand deaths, a brave man only once. A thousand to one....That's a pretty good advantage."

"There's only one thing more important than money, and that's more money."

MAKING UP WORDS

Mrs. Uncle John made up a word to describe Uncle John when he's working late to finish a book: *!#?@$*. Here are some recently-coined words that we can print.

"Getting jiggy wit it is like, the next level of cool. It's cool to the eighth power. Some people are fly, some people are kind of hot. But when you the jiggiest, you exhume jiggy-essence. It's the acme of cool."

—**Will Smith**

"I love those fake jewelry names on QVC. 'Diamonique, the only diamond in the world made from crystal!' And the ring isn't gold either, it's 'a Goldine finish on genuine steel!' People buy this crap. You can call crap anything; they'll buy it. Would you buy a steak with a genuine beefinque finish? And God help us if the Pentagon starts talking this way: 'It's not war, it's a warette! We drop a few bombiniques; it'll be over. Then we'll set up a one-party government with a genuine Democracine finish.'"

—**Daniel Liebert**

LAME EXCUSES

What's your excuse for not reading this page sooner?

Offender: Edward G. Edwards

Offense: The Louisiana gubernatorial candidate suffered an embarrassing loss in a debate shortly before the 1992 election.

Lame Excuse: "I deliberately fumbled around and didn't do as good as I could. I gave that guy a false sense of security and he fell for it hook, line, and sinker."

Offender: Texas State Senator Bill Moore

Offense: Critics charged that he would personally profit from a bill he was backing.

Lame Excuse: "I'd just make a little bit of money. I wouldn't make a whole lot."

Offender: Demi Moore

Offense: She changed the ending of *The Scarlet Letter* from sad to happy.

Lame Excuse: "Not many people have read the book."

Offenders: Two operators at Dresden Nuclear Power Plant

Offense: They were caught sleeping on the job. John Hogan, the Commonwealth Edison supervisor of news information, explained it to reporters.

Lame Excuse: "It depends on your definition of asleep. They weren't stretched out. They had their eyes closed. They were seated at their desks with their heads in a nodding position."

Offender: Ozzy Osbourne

Offense: The hard rocker bit the head off of a dead dove at a CBS Records meeting.

Lame Excuse: "I wanted them to remember me."

Offender: Jim Morrison

Offense: Revealing himself while on stage

Lame Excuse: "I just wanted to see what it looked like in the spotlight."

*　　*　　*

"It is better to offer no excuse than a bad one."

—**George Washington, letter to his niece Harriet Washington, October 30, 1791**

"This is on me." —Dorothy Parker's tombstone

BOBBY AND JFK

America's had several political dynasties. Here are some quotes from one of the most prominent.

"Progress is nice. But change is its motivator. And change has its enemies."
—**Robert F. Kennedy**

"Those who make peaceful revolution impossible will make violent revolution inevitable."
—**John F. Kennedy**

"Only those who dare to fail greatly can ever achieve greatly."
—**Robert F. Kennedy**

"Take time to repair the roof when the sun is shining."
—**John F. Kennedy**

"Tragedy is a tool for the living to gain wisdom, not a guide by which to live."
—**Robert F. Kennedy**

ANONYMOUS WHO?

*We have no idea who this person is or was,
but he or she sure was a prolific speaker.*

"She's too young for Medicare and too old for me to care."
—**Anonymous**

"A conscience is what hurts when all your other parts feel so good."
—**Anonymous**

"You laugh at me because I am different, but I laugh at you because you are all the same."
—**Anonymous**

"Thinking is the greatest torture in the world for most people."
—**Anonymous**

"A good scare is worth more to a man than good advice."
—**Anonymous**

"Some people have a large circle of friends while others have only friends that they like."
—**Anonymous**

"Living on Earth may be expensive, but it includes an annual free trip around the Sun."
—**Anonymous**

"Everything is okay in the end. And if it's not okay, then it's not the end."
—**Anonymous**

"Wear the old coat and buy the new book."
—**Anonymous**

"Write a wise saying and your name will live forever."
—**Anonymous**

"Does anal retentive have a hyphen?" —seen on a T-shirt

CONAN O'BRIEN

A few words from the king of late, late, late-night television.

"A new study reveals U.S. students have very little knowledge of American history. In fact, test scores are the lowest since the Lincoln-Kennedy debates."

"The price of Prozac went up 50 percent last year. When they asked Prozac users how they felt about this they said, 'Whatever.'"

"The pope was a soccer goalie in his youth. So apparently, even as a young man, he tried to stop people from scoring."

"Bill Gates was in India for four days…because sometimes he just likes to feel even richer."

"Good news: The FDA has approved pills that help you lose weight by making you feel full. The recommended dosage is five thousand pills a day."

"American and British troops handed out food to hundreds of Iraqis. Not surprisingly, Iraqis handed the British food back."

"A former classmate of Pamela's [Anderson] said that in high school, she was flat-chested. That's shocking—I had no idea she graduated from high school."

"CBS news anchor Dan Rather has interviewed Iraqi dictator Saddam Hussein. When asked what it was like to talk to a crazy man, Saddam said, 'It's not so bad.'"

"In West Virginia yesterday, a man was arrested for stealing several blow-up dolls. Reportedly, police didn't have any trouble catching the man because he was completely out of breath."

"Scientists announced that they have located the gene for alcoholism. Scientists say they found it at a party, talking way too loudly."

"Apparently the new high-tech *Star Wars* toys will be in stores any day now. The toys can talk and are interactive, so they can be easily distinguished from *Star Wars* fans."

COACHES' CORNER

All right, team, listen up! I want you to read this page and read it good. Anyone who doesn't can drop and give me 20!

"Managing is getting paid for homeruns someone else hits."
—Casey Stengel

"I wouldn't say that Joe has a sore arm, per se, but his arm is kind of sore."
—Weeb Ewbank

"Our strength is that we don't have any weaknesses. Our weakness is that we don't have any real strengths."
—Frank Boyles

"John didn't flunk his physical, he just didn't pass it."
—Steve Ortmayer

"If we hadn't given them those first four touchdowns, it might have been different."
—"Cootie" Reeves, Hokes Bluff, Alabama, high school football coach, after his team lost 53–0

"It's not how good you can play when you play good. It's how good you play when you play bad and we can play as bad as anyone in the country."
—Hugh Durham

"I don't think there's anybody in this organization not focused on the 49ers—I mean Chargers."
—Bill Belichick

"He wants Texas back."
—Tommy Lasorda, on what Mexican-born pitching sensation Fernando Valenzuela might demand in upcoming contract negotiations

"I've only heard what I've read in the papers."
—Frank Burns

"I have nothing to say. And I'll say it only once."
—Floyd Smith

"I'm as nauseous as I've ever been. I have a terrible headache. My head is pounding. I feel like throwing up and I'm having trouble swallowing. And the beauty of it is, you want to feel like this every day."
—Tony LaRussa, during the 1996 NL Central Division title race

---

In the average film, male actors utter 10 times as many profanities as female actors.

FAMILY VALUES

*Just because someone is related to you doesn't
mean they know what they're talking about.*

"My mom always said men are like linoleum floors. Lay 'em right and you can walk all over them for thirty years."
—Brett Butler

"It's true that I did get the girl, but then my grandfather always said, 'Even a blind chicken finds a few grains of corn now and then.'"
—**Lyle Lovett, on marrying Julia Roberts, 1994**

"My mother said this: 'Sex is a dirty, disgusting thing you save for somebody you love.'"
—**Carol Henry**

Arthur Dent: You know, it's a time like this, when I'm stuck in a Volgon airlock with a man from Betelgeuse, about to die of asphyxiation in deep space, that I really wish I'd listened to what my mother told me when I was young.
Ford Perfect: Why? What did she tell you?
Arthur Dent: I don't know. I didn't listen.
—*The Hitchhiker's Guide to the Galaxy*

"My mother always said to me, 'Son, look the devil in the eye and meet him straight on. You can't wrestle him to the ground unless you got ahold of him first.' ...My mother was a babbling fool."
—Benson, *Soap*

"My pa always said every man is your friend until he shows you otherwise."
—Hoss, *Bonanza*

"And always remember the last words of my grandfather, who said, 'A *truck!*'"
—Emo Philips

*   *   *

"The only thing my mother told me about sex was that I was never going to get any."
—Doug Graham

NO SWEAT!

Copy this page and tape it to your fridge.
It won't help you lose weight, but it
might make you feel better.

"I exercise every morning without fail. One eyelid goes up and the other follows."
—Pete Postlethwaite

"Joined a health club last year, spent four hundred bucks. Haven't lost a pound. Apparently, you have to show up."
—Rich Ceisler

"I believe every human has a finite number of heartbeats. I don't intent to waste any of mine running around doing exercises."
—Neil Armstrong

"My problem with most athletic challenges is training. I'm lazy and find that workouts cut into my drinking time."
—Dave Barry

"I'm not into working out. My philosophy: no pain, no pain."
—Carol Leifer

"They say the best exercise happens in the bedroom. I believe it, because that's where I get the most resistance."
—Jeff Shaw

"I've been doing leg lifts faithfully for about fifteen years. The only thing that's gotten thinner is the carpet where I've been doing the leg lifts."
—Rita Rudner

"It is unnatural for people to run around city streets unless they are thieves or victims."
—Mike Royko

"Another good reducing exercise consists in placing both hands against the table edge and pushing back."
—Robert Quillen

"Exercise is bunk. If you are healthy, you don't need it. If you are sick, you shouldn't take it."
—Henry Ford

"I take my only exercise acting as pallbearer at the funerals of my friends who exercise regularly."
—Mark Twain

"They say exercise and a proper diet are the keys to a longer life. Oh, well."
—Drew Carey

Couch Potatoes: 25% of American adults say they never exercise.

YOU'RE HISTORY!

More quotes about the past.

"Throughout history, it has been the inaction of those who could have acted, the indifference of those who should have known better, the silence of the voice of justice when it mattered most, that has made it possible for evil to triumph."
—**Haile Selassie**

"One of the lessons of history is that nothing is often a good thing to do and always a clever thing to say."
—**Will Durant**

"Does history record any case in which the majority was right?"
—**Robert A. Heinlein**

"The past is not dead. In fact, it's not even past."
—**William Faulkner**

"The most significant fact of modern history is that America speaks English."
—**Ludwig von Bismarck**

"Whoever wishes to foresee the future must consult the past; for human events ever resemble those of preceding times. This arises from the fact that they are produced by men who ever have been, and ever shall be, animated by the same passions, and thus they necessarily have the same results."
—**Niccolo Machiavelli**

"Study history, study history. In history lies all the secrets of statecraft."
—**Winston Churchill**

"If you would understand anything, observe its beginning and its development."
—**Aristotle**

"Myth, memory, history— these are three alternative ways to capture and account for an elusive past, each with its own persuasive claim."
—**Warren I. Susman**

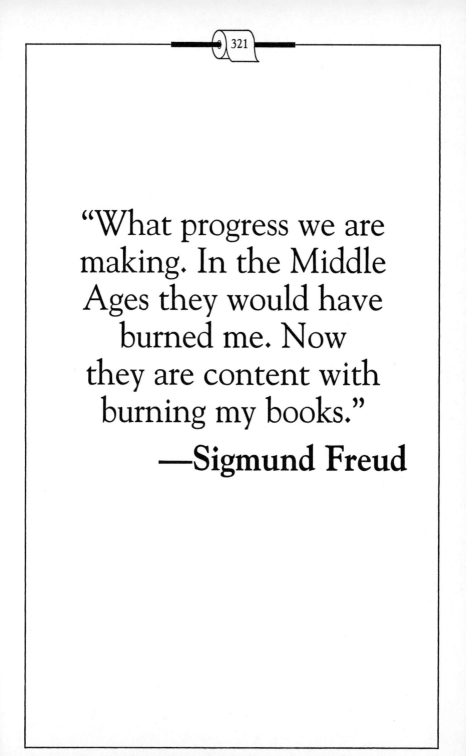

"What progress we are making. In the Middle Ages they would have burned me. Now they are content with burning my books."
—**Sigmund Freud**

OVERLY OPTIMISTIC

*These dumb predictions probably sounded pretty good
at the time, but with hindsight, they're pretty funny.*

"God himself could not sink this ship."
—**Deckhand on the *Titanic***

"Before man reaches the moon, your mail will be delivered within hours from New York to Australia by guided missiles. We stand on the threshold of rocket mail."
—**Arthur Summerfield, US Postmaster General, 1959**

"Automobiles will start to decline almost as soon as the last shot is fired in World war II. Instead of a car in every garage, there will be a helicopter."
—**Harry Bruno, Aviation publicist, 1943**

"Where a calculator on the ENIAC is equipped with 18,000 vacuum tubes and weighs 30 tons, computers in the future may have only 1,000 vacuum tubes and weigh only 1.5 tons."
—***Popular Mechanics*, 1949**

"We just won't have arthritis in 2000."
—**Dr. William Clark, president of the Arthritis Foundation, 1966**

"I see no good reasons why the views given in this volume should shock the religious sensibilities of anyone."
—**Charles Darwin, in a preamble to *The Origin of the Species***

"Color and stereoscopy will make the cinema into the greatest art in the world. Bad films will be impossible."
—**Sir John Betjeman, Poet Laureate, 1935**

LIBERALS AND CONSERVATIVES

*Some of Uncle John's friends say he's a liberal Conservative.
But that's a lot of crap: he's a conservative Liberal—
ask anyone who knows him.*

"Conservative: a statesman who is enamoured of existing evils, as distinguished from the Liberal, who wishes to replace them with others."

—Ambrose Bierce

"The Democrats seem to be basically nicer people, but they have demonstrated time and again that they have the management skills of celery. They're the kind of people who'd stop to help you change a flat, but would somehow manage to set your car on fire. I would be reluctant to entrust them with a Cuisinart, let alone the economy. The Republicans, on the other hand, would know how to fix your tire, but they wouldn't bother to stop because they'd want to be on time for Ugly Pants Night at the country club."

—Dave Barry

"Any man who is under 30, and is not a liberal, has no heart; and any man who is over 30, and is not a conservative, has no brains."

—Winston Churchill

"There is a nickel's worth of difference between Democrats and Republicans. If you put a nickel on the table, the Democrat will steal it from you and the Republican will kill you for it."

—Barry Crimmins

"May you be as rich as a Republican and have the sex life of a Democrat."

—Johnny Carson

GOVSPEAK

Can you speak out of both sides of your mouth at the same time? Good news! There will always be room in the government for you.

"We don't necessarily discriminate. We simply exclude certain types of people."
—Colonel Gerald Wellman, Reserve Officer Training Corps

"I haven't committed a crime. What I did was fail to comply with the law."
—David Dinkins, New York City mayor

"As we know, there are known knowns. There are things we know we know. We also know there are known unknowns."
—Donald Rumsfeld

"The private enterprise system indicates that some people have higher incomes than others."
—Jerry Brown

"I have opinions of my own—strong opinions—but I don't always agree with them."
—George H. W. Bush

"I do not like this word 'bomb.' It is not a bomb. It is a device which is exploding."
—Jacques Le Blanc, French ambassador to New Zealand, describing France's nuclear testing in 1995

"Those who survived the San Francisco earthquake said, 'Thank God, I'm still alive.' But, of course, those who died, their lives will never be the same again."
—Sen. Barbara Boxer

"We are not without accomplishment. We have managed to distribute poverty equally."
—Nguyen Co Thatch, Vietnamese foreign minister

"First, it was not a strip bar, it was an erotic club. And second, what can I say? I'm a night owl."
—Marion Barry

"For I am a bear of very little brain and long words bother me." —Winnie the Pooh

CELEBRITY KIDS SPEAK

Celebrities are people too. How do we know? Because they reproduce.

"I asked the hairdressers, 'Do I need to be in the first shot?' and she said, 'Yeah, we asked and you definitely have to be in it.' So it's like, 'Daaadddy, do I have to be in the first shot?' And he's like, 'Nope.' It was great."
—**Gwyneth Paltrow, on starring in** *Duets*, **directed by father Bruce Paltrow**

"I still have slumber parties with my father where we do beauty treatments. It's really cool because he has all the good creams and stuff."
—**Liv Tyler, daughter of Steven Tyler**

"He stands there groping himself, and he is 46 years old. It disgusts me, but he tells me that the kids like it."
—**Mia Tyler, another daughter of Steven Tyler**

"It was hard growing up seeing all the press against your mother. I'd be sitting next to a girl in chemistry class and she'd say, 'You're mother's a commie.'"
—**Natasha Richardson, on mother Vanessa Redgrave**

"Wouldn't you know it? I finally got my sh*t together. I stopped drinking. I stopped smoking. I stopped fighting the fact that Bing Crosby was my father. And now look what's happened."
—**Gary Crosby, two weeks before dying of lung cancer**

"My only complaint about having a father in fashion is that every time I go to bed with a guy I have to look at my dad's name all over his underwear."
—**Marci Klein, daughter of Calvin Klein**

"It was no great tragedy being Judy Garland's daughter. I had tremendously interesting childhood years—except they had little to do with being a child."
—**Liza Minelli**

UNCLE JOHN'S QUOTATIONARY

Here's Part 8 of our quotation dictionary.
(Part 7 begins on page 292.)

PAINTING: an activity that's easy if you don't know how to do it, but difficult when you do. (Edgar Degas)

PARADISE: utility is when you have one telephone, luxury is when you have two, opulence is when you have three—and paradise is when you have none. (Doug Larson)

PARADOX: truth standing on her head to get attention. (G. K. Chesterson)

PARENTS: the bones on which children sharpen their teeth. (Peter Ustinov)

PEACE: a continuation of war by other means. (Vo Nguyen Giap)

PESSIMIST: a man that thinks every man is as nasty as himself and hates them for it. (George Bernard Shaw)

PHILOSOPHY: what you don't know. (Bertrand Russell)

PICTURES (films): the only business where you can sit out front and applaud yourself. (Will Rogers)

PITCHING: the art of instilling fear by making a man flinch. (Sandy Koufax)

PLATITUDE: an idea (a) that is admitted to be true by everyone, and (b) that is not true. (H. L. Mencken)

PLAYBOY: a man who believes in wine, women, and so long. (John Travolta)

POETRY: the impish attempt to paint the color of the wind. (Maxwell Bodenheim)

POLITENESS: half good manners and half good lying. (Mary Wilson Little)

POLITICIAN: a fellow who will lay down your life for his country. (Texas Guinan)

POLITICS: the skilled use of blunt objects. (Lester B. Pearson)

PONDER: to arrive at a stupid decision slowly. (Herbert Prochnov)

POVERTY: the mother of crime. (Marcus Aurelius)

POWER: the ability not to have

"America is a place where Jewish merchants sell Zen love beads...

to please. (Elizabeth Janeway)

PREJUDICES: what fools use for reason. (Voltaire)

THE PRESENT: the now, the here, through which all future plunges to the past. (James Joyce)

PRIVACY: one of those precious modern constructions that we've dressed up as a fundamental right when it's really a frilly privilege that comes with being so affluent that we can ignore the neighbors and pretend we don't need anyone else. (Mark Fisher)

PROBLEM: a chance for you to do your best. (Duke Ellington)

PROCRASTINATION: putting off tomorrow what you put off yesterday until today. (Laurence J. Peter)

PROFESSOR: one who talks in someone else's sleep. (W. H. Auden)

PROGRESS: the exchange of one nuisance for another. (Havelock Ellis)

PROPHECY: the most gratuitous form of error. (George Eliot)

PROVERB: one man's wit and all men's wisdom. (Lord John Russell)

PSYCHIATRIST: a man who asks you a lot of expensive questions your wife will ask you for free. (Sam Bardell)

PSYCHOANALYSIS: confession without absolution. (G. K. Chesterson)

PUBLIC LIFE: the paradise of voluble windbags. (George Bernard Shaw)

PUBLISHERS: people who kill good trees to put out bad newspapers. (James G. Watt)

PUNCTUALITY: the virtue of the bored. (Evelyn Waugh)

PUNDIT: an expert on nothing but an authority on everything. (William Safire)

PUNK ROCK: a newborn baby, crying. (Thurston Moore, of Sonic Youth)

PURITANISM: the haunting fear that someone, somewhere, may be happy. (H. L. Mencken)

QUALITY: doing it right when no one is looking. (Henry Ford)

QUEEN: a woman by whom the realm is ruled when there is a king, and through whom it is ruled when there is not. (Ambrose Bierce)

QUOTING: the act of repeating erroneously the words of another. (Ambrose Bierce)

RACEHORSE: the only animal that can take thousands of people for a ride at the same time. (Herbert Prochnov)

RACIAL PREJUDICE: a pigment of the imagination. (Nigel Rees)

RAP MUSIC: the CNN of young black America. (Chuck D)

REALITY: a crutch for people who can't cope with drugs. (Lily Tomlin)

REDUNDANCY: an airbag in a politician's car. (Larry Hagman)

RELIGIONS: all the same—basically guilt, with different holidays. (Cathy Ladman)

RESTAURANT: mouth brothel. (Frederic Raphael)

RETIREMENT: twice the husband on half the money. (Sean McCarthy)

RICH MAN: nothing but a poor man with money. (W. C. Fields)

ROCK JOURNALISM: people who can't write interviewing people who can't talk for people who can't read. (Frank Zappa)

ROCK 'N' ROLL: monotony tinged with hysteria. (Vance Packard)

ROMANCE: a love affair in other than domestic surroundings. (Sir Walter Raleigh)

RUDENESS: the weak man's imitation of strength. (Eric Hoffer)

For more, see page 374.

*　　*　　*

We are unable to announce the weather. We depend on weather reports from the airport, which is closed, due to the weather. Whether we will be able to give you the weather tomorrow will depend on the weather.

—from the *Arab News*

"The fool doth think he is wise, but the wiseman knows himself to be a fool." —*As You Like It*

NEW YORK, NEW YORK

*Hey, youse guys! Here are some thoughts on the city that
never sleeps. Now shut up and read, already!*

"When you leave New York, you are astonished at
how clean the rest of the world is. Clean is not
enough."
—**Fran Lebowitz**

"New York is not the center of the goddamn universe. I grant you it's an exciting, vibrant, stimulat-
ing, fabulous city, but it is not Mecca. It just smells
like it."
—**Neil Simon**

"New York is a narrow island off the coast of New
Jersey devoted to the pursuit of lunch."
—**Raymond Sokolov**

"New York is that unnatural city where everyone is
an exile, none more so than the American."
—**Charlotte Perkins Gilman**

"Traffic signals in New York are just rough guide-
lines."
—**David Letterman**

"I took a bus in San Francisco. The sign above the
driver says, 'Information gladly given, but safety
requires avoiding unnecessary conversation.' In
New York, it's 'Don't talk to the freakin' driver. He
could snap.'"
—**Norman K.**

MENCKEN'S MUSINGS

*Known as the "Sage of Baltimore," H. L. Mencken was considered
one of the greatest writers—and cynics—of the 20th century.*

"Morality is the theory that every human act must be either right or wrong, and that 99 percent of them are wrong."

"There's no underestimating the intelligence of the American public."

"Love is the triumph of imagination over intelligence."

"Public opinion, in its raw state, gushes out the immemorial form of the mob's fear. It is piped into central factories, and there it is flavored and colored, and put into cans."

"There is only one honest impulse at the bottom of Puritanism, and that is to punish the man with a superior capacity for happiness."

"On one issue, at least, men and women agree: they both distrust women."

"An idealist is one who, on noticing that a rose smells better than a cabbage, concludes that it will also make better soup."

"It is impossible to imagine the universe run by a wise, just, and omnipotent God, but it is quite easy to imagine it run by a board of gods. If such a board actually exists, it operates precisely like the board of a corporation that is losing money."

"For every problem there is an answer that is clear, simple, and wrong."

"The harsh, useful things of the world, from pulling teeth to digging potatoes, are best done by men who are as starkly sober as so many convicts in the death-house, but the lovely and useless things, the charming and exhilarating things, are best done by men with, as the phrase is, a few sheets in the wind."

"Only presidents, editors, and people with tapeworms have the right to use the editorial 'we.' "

"A cynic is a man who, when he smells flowers, looks around for a coffin."

"Reality is merely an illusion, albeit a very persistent one." —Albert Einstein

CHIASMUS

When you use the same phrase backward and forward in the same sentence, you're creating a "chiasmus." Here are a few examples.

"It's not the size of the dog in the fight, its the size of the fight in the dog."
—Mark Twain

Laura Holt: "Some questions are best left unanswered."
Remington Steele: "And some answers are best left unquestioned."
—*Remington Steele*

"Real pain for your sham friends and champagne for your real friends."
—Anonymous

"The gambling known as business looks with austere disfavor upon the business known as gambling."
—Ambrose Bierce

"Money will not make you happy, and happy will not make you money."
—Groucho Marx

"Don't sweat the petty things, and don't pet the sweaty things."
—George Carlin

"Don't count the days, make the days count."
—Muhammad Ali

"You don't get ulcers from what you eat. You get them from what's eating you."
—Vicki Baum

"Everyone wants to live at the expense of the State. They forget that the State lives at the expense of everyone."
—Frédéric Bastiat

"I'd rather have a bottle in front of me, than a frontal lobotomy."
—Tom Waits

"People need a leader more than a leader needs people."
—Bob Dylan

COME ON DOWN!

Deep thoughts from the highbrow world of television game shows.

Jack Barry: "What do you want to be when you grow up?"
Kid: "A game show host."
Jack: "Oh, you mean like me?"
Kid: "No, like Bob Barker."
—*Joker Joker Joker*

"It's not as easy as it looks, being on all the time. I mean, what happens if I'm in a bad mood?"
—**Vanna White**

Contestant: "I'd like to buy a vowel, Regis."
Regis Philbin: "I think you mean lifeline."
Contestant: "Yeah, that."
—*Who Wants to Be a Millionaire*

Anne Robinson: "Rob, do you still think I'm sexy?"
Rob Schneider: "Yes, I do."
Anne Robinson: "Good, because I still think you're stupid."
—*The Weakest Link*

"Lisa, from where I'm standing, you have some nice prizes."
—**Ken Ober,** *Remote Control*

Richard Dawson: "Name a fruit that begins with 'A.'"
Contestant: "Orange."
—*Family Feud*

Richard Dawson: "Name the first article of clothing that you take off when you get home from work."
Female Contestant: "My underwear."
Richard Dawson: "Next question, what time do you get off work?"
—*Family Feud*

"I'd like to buy an owl."
—Contestant on *Wheel of Fortune*

A contestant on *Wheel of Fortune* had gotten all of the letters but one in the following puzzle:

"_T TAKES ONE TO KNOW ONE"

Contestant: "I'd like to solve the puzzle."
Pat Sajak: "This shouldn't be too hard. Go ahead."
Contestant: "E.T. takes one to know one."
Pat Sajak: "Uhh… really?"

"A little nonsense now and then is relished by the wisest men." —Roald Dahl

SILVER SCREEN DIVAS

A few thoughts from some women who are larger than life.

"Happiness is good health and a bad memory."
—Ingrid Bergman

"My heart is as pure as the driven slush."
—Tallulah Bankhead

"They say that movies should be more like life. I think life should be more like the movies."
—Myrna Loy

"I did a picture in England one winter and it was so cold I almost got married."
—Shelley Winters

"I've never yet met a man who could look after me. I don't need a husband. What I need is a wife."
—Joan Collins

"From the moment I was six I felt sexy. And let me tell you it was hell, sheer hell, waiting to do something about it."
—Bette Davis

"Any girl can be glamorous. All you have to do is stand still and look stupid."
—Hedy Lamarr

"I love animals and children. People I could do without."
—Zsa Zsa Gabor

"If I had to live my life again, I'd make all the same mistakes, only sooner."
—Tallulah Bankhead

"Deep down, I'm pretty superficial."
—Ava Gardner

"I've been through it all, baby. I'm Mother Courage."
—Elizabeth Taylor

"I dress for women, and undress for men."
—Angie Dickinson

"I don't remember anybody's name. How do you think the "dahling" thing got started?"
—Zsa Zsa Gabor

"Yes, but what about the deaf ones?"
—Katharine Hepburn, while filming *The African Queen,* after being reassured that the alligators swimming in the river where she was filming would be scared away by gunfire

CHILLIN' WITH DYLAN

"Can you imagine what a world it would be if we didn't have a Bob Dylan? It would be awful." —George Harrison

"When I first heard Elvis' voice, I just knew that I wasn't going to work for anybody; and nobody was going to be my boss....Hearing him for the first time was like busting out of jail."

"Soon the new generation will rebel against me just like I rebelled against the older generation."

"Great paintings shouldn't be in museums. Museums are cemeteries. Paintings should be on the walls of restaurants, in dime stores, in gas stations, in men's rooms....It's not the bomb that has to go, man, it's the museums."

"He not busy being born is busy dying."

"If I told you what our music is really about we'd probably all get arrested."

"I always needed a song to get by. There's a lot of singers who don't need songs to get by. A lot of 'em are tall, good-looking, you know. They don't need to say anything in order to grab people. Me, I had to make it something other than my looks or my voice."

"The world don't need any more songs. If nobody wrote any songs from this day on, the world ain't gonna suffer it."

"Being noticed can be a burden. Jesus got himself crucified because he got himself noticed. So I disappear a lot."

"Just because you like my stuff doesn't mean I owe you anything."

"God, I'm glad I'm not me."

FASHION STATEMENTS

*If you still have your Nehru jacket, your love beads, and your
go-go boots, this page will go right over your head.*

"A dress has no meaning unless it makes a man want to take it off."
—Francoise Sagan

"Speedo is a crime against democracy. It undercuts my freedom not to look at your ass region."
—Janeane Garofalo

"Although a life-long fashion dropout, I have absorbed enough by reading *Harper's Bazaar* while waiting at the dentist's to have grasped the purpose of fashion is to make A Statement. My own modest Statement, discerned by true cognoscenti, is, 'Woman Who Wears Clothes So She Won't Be Naked.' "
—Molly Ivins

"Women who are not vain about their clothes are often vain about not being vain about their clothes."
—Cyril Scott

"It takes up to forty dumb animals to make a fur coat, but only one to wear it."
—Bryn James

"I don't know who invented the high heel, but all women owe him a lot."
—Marilyn Monroe

"If high heels were so wonderful, men would be wearing them."
—Sue Grafton,
I is for Innocence

"I just accepted them [my breasts] as a great accessory to every outfit."
—Jennifer Love Hewitt

"Fashion is a form of ugliness so intolerable that they have to alter it every six months."
—Oscar Wilde

"I base most of my fashion taste on what doesn't itch."
—Gilda Radner

"Does fashion matter? Always—though not quite as much after death."
—Joan Rivers

"Say what you want about long dresses, but they cover a multitude of shins."
—Mae West

"Plan for the future because that's where you're going to spend the rest of your life." —Mark Twain

CONGRESSIONAL FOLLIES

Members of Congress say the damnedest things.

"Wait a minute! I'm not interested in agriculture. I want the military stuff."
**—Sen. William Scott,
during a briefing in which officials
began telling him about missile silos**

"The only way we'll ever get a voluntary army is to draft them."
—Rep. F. Edward Herbert

"We have got an awful lot of members who don't understand that harass is one word, not two."
—Rep. Pat Schroeder

"We are going to push health care legislation through no matter what the people want."
—Sen. John D. Rockefeller, IV

"Capital punishment is our society's recognition of the sanctity of human life."
—Sen. Orrin Hatch

*   *   *

"Can any of you seriously say the Bill of Rights could get through Congress today? It wouldn't even get out of committee."
—F. Lee Bailey

MORE CRAZY TALK

Uncle John wanted to take this page out…but Mr. Glug-Glug—the man in the toilet tank—told him to leave it in.

"I became insane, with long intervals of horrible sanity."
—Edgar Allan Poe

"Insanity: a perfectly rational adjustment to the insane world."
—R. D. Laing

"The statistics on sanity say that one out of every four Americans is suffering from mental illness. Think of your three best friends. If they're okay, then it's you."
—Rita Mae Brown

"Some people hear their own inner voices with great clearness. And they live by what they hear. Such people become crazy…or they become legend."
—Jim Harrison

"Anyone who needs psychiatry is sick in the head."
—Frank Burns, M*A*S*H

"You know, a long time ago, being crazy meant something. Nowadays, everybody's crazy."
—Charles Manson

"Better mad with the rest of the world than wise alone."
—Baltasar Gracian

"Insanity is hereditary: you can get it from your children."
—Sam Levenson

WHAT THE KRUK?

John Kruk was as famous for his remarks as he was for his career as a firstbaseman for the Philadelphia Phillies.

"I try to dumb down out there. They tell you to stay within yourself, so that's what I do. Mentally, I'm not gonna out-think myself too often."
—on being chosen as an All-Star starter in 1993

"It's amazing that fans want to see me play. What is our society coming to?"

"It's the first letter I ever got from Bill White that wasn't asking me to pay a fine. It's the first one that doesn't start out, 'Please make check payable to…'"
—on receiving a congratulatory letter from the National League president for making the All-Star team

"I would think I drive most hitting coaches crazy. During one single at-bat, I used six different stances on six pitches. Oh yeah, I also struck out. So what do I know?"

"No mascots on the field. Shoot anything that looked like it escaped from *Sesame Street*."
—on how he would change baseball

"I wanted to kill Mitch. But they told me I couldn't. It was illegal."
—on Mitch Williams, after the Phillies closer blew a save and the game stretched on for six hours

"I ain't an athlete, lady. I'm a professional baseball player."

MITCH HEDBERG

Who's Mitch Hedberg? He's one of the funniest up and coming comedians we've seen in quite a while.

"I got my hair highlighted because I felt that some strands were more important than others."

"I got an ant farm. Them fellas didn't grow *sh*t*."

"I type 101 words a minute. But it's in my own language."

"I bought a doughnut and they gave me a receipt for the doughnut. I can't imagine a scenario that I would have to prove to some skeptical friend that I bought a doughnut. 'Don't even act like I didn't buy a doughnut. I've got the documentation right here…'"

"I don't have a girlfriend. But I do know a woman who'd be mad at me for saying that."

"I'm against picketing, but I don't know how to show it."

"I have a cheese-shredder at home, which is its positive name. They don't call it by its negative name, which is sponge-ruiner."

"My sister wanted to be an actress, but she never made it. She does live in a trailer. She got half way. She's an actress, she just never gets called to the set."

"One time a guy handed me a picture of himself, and said, 'Here's a picture of me when I was younger.' Every picture of you is of when you were younger."

"I went to the store to buy a candle holder, but they didn't have any, so I got a cake instead."

"The depressing thing about tennis is that no matter how much I play, I'll never be as good as a wall. I played a wall once. They're f**king relentless."

"My friend said to me, 'You know what I like? Mashed potatoes.' I was like, 'Dude, you have to give me time to guess. If you're going to quiz me you have to insert a pause.'"

Real newspaper headline: "Mortuary Adds Drive-Through"

FRACTURED PHRASES

Variations on a phrase.

> **"If God had intended us to fly,
> He'd have given us wings."**

"If God had really intended man to fly, He'd make it easier to get to the airport."
—Jonathan Winters

"If God had intended us to drink beer, He would have given us stomachs."
—David Daye

"If God had intended us to have group sex, He'd have given us more organs."
—Malcolm Bradbury

"If God had meant for us not to fly, he wouldn't have given us marijuana."
—Patrick Marlowe

"If God had wanted us to vote, he would have given us candidates."
—Jay Leno

"I'm Jewish. I don't work out. If God had wanted us to bend over, He would have put diamonds on the floor."
—Joan Rivers

"Sex was never dirty to me. After all, God gave us the equipment and the opportunity. There's that old saying, 'If God had meant for us to fly, He'd have given us wings.' Well, look what He did give us."—Dolly Parton

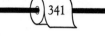

SUCCESS!

*One measure of success: if your name appears
on this quote page, you're successful.*

"Every material possession you acquire becomes a stick to beat you with."
—Roseanne Cash

"I figure as an artist the best thing you can do is just follow your heart—and if your heart is marketable, then you win."
—Rodney Crowell

"I couldn't wait for success, so I went ahead without it."
—Jonathan Winters

"As soon as you find the key to success, someone always changes the lock."
—Tracey Ullman

"Success and failure are both difficult to endure. Along with success come drugs, divorce, fornication, bullying, travel, medication, depression, neurosis, and suicide. With failure comes failure."
—Joseph Heller

"You have reached the pinnacle of success as soon as you become uninterested in money, compliments, or publicity."
—Thomas Wolfe

"Five years ago, I would get annoyed when my [welfare] check arrived a day late. The next thing I know, I'm getting pissed off if my limo didn't turn up."
—Seal

"There is no point at which you can say, 'Well, I'm successful now. I might as well take a nap.'"
—Carrie Fisher

"Success didn't spoil me, I've always been insufferable."
—Fran Lebowitz

"Formula for success: under-promise and overdeliver."
—Tom Peters

"Success is having to worry about every darned thing in the world except money."
—Johnny Cash

"The worst part about success is trying to find someone who is happy for you."
—Bette Midler

"It is not enough to succeed; others must fail."
—Gore Vidal

BATTLE OF THE SEXES: ROUND 3

*When we're finshed reading this
page, let's kiss and make up.*

"Nothing men do surprises me.
I'm ready for them. I know
how to whack below the belt."
—**Patsy Cline**

"Three things have been difficult to tame: the oceans, fools,
and women. We may soon be
able to tame the oceans; fools,
and women will take a little
longer."
—**Spiro Agnew**

"Men are such idiots—and I
married their king."
—**Peg Bundy,
Married...with Children**

"A woman is like an appen-
dix...she's something a man is
better off without."
—**Popeye the Sailor**

"There's a commercial where
guys sit around drinking beer,
cleaning fish, wiping their
noses on their sleeves, and saying, 'It doesn't get any better
than this.' That's not a commercial. That's a warning."
—**Diane Jordan**

"I know I'm not going to
understand women. I'll never
understand how you can take
boiling hot wax, pour it onto
your upper thigh, rip the hair
out by the root...and still be
afraid of spiders."
—**Jerry Seinfeld**

"Beware of the man who
denounces women writers; his
penis is tiny and he cannot
spell."
—**Erica Jong**

"Women are the root of all
evil. I ought to know, I'm
Evel."
—**Evel Knievel**

"Guys would sleep with a
bicycle if it had the right color
lip gloss on. They have no
shame."
—**Tori Amos**

"I think women rule the world
and that no man has ever
done anything that a woman
hasn't allowed him to do or
encouraged him to do."
—**Bob Dylan**

"The great question that has never been answered, and which I have not yet been able to answer, despite my 30 years of research into the feminine soul, is 'What does a woman want?'"

—Sigmund Freud

MAE WEST

Mae West was one of Hollywood's original vixens…

"Give a man a free hand and he'll run it all over you."

"When choosing between two evils, I always like to try the one I've never tried before."

"Too much of a good thing can be wonderful."

"If I asked for a cup of coffee, someone would search for the double meaning."

"Save a boyfriend for a rainy day—and another, in case it doesn't rain."

"A hard man is good to find."

"I used to be Snow White… but I drifted."

"To err is human—but it feels divine."

"Sex is an emotion in motion."

"I feel like a million tonight, but one at a time."

"Ten men at my door? I'm tired. Send one of them away."

"When I'm good, I'm very good; when I'm bad, I'm better."

"I may be good for nothing, but I'm never bad for nothing."

"I only have 'yes' men around me. Who needs 'no' men?"

"I believe in censorship. I made a fortune out of it."

"I never worry about diets. The only carrots that interest me are the number you get in a diamond."

"A man in love is like a clipped coupon: it's time to cash in."

"It's not the men in my life that count, it's the life in my men."

"Virtue has its own reward, but no box office."

"When women go wrong, men go right after them."

"It's hard to be funny when you have to be clean."

Mae West was only 5'1". To compensate on screen, she wore high platform shoes.

OOO LA LA!

Why is it that people get so much pleasure out of making fun of the French? Oh well, it makes for interesting bathroom reading. Bon Apetit!

"Frenchman are like gunpowder, each by itself smutty and contemptible, but mass them together and they are terrible indeed!"
—**Samuel Taylor Coleridge**

"You know why the French don't want to bomb Saddam Hussein? Because he hates America, he loves mistresses, and wears a beret. He IS French, people."
—**Conan O'Brien**

"France has neither winter nor summer nor morals. Apart from these drawbacks, it is a fine country. France has usually been governed by prostitutes."
—**Mark Twain**

"Germans with good food."
—**Fran Lebowitz**

"Going to war without France is like going deer hunting without your accordion."
—**Norman Schwartzkopf**

"We can stand here like the French, or we can do something about it!"
—**Marge Simpson**

"How can you govern a country which produces 246 different kinds of cheese?"
—**Charles de Gaulle**

"France is a country where the money falls apart in your hands and you can't tear the toilet paper."
—**Billy Wilder**

"What kind of country puts up more resistance to Disney than they did to the Nazis?"
—**Conan O'Brien**

*　　*　　*

...and now for an opposing view:
"I adore the French because they're very honest in their snot. They don't pretend to like anybody but themselves. I love that. I love the French restaurant and the French shop where everyone is addressed as Monsieur or Madame, regardless of their social class."
—**Paul Fussell**

"The most exciting phrase to hear in science is not 'Eureka!', but 'That's funny.'" —Isaac Asimov

THE FUTURE

Are we there yet?

"We drive into the future using only our rearview mirror."
—**Marshall McLuhan**

"The future ain't what it used to be."
—**Yogi Berra**

"Plan for the future, because that's where you are going to spend the rest of your life."
—**Mark Twain**

"Never let the future disturb you. You will meet it, if you have to, with the same weapons of reason which today arm you against the present."
—**Marcus Aurelius**

"Prediction is very difficult, especially of the future."
—**Niels Bohr**

"The future is something which everyone reaches at the rate of sixty minutes an hour, whatever he does, whoever he is."
—**C. S. Lewis**

"Your future depends on many things, but mostly on you."
—**Frank Tyger**

"Tomorrow, every fault is to be amended; but tomorrow never comes."
—**Benjamin Franklin**

"Every moment that I am centered in the future, I suffer a temporary loss of this life."
—**Hugh Prather**

"We can chart our future clearly and wisely only when we know the path which has led to the present."
—**Adlai E. Stevenson**

"Change is the law of life. And those who look only to the past or present are certain to miss the future."
—**John F. Kennedy**

"Life lived for tomorrow will always be just a day away from being realized."
—**Leo Buscaglia**

"The wave of the future is coming and there is no fighting it."
—**Anne Morrow Lindbergh**

"Well, the future for me is already a thing of the past."
—**Bob Dylan**

MORE CARTOON COMEDY

Fry: "Did you build the Smelloscope?"

Professor Farnsworth: "Go ahead, try it. You'll find that every heavenly body has its own particular scent. Here, I'll point it at Jupiter."

Fry: "Smells like strawberries."

Professor: "Exactly. And now, now Saturn."

Fry: "Pine needles. Oh, man, this is great…as long as you don't make me smell Uranus."

Leela: "I don't get it."

Professor: "I'm sorry, Fry, but astronomers renamed Uranus in 2620 to end that stupid joke once and for all."

Fry: "Oh. What's it called now?"

Professor: "Urrectum."

—*Futurama*

THE GREAT COMMUNICATOR

Heck, even Ronald Reagan had trouble communicating once in a while.

"Now we are trying to get unemployment to go up, and I think we are going to succeed."

"My goal is an America where something or anything that is done to or for anyone is done neither because of nor in spite of any difference between them, racially, religiously, or ethnic-origin-wise."

"There is a mandate to impose a voluntary return to traditional values."

"I've talked to you on a number of occasions about the economic problems our nation faces, and I am prepared to tell you it's in a hell of a mess— we're not connected to the press room yet, are we?"

"Politics is not a bad profession. If you succeed there are many rewards, if you disgrace yourself, you can always write a book."

—Ronald Reagan

The world is a book, and those who do not travel, read only a page." —Saint Augustine

MORE DUMB JOCKS

Uncle John was lousy at sports in high school. Revenge!

"You guys line up alphabetically by height."
    —Bill Peterson, a Florida State football coach

"He treats us like men. He lets us wear earrings."
    —Torrin Polk, University of Houston receiver, on his coach, John Jenkins, 1991

"I don't care what the tape says. I didn't say it."
    —Football coach Ray Malavasi

"I may be dumb, but I'm not stupid."
    —Terry Bradshaw

"It's basically the same, just darker."
    —Alan Kulwicki, stock car racer, on racing Saturday nights as opposed to Sunday afternoons

"I want to rush for 1,000 or 1,500 yards, whichever comes first."
    —George Rogers

"I'll always be number 1 to myself."
    —Moses Malone

"Sometimes they write what I say and not what I mean."
    —Baseball player Pedro Guerrero, on sportswriters

"Left hand, right hand, it doesn't matter. I'm amphibious."
    —Charles Shackleford of the NCSU basketball team

"I can't really remember the names of the clubs that we went to."
    —Shaquille O'Neal, on whether he had visited the Parthenon during his visit to Greece

"Guys aren't able to get $15 or $20 million anymore, so you have to play for the love of the game."
    —Penny Hardaway, NBA basketball player

"My sister's expecting a baby, and I don't know if I'm going to be an uncle or an aunt."
    —Chuck Nevitt, North Carolina State basketball player, explaining to Coach Jim Valvano why he appeared nervous at practice

FREEDOM AND LIBERTY

You can't see them. You can't hold them in your hand.
But they're the most precious possessions you own.

"Liberty doesn't work as well in practice as it does in speeches."
—**Will Rogers**

"Liberty means responsibility; that is why most men dread it."
—**George Bernard Shaw**

"The way to final freedom is within thy self."
—*The Book of the Golden Precepts*

"You can only be free if I am free."
—**Clarence Darrow**

"The right to be let alone is indeed the beginning of all freedom."
—**Justice William O. Douglas**

"Is life so dear, or peace so sweet, as to be purchased at the price of chains and slavery? Forbid it, Almighty God! I know not what course others may take; but as for me, give me liberty or give me death!"
—**Patrick Henry**

"Disobedience is the true foundation of liberty. The obedient must be slaves."
—**Henry David Thoreau**

"Freedom is not an ideal, it is not even a protection, if it means nothing more than freedom to stagnate, to live without dreams, to have no greater aim than a second car and another television set."
—**Adlai Stevenson**

"We are so concerned to flatter the majority that we lose sight of how often it is necessary, in order to preserve freedom for the minority, to face that majority down."
—**William F. Buckley, Jr.**

PANNING THE CRITICS

More criticism of critics.

"In judging others, folks will work overtime for no pay."
—**Charles Carruthers**

"A critic is a gong at a railroad crossing clanging loudly and vainly as the train goes by."
—**Christopher Morley**

"A good review from the critics is just another stay of execution."
—**Dustin Hoffman**

"A bad review is like baking a cake with all the best ingredients and having someone sit on it."
—**Danielle Steele**

"A critic is someone who's at his best when you're at your worst."
—**Tony Pettito**

"I just read your lousy review buried in the back pages. You sound like a frustrated old man who never made a success, an eight-hour man on a four-ulcer job and all four ulcers working."
—**Harry S Truman, from a letter to critic Paul Hume, who gave Truman's daughter's play a bad review**

"I've always felt those articles somehow reveal more about the writers than they do about me."
—**Marilyn Monroe**

"We are not trying to entertain the critics. I'll take my chances with the public."
—**Walt Disney**

*　　*　　*

"Honest criticism is hard to take, particularly from a relative, a friend, an acquaintance, or a stranger."
—**Franklin P. Jones**

"It may be that all games are silly—but then, so are humans." —Robert Lynd

THEM'S DRINKIN' WORDS

Humans have been consuming alcohol since the beginning of civilization. Maybe that's why civilization is so weird.

"You sit back in the darkness, nursing your beer, breathing in that ineffable aroma of the old-time saloon: dark wood, spilled beer, good cigars, and ancient whiskey—the sacred incense of the drinking man."
—**Bruce Aidells**

"First you take a drink, then the drink takes a drink, then the drink takes you."
—**F. Scott Fitzgerald**

"One tequila, two tequila, three tequila, floor."
—**George Carlin**

"Work is the curse of the drinking class."
—**Oscar Wilde**

"I feel sorry for people who don't drink. When they wake up in the morning, that's as good as they're going to feel all day."
—**Frank Sinatra**

"A woman drove me to drink, and I didn't even have the decency to thank her."
—**W. C. Fields**

"I believe, if we take habitual drunkards as a class, their heads and their hearts will bear an advantageous comparison with those of any other class. There seems ever to have been a proneness in the brilliant and warm-blooded to fall into this vice."
—**Abraham Lincoln**

"I've been SOBER a while. To me, SOBER stands for 'Son-of-a-Bitch, Everything's Real.' "
—**Kathy G**

"Women and drink. Too much of either can drive you to the other."
—**Michael Still**

"I find the more I drink the more interesting others become."
—**Tom Ralphs**

"If you are young and you drink a great deal it will spoil your health, slow your mind, make you fat. In other words, turn you into an adult."
—**P. J. O'Rourke**

PRIMETIME PROVERBS

More TV comments about everyday life.

ON HEROES...

"My heroes are Larry Bird, Admiral Byrd, Lady Bird, Sheryl Crow, Chick Corea, the inventor of bird seed, and anyone who reads to you even if she's tired."
—**Big Bird, *Sesame Street***

ON SEX APPEAL...

"I always get the feeling that when lesbians look at me, they're thinking, 'That's why I'm not a heterosexual.'"
—**George Costanza, *Seinfeld***

ON COURAGE...

"He who chickens out and runs away will chicken out another day."
—**Robot, *Lost in Space***

ON COPS...

"When a man carries a gun all the time, the respect he thinks he's getting might really be fear. So I don't carry a gun because I don't want the people of Mayberry to fear a gun; I'd rather they would respect me."
—**Sheriff Andy Taylor, *The Andy Griffith Show***

Det. Cruz: "You and I are on the same street, you know. Just different sides."
Jordan: "That doesn't make us pals. So far—not a big fan."
Det. Cruz: "Don't worry. I grow on people."
Jordan: "So does fungus."
—***Crossing Jordan***

"You know, I'm violently opposed to police brutality."
—**Commissioner Gordon, *Batman***

ON BEAUTY...

Cosmetic Saleslady: "What kind of powder does your mommy use?"
Wednesday: "Baking powder."
Saleslady: "I mean, on her face."
Wednesday: "Baking powder."
—***The Addams Family***

ON POLITICS...

"Where would we be without the agitators of the world attaching the electrodes of knowledge to the nipples of ignorance?"
—**Dick, *3rd Rock from the Sun***

TAKE OUR ADVICE: READ THIS PAGE

*A few pages of people telling you
what they think you should do.*

"What I am saying to all you songwriters is to get yourself a good lawyer before you sign anything, no matter how much the company says they love you." —Willie Nelson

"A word of advice: don't give it." —A. J. Volicos

"Be a fountain, not a drain." —Rex Hudler

"When the other person nods his head affirmatively but says nothing, it's time to stop talking." —Henry S. Haskins

"When a thing is done, it's done. Don't look back. Look forward to your next objective." —George C. Marshall

"Oh, grow up!" —Joan Rivers

*　　*　　*

"The single most important conclusion I reached, after traveling through Japan, as well as countless hours reading, studying, and analyzing this fascinating culture, is that you should always tighten the cap on the shampoo bottle before you put it in your suitcase." —Dave Barry

"Finish every day and be done with it. You have done what you could; some blunders and absurdities crept in; forget them as soon as you can. Tomorrow is a new day. You shall begin it serenely and with too high a spirit to be encumbered with your old nonsense."

—Ralph Waldo Emerson

...Lucy Ricardo: "I do not. I just want to see what I haven't got that I don't want."

LAST WORDS

We're all going to go, but it would be nice to have something clever to say when you do.

"I should have never switched from scotch to martinis."
—**Humphrey Bogart**

"Only one man ever understood me. And he didn't understand me."
—**George Wilhelm Hegel**

"Boys, boys, you wouldn't hang your sheriff, would you?"
—**Henry Plummer,** *sheriff of Bannock, Washington, in 1884*

"Codeine…bourbon."
—**Tallulah Bankhead,** *when asked if there was any final thing she wanted*

"Qualis artifex pereo!" ("What an artist dies in me!")
—**Roman Emperor Nero**

"Am I dying, or is it my birthday?"
—**Nancy, Lady Astor,** *upon seeing her entire family gathered around her sick bed*

"Don't let it end like this. Tell them I said something."
—**Pancho Villa**

"I don't feel good."
—**Luther Burbank**

"I have offended God and mankind because my work did not reach the quality it should have."
—**Leonardo da Vinci**

"They couldn't hit an elephant at this dist—"
—**General John Sedgwick**

"Ask her to wait a moment—I am almost done."
—**Carl Friedrich Gauss,** *on hearing his wife was dying*

"Show my head to the people. It is worth seeing."
—**Georges Danton,** *to his executioner*

"Dear World: I am leaving you because I am bored, I am leaving you with your worries in this sweet cesspool."
—**George Sanders'** suicide note

"Quick! Serve the dessert! I think I'm dying!"
—**Paulette Brillat-Savarin,** *at a meal in her 100th year*

In 1946 W. C. Fields was lying in his deathbed. His friend and fellow actor Thomas Mitchell entered the room and was surprised to see the old coot reading the Bible. Mitchell asked Fields—who had led a proud life of sin and debauchery—why on Earth he was reading the Bible, and Fields explained: "Looking for loopholes."

"USE THE FORCE, LUKE!"

More famous movie lines to keep you busy.

1. "Do. Or do not. There is no try."

a. *Ace Ventura*

2. "Why, oh, why, didn't I take the blue pill?"

b. *Caddyshack*

3. "I'm having an old friend for dinner."

c. *Hannibal*

4. "Be the ball."

d. *Babe*

5. "We're on a mission from God."

e. *The Shawshank Redemption*

6. "Get busy living, or get busy dying."

f. *The Blues Brothers*

7. "All righty then!"

g. *The Empire Strikes Back*

8. "Hello, my name is Inigo Montoya. You killed my father. Prepare to die."

h. *The Sixth Sense*

9. "That'll do, pig."

i. *The Matrix*

10. "I see dead people."

j. *The Princess Bride*

Answers

1. g; 2. i; 3. c; 4. b; 5. f; 6. e; 7. a; 8. j; 9. d; 10. h

In 1946, Henrietta Radner saw the movie *Gilda*, starring Rita Hayworth. She loved...

REMEMBERING GILDA

A few lines from Gilda Radner, the first performer cast on Saturday Night Live in 1975...and easily one of the funniest. She passed away from cancer in 1989 when she was only 42.

"I'd rather be a woman than a man. Women can cry, they can wear cute clothes, and they're the first to be rescued off sinking ships."

"I think I'd be a neat old woman—if I ever make it that far. I once said that to a guy I was going out with, and he said, 'You already are.'"

"I'm so full I can't hear."

"If humor was the foundation of my life, men were definitely the first floor."

"Fame changes a lot of things, but it can't change a light bulb."

*　　*　　*

Shortly after she finished Saturday Night Live:
"I feel with my life, somebody's been so generous with experiences for me—whoever is controlling it. I mean, I've enjoyed a real generosity there. So maybe I feel I'm getting all this now and quickly because there's not going to be a whole lot later. I mean, maybe I'm going to die or something. I know that's an awful way to think, but I have been real fortunate. Real lucky."

After being diagnosed with cancer:
"The goal is to live a full, productive life even with all that ambiguity. No matter what happens, whether the cancer never flares up again or whether you die, the important thing is that the days that you have had you will have lived."

ENDANGERED FECES

Gilda Radner's break-out characters on Saturday Night Live
were Roseanne Roseannadana, a consumer affairs reporter
who gave way too much information, and Emily Litella,
a social activist with a hearing problem. Both got to
speak their minds on "Weekend Update."

Roseanne Roseannadana: "Let me ask you this: Did you ever eat a hamburger and there's a hard thing in it? It's a toenail. You know it's not part of the hamburger, but you separate the meat and the lettuce and the pickle to one side of your mouth—and you come around with your tongue and you take out this thing and it's like a bone. But it's not a bone. I keep asking myself, 'Roseanne Roseannadana, if they can make coffee I like with no caffeine, how come they can't make a hamburger I like with no toenails?'"

*   *   *

Emily Litella: "What's all this fuss I hear about endangered feces? That's outrageous. Why is feces endangered? How can you possibly run out of such a thing? Just look around you—you can see it all over the place. And besides, who wants to save that anyway?"

Jane Curtin: "Umm, Emily, the issue is actually endangered *species*, not feces."

Emily: "Oh…that's different. Never mind."

EAT YOUR VEGGIES

Vegetables. Some people love 'em, some people hate 'em.

"Vegetables are interesting but lack a sense of purpose when unaccompanied by a good cut of meat."
—Fran Lebowitz

"An onion can make people cry, but there's never been a vegetable that can make people laugh."
—Will Rogers

"In some circles, I'm as famous for my Caesar salads as I am for my breasts."
—Jamie Lee Curtis

"Eating garlic and onions cuts your risk of prostate cancer in half. Of course, you smell like you're dead."
—Jay Leno

"There is no such thing as a little garlic."
—Arthur 'Bugs' Baer

"I'm a Jewish girl raised in a vegetarian family. My dream is to open a restaurant called 'Soy Vey.'"
—Margo Black

"I don't like spinach, and I'm glad I don't, because if I liked it I'd eat it, and I just hate it."
—Clarence Darrow

"After all the trouble you go to, you get about as much actual 'food' out of eating artichokes as you would licking 30 or 40 postage stamps. Have the shrimp cocktail instead."
—Miss Piggy

"Sex is good, but not as good as fresh, sweet corn."
—Garrison Keillor

"Vegetarianism is harmless enough, though it is apt to fill a man with wind and self-righteousness."
—Robert Hutchinson

"Vegetables are a must on a diet. I suggest carrot cake, zucchini bread, and pumpkin pie."
—Garfield

"Tomatoes and oregano make it Italian; wine and tarragon make it French; lemon and cinnamon make it Greek. Soy sauce makes it Chinese; garlic makes it good."
—Alice May Brock

"I am not a vegetarian because I love animals. I am a vegetarian because I hate plants."
—A. Whitney Brown

OVERLY OPTIMISTIC

*These dumb predictions probably sounded pretty good
at the time, but with hindsight, they're pretty funny.*

"There is no doubt that soccer will one day challenge football and baseball as the number one sport in America."

**—Phil Woosman, commissioner of the
North American Soccer League, 1982**

"That's what I'm going to do—kick Jay's ass."

**—Arsenio Hall,
on the *Tonight Show with Jay Leno***

"We're going to make everybody forget the Beatles."

**—Barry Gibb, on the Bee Gee's 1976 movie
version of *Sgt. Pepper's Lonely Hearts Club Band***

"By 2000, politics will simply fade away. We will not see any political parties."

—Buckminster Fuller, 1966

"The culminating and final war for human liberty."

**—President Woodrow Wilson,
on World War I, 1918**

"In the year 2024, the most important thing which the cinema will have helped in a large way to accomplish will be that of eliminating from the face of the civilized world all armed conflict."

—D. W. Griffith, 1924

MORE LAME EXCUSES

We had another page of these, but our dog ate it.

Offender: Johnny Depp
Offense: After a fight with his girlfriend, Depp smashed up a hotel room.
Lame Excuse: "There was a bug in the place that I was trying to kill. This thing had tried to attack me and tried to suck my blood—a big cockroach. And I tried to get it; I tried to whack it. I'd miss and smash a lamp."

Offender: Saquib Bashir, a taxi driver in Derby, England
Offense: During a fuel shortage in 2000, Bashir bought 80 liters of gas and stored it in his house. The fuel melted the plastic bottles, leaked all over the house, and the entire street had to be evacuated while firefighters cleaned up the dangerous mess. Total cost: £100,000.
Lame Excuse: "I didn't know petrol was flammable."

Offender: Tanya Tucker
Offense: At an Epic Records industry party in 1997, she had a couple of drinks. After shouting back and forth with Ty Herndon, who was onstage performing at the time, she lifted her shirt and flashed the entire place—and was asked to leave.
Lame Excuse: "It was very hot and I lifted up my sweater to get some air in there. I didn't think people would make such a big deal out of it."

Offender: Gary Hart
Offense: While running for president, Hart was captured by a photographer with a beautiful blonde woman (not his wife) sitting in his lap.
Lame Excuse: "It was suggested that I have this picture taken with Miss Rice. This attractive lady, whom I had only recently been introduced to, dropped in my lap. I was embarrassed. I chose not to dump her off and the picture was taken."

Offender: George H. W. Bush
Offense: During his first presidential campaign, Bush promised that there would be no loss of wetlands. He didn't keep his promise, but Richard Darman, director of the Office of Management and Budget, came to his defense.
Lame Excuse: "He didn't say that. He read what was given to him in a speech."

"Over my dead body." —George S. Kaufman's tombstone

HOLLYWOOD SQUARES

*Some lines from a few celebrities who get paid
to sit inside a box and think outside the box.*

Peter Marshall: "In the days of Catherine the Great, at parties, men had to wait until 9 o'clock before doing something. Doing what?"
Charley Weaver: "Catherine the Great."

John Davidson: "One-third of all ice cream sold in the United States is…?"
Louie Anderson: "In my freezer."

Tom Bergeron: "In karate, what do you get after a white belt."
Jason Alexander: "Your ass kicked."

Peter Marshall: "Jackie Gleason recently revealed that he firmly believes in them and that he has actually seen them on two occasions. What are they?"
Charley Weaver: "His feet."

Tom Bergeron: "What does Kenny G. hold the world's record for doing longer than anyone else?"
Kathy Griffin: "Sucking?"

* * *

"I watch game shows. I was a big fan of *Family Feud*. In fact, the high point of my career was having an episode of *Family Feud* dedicated to me on the air. The producer called my agent and said they had noticed how often I said I liked it and that they were going to dedicate a show to me on the air. They did and I watched it and to me it was the Nobel Prize."
—**Fran Lebowitz**

"A man's got to take a lot of punishment to write a really funny book." —Ernest Hemingway

CAT CALLS

More catty comments.

"I'm used to dogs. When you leave them in the morning, they stick their nose in the door crack and stand there like a portrait until you turn the key eight hours later. A cat would never put up with that kind of rejection. When you returned, she'd stalk you until you dozed off and suck the air out of your body."
—Erma Bombeck

"A cat is a puzzle for which there is no solution."
—Hazel Nicholson

"Even the stupidest cat seems to know more than any dog. "
—Eleanor Clark

"There are two means of refuge from the miseries of life: music and cats."
—Albert Schweitzer

"If I die before my cat, I want a little of my ashes put in his food so I can live inside him."
—Drew Barrymore

"Nature abhors a vacuum, but not as much as cats do."
—Nelson A. Crawford

"Happiness is like a cat. If you try to coax it or call it, it will avoid you; it will never come. But if you pay no attention to it and go about your business, you'll find it rubbing against your legs and jumping into your lap."
—William John Bennett

"A kitten is a rosebud in the garden of the animal kingdom."
—Robert Southey

"If you hold a cat by the tail you learn things you cannot learn any other way."
—Mark Twain

"To bathe a cat takes brute force, perseverance, courage of conviction—and a cat. The last ingredient is usually hardest to come by."
—Stephen Baker

"Cats are intended to teach us that not everything in nature has a purpose."
—Garrison Keillor

"To err is human, to purr, feline."
—Robert Byrne

ACTORS ON ACTING

Acting is a strange profession, so it figures that strange people would get into it. Here's what some of them say about their "craft."

"One of the things about acting is it allows you to live other people's lives without having to pay the price. I've never been one of those actors who has touted myself as a fascinating human being. I had to decide early on whether I was to be an actor or a personality."
—Robert De Niro

"When actors talk about the balance between art and commerce, they're usually on their way to hell."
—Sean Penn

"You'd think it is something one would grow out of. But you grow into it. The more you do, the more you realize how painfully easy it is to be lousy and how very difficult to be good."
—Glenda Jackson

"Acting has destroyed my ego. I have very little self-respect now. I don't particularly admire actors, and so to be one is something I don't particularly admire."
—Hugh Grant

"I'm no actor, and I have sixty-four pictures to prove it."
—Victor Mature

"Every actor has a natural animosity toward every other actor, past or present, living or dead."
—Louise Brooks

"Acting is the most minor gift and not a very high-class way to earn a living. After all, Shirley Temple could do it at age four."
—Katharine Hepburn

"My dream role would probably be a psycho killer, because the whole thing I love about movies is that you get to do things you could never do in real life, and that would be my way of vicariously experiencing being a psycho killer. Also, it's incredibly romantic."
—Christina Ricci

"If I ever start talking about my 'craft' and my 'instrument,' you have permission to shoot me point blank."
—Drew Barrymore

"I have
always hated that
damn James Bond.
I'd like to kill him."
—**Sean Connery**

"I never disliked Bond,
as some have thought.
Creating a character
like that does take
a certain craft."
—**Sean Connery**

IT'S ABOUT TIME

What better way to spend your time than to read about it.

"Time is the only critic without ambition."
—John Steinbeck

"Time would become meaningless if there were too much of it."
—Ray Kurzweil

"Only time can heal your broken heart, just as only time can heal his broken arms and legs."
—Miss Piggy

"Tobacco, coffee, alcohol, hashish, prussic acid, strychnine, are weak dilutions; the surest poison is time."
—Ralph Waldo Emerson

"Time is the fire in which we burn."
—Malcolm McDowell,
Star Trek: Generations

"At my back I often hear Time's winged chariot changing gear."
—Eric Linklater

"Time is not a line, but a series of now points."
—Taisen Deshimaru

"Time is the coin of your life. It is the only coin you have, and only you can determine how it will be spent. Be careful lest you let other people spend it for you."
—Carl Sandburg

"Time is an illusion. Lunchtime doubly so."
—Douglas Adams

"An unhurried sense of time is in itself a form of wealth."
—Bonnie Friedman

"Time is a sort of river of passing events, and strong is its current; no sooner is a thing brought to sight than it is swept by and another takes its place, and this, too, will be swept away."
—Marcus Aurelius

FRACTURED PHRASES

More variations on a phrase.

**He who laughs last,
laughs best.**

"He who laughs, lasts."
—Mary Poole

"He who laughs last, thinks slowest."
—Troy Owens

"He who laughs last didn't get it."
—Helen Giangregorio

"He who laughs has not yet heard the bad news."
—Bertolt Brecht

**To err is human,
to forgive divine.**

"To err is human, and to blame it on a computer is even more so."
—Robert Orben

**If at first you don't
succeed, try, try again.**

"If at first you don't succeed, failure may be your style."
—Quentin Crisp

"If at first you don't succeed, quit, quit at once."
—Stephen Leacock

"If at first you don't succeed, find a gap in the fence, or a civil servant who could use a double sawbuck."
—Will Durst

"If at first you don't succeed, call in an air strike."
—Military Law of Combat

"If at first you don't succeed, you're fired."
—Lew Grade,
British media tycoon

"If at first you don't succeed, your skydiving days are over."
—Milton Berle

CLASSIC COMICS

Your grandparents laughed at these jokes. Now you can, too.

"My wife will buy anything marked down. Yesterday, she tried to buy an escalator."
—Joey Bishop

"The other day I went into a feminist bookstore. How did I know? It didn't have a humor section."
—Bob Hope

"I told the doctor I broke my leg in two places. He told me to quit going to those places."
—Henny Youngman

"My brother is very superstitious. He won't work any week that has a Friday in it."
—Milton Berle

"Give me golf clubs, fresh air, and a beautiful partner, and you can keep the clubs and the fresh air."
—Jack Benny

"Health nuts are going to feel stupid someday, lying in hospitals dying of nothing."
—Redd Foxx

"The Steinway people have asked me to announce that this is a Baldwin piano."
—Victor Borge

"If your parents never had children, chances are you won't either."
—Dick Cavett

"I said to my wife, 'Where do you want to go for our anniversary?' She said, 'Somewhere I've never been before.' I said, 'Try the kitchen.'"
—Henny Youngman

"Never raise your hand to your children—it leaves your midsection unprotected."
—Fred Allen

"The best car safety device is a rear-view mirror with a cop in it." —Dudley Moore

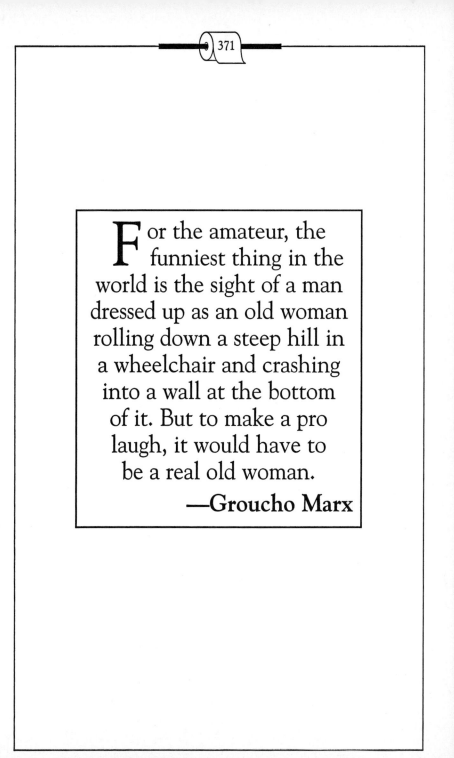

For the amateur, the funniest thing in the world is the sight of a man dressed up as an old woman rolling down a steep hill in a wheelchair and crashing into a wall at the bottom of it. But to make a pro laugh, it would have to be a real old woman.

—**Groucho Marx**

UNCLE JOHN'S
QUOTATIONARY

Here's Part 9 of our quote dictionary. (Part 8 is on page 326.)

SAINT: A dead sinner, revised and edited. (Ambrose Bierce)

SANITY: madness put to good use. (George Santayana)

SCIENCE FICTION: the archaeology of the future. (Clifton Fadiman)

SCIENTIST: a peeping Tom at the keyhole of eternity. (Arthur Koestler)

SELF-ESTEEM: regarding yourself as a grownup. (Susan Faludi)

SEX: the thing that takes the least amount of time and causes the most amount of damage. (John Barrymore)

SEX APPEAL: fifty percent what you've got and fifty percent what people think you've got. (Sophia Loren)

SEXUAL INTERCOURSE: kicking death in the ass while singing. (Charles Bukowski)

SHORTCUT: the longest distance between two points. (Charles Issawi)

SILENCE: argument carried on by other means. (Che Guevara)

SILK: material invented so women could go naked in clothes. (Muhammad Ali)

SKEPTICISM: the first step toward truth. (Dennis Diderot)

SLANG: a language that rolls up its sleeves, spits on its hands, and goes to work. (Carl Sandburg)

SLAVERY: government without the consent of the governed. (Jonathan Swift)

SLEEP: death without the responsibility. (Fran Leibowitz)

SMOKING: one of the leading causes of statistics. (Fletcher Knebel)

SOLUTIONS: the chief causes of problems. (Peter Dickson)

SPARKLERS: the gay cousins of the fireworks family. (Dave Attell)

SPORTS: the toy department of human life. (Howard Cosell)

STATESMAN: any politician it's considered safe to name a school after. (Bill Vaughan)

STATISTICS: the science of producing unreliable facts from

reliable figures. (Evan Esar)

STATUS QUO: Latin for the mess we're in. (Jeve Moorman)

STIGMA: what you beat a dogma with. (Philip Guedalla)

STOCK MARKET: a weapon that destroys people but leaves buildings still standing. (Jay Leno)

STRENGTH: the capacity to break a chocolate bar into four pieces with your bare hands—and then eat just one of the pieces. (Judith Viorst)

STYLE: knowing who you are, what you want to say, and not giving a damn. (Gore Vidal)

SUBURBIA: where they cut down the trees and name the streets after them. (Bill Vaughan)

SURF-N-TURF: a tiny, aquatic Hereford that has horns and a shell—a beast that moves through the depths slowly, in herds, and both moos and draws flies under water. (Calvin Trillin)

SWEAT: the cologne of accomplishment. (Heywood Broun)

SWEATER: a garment worn by a child when his mother feels chilly. (Alma Denny)

TACT: the ability to describe others as they see themselves. (Abraham Lincoln)

TAKE: to acquire, frequently by force but preferably by stealth. (Ambrose Bierce)

TAXES: the price society pays for civilization. (Oliver Wendell Holmes, Jr.)

TEAM EFFORT: a lot of people doing what I say. (Michael Winner)

TECHNOLOGY: a queer thing—it brings you great gifts with one hand, and it stabs you in the back with the other. (Carrie P. Snow)

TELEVISION: chewing gum for the eyes. (Frank Lloyd Wright)

THOUGHT: the ancestor of every action. (Ralph Waldo Emerson)

TIME: a storm in which we all are lost. (William Carlos Williams)

TODAY: the tomorrow you worried about yesterday. (Mort Sahl)

TRADITION: a guide and not a jailer. (W. Somerset Maugham)

TRADITIONALISTS: pessimists about the future and optimists about the past. (Lewis Mumford)

TRAGEDY: undeveloped comedy. (Paddy Kavanaugh)

TRUTH: what stands the test of experience. (Albert Einstein)

For more, see page 400.

For more, see page 400.

Thank you for calling the suicide hotline. Please hold.

SMART QUOTES

Toward the end of his life, Josh Billings had this epiphany: "I have finally come to the conclusion that a good reliable set of bowels is worth more to a man than any quantity of brains." Not everyone agrees with that...these folks, for example.

"Everyone is born a genius, but the process of living de-geniuses them."
—R. Buckminster Fuller

"The brain is a wonderful organ. It starts working the moment you get up in the morning and does not stop until you get into the office."
—Robert Frost

"Think about how stupid the average person is, then realize that half the population is stupider."
—George Carlin

"Even more exasperating than the guy who thinks he knows it all is the one who really does."
—Al Bernstein

"A great many people think they are thinking when they are actually rearranging their prejudices."
—William James

"'Tis not knowing much, but what is useful, that makes a wise man."
—Thomas Fuller

"Most people would sooner die than think; in fact, they do so."
—Bertrand Russell

"Everybody gets so much information all day long that they lose their common sense."
—Gertrude Stein

"Ignorance is no excuse—it's the real thing."
—Jean Kerr

"Artificial intelligence is no match for human stupidity."
—Red Green

"Genius is 1% inspiration and 99% perspiration."
—Thomas Edison

"Some folks are wise, and some are otherwise."
—Thomas Smollett

"I'd like to become more of a bimbo if I could, because the less you think, the easier it is. Thinking is fatal. It's better just to look nice, have your mouth a little open and say, 'Yeah.'"
—Rupert Everett

JUST PLAIN DUMB

Karl Kraus once said, "Stupidity is an elemental force for which no earthquake could match." These folks register a 9.5 on the Richter scale.

"You mean, like a book?"
—Justin Timberlake, when asked what was the best thing he had read all year

"I know nothing about nothing."
—Anna Nicole Smith

"It's like the Roman Empire. Wasn't everybody running around just covered with syphilis? And then it was destroyed by the volcano."
—Joan Collins

"Whoever wrote this doesn't understand comedy."
—Kim Basinger, on a screenplay by Neil Simon

"You get to meet important people from all walks of life—from Joe DiMaggio to Barry Bonds."
—Michael Bolton, on the advantages of being famous

"I've got taste. It's inbred in me."
—David Hasselhoff

"It's a drag having to wear socks during matches, because the tan, like, stops at the ankles. I can never get my skin, like, color coordinated."
—Monica Seles, tennis pro

"Rome wasn't burned in a day."
—Abe Hirschfield, New York businessman

"Sometimes poor people don't smell so good, so love can have no nose."
—Tammy Faye Bakker

"After finding no qualified candidates for the position of principal, the school board is extremely pleased to announce the appointment of David Steele to the post."
—Philip Streifer, Superintendent of Schools, Barrington, Rhode Island

POLI-TALKS

Bob Dylan once said, "I think politics is an instrument of the devil." Not everyone is that cynical. Here's what some other people have to say about it.

"The president doesn't have any yes-men and yes-women around him. When he says no, we all say no."
—**Elizabeth Dole, then aide to Ronald Reagan**

"Life is indeed precious. And I believe the death penalty helps to affirm this fact."
—**Ed Koch**

"A government is the only known vessel that leaks from the top."
—**James Reston**

"In politics, people give you what they think you deserve, and deny you what you think you want."
—**Cecil Parkinson**

"Put a federal agency in charge of the Sahara Desert and it would run out of sand."
—**Peggy Noonan**

"The American political system is like fast food: mushy, insipid, made out of disgusting parts of things—and everybody wants some."
—**P. J. O'Rourke**

"Politics is not the art of the possible. It consists in choosing between the disastrous and the unpalatable."
—**John Kenneth Galbraith**

"We already know the winners of the next election. They'll be old white men who don't care about you or your problems."
—**Craig Kilborn**

"You can't trust politicians. It doesn't matter who makes a political speech. It's all lies... and it applies to any rock star who wants to make a political speech, as well."
—**Bob Geldof**

"When you're as rich as I am, you don't have to be political."
—**Sting**

"In political discussion, heat is in inverse proportion to knowledge."
—**J. G. Minchin**

"Politicians are people who, when they see a light at the end of the tunnel, order more tunnel."
—**Sir John Quinton**

DIALOGUES WITH WORLD LEADERS

Here are some unofficial exchanges involving heads of state at official state functions.

Queen Elizabeth II: How do you do, Mr. King?

Alan King: How do you do, Mrs. Queen?

President Nixon: You dress pretty wild, don't you?

Elvis Presley: Mr. President, you got your show to run and I got mine.

At an old folks home, President Bush approaches an old lady.

George H. W. Bush: Do you know who I am?

Old Lady: No, but if you ask in reception I'm sure they will be able to tell you.

At French President Charles de Gaulle's retirement luncheon:

English guest: Madame de Gaulle, what are you looking forward to in the years ahead?

Madame de Gaulle: A penis....

...embarrassing silence...

Charles de Gaulle: My dear, I don't think the English pronounce the word like that. It is 'appiness.'

George H.W. Bush: Tell me, General, how dead is the Dead Sea?

General Zayid bin Shakr: Very dead, sir.

Gladstone: I predict, Sir, that you will die either by hanging or by of some vile disease.

Disraeli: That all depends, Sir, upon whether I embrace your principles or your mistress.

Woman at dinner party: You must talk to me, Mr. Coolidge. I made a bet with someone that I could get more than two words out of you.

Calvin Coolidge: You lose.

"A body of men holding themselves accountable to nobody ought not to be trusted by anybody."
—**Thomas Paine**

WHEN CELEBRITIES ATTACK

Celebrities are often at their funniest when they're attacking other celebrities.

"I'm not a Julie Andrews fan, no. I'm a diabetic."
—**David Jannsen**

"Prince looks like a dwarf that fell into a vat of pubic hair."
—**Boy George on Prince**

"Marlon [Brando] is the most overrated actor in the world."
—**Frank Sinatra**

"Zsa Zsa the-Bore. Did I spell that right?"
—**Elayne Boosler**

"If Kathleen Turner had been a man, I would have knocked her out long ago."
—**Burt Reynolds**

"Jeremy Irons has no sex appeal….He's perfect for horror movies—or science fiction. He's an iceberg with an accent."
—**Andy Warhol**

"Where else but in America could a poor black boy like Michael Jackson grow up to be a rich white woman?"
—**Red Buttons**

"Charlton Heston—a graduate of the Mt. Rushmore school of acting."
—**Edward G. Robinson**

"Peter O'Toole looks like he's walking around just to save the funeral expenses."
—**John Huston**

"Sylvester Stallone's got two bodyguards who look exactly like him walking around on the beach, so I guess he figures that cuts the odds of being assassinated to one in three."
—**Jack Lemmon**

"I am fascinated by Courtney Love, the same way I am by someone who's got Tourette's syndrome walking in Central Park."
—**Madonna**

"In truth, he's [Michael Caine] an overfat, flatulent, 62-year-old windbag, a master of inconsequence now masquerading as a guru, passing off his vast limitations as pious virtues."
—**Richard Harris**

"The freethinking of one age is the common sense of the next." —**Matthew Arnold**

DEEP THOUGHTS

Hey! Someone goofed—these really are deep.

"Who looks outside, dreams; who looks inside, awakes."
—Carl Gustav Jung

"When all you have is a hammer, all your problems start to look like nails."
—Abraham Maslow

"There is only one thing more powerful than all the armies of the world, that is an idea whose time has come."
—Victor Hugo

"Well done is better than well said."
—Benjamin Franklin

"Usually when people are sad, they don't do anything. They just cry over their condition. But when they get angry, they bring about a change."
—Malcolm X

"Every great mistake has a halfway moment, a split second when it can be recalled and perhaps remedied."
—Pearl S. Buck

"Just because something doesn't do what you planned it to do doesn't mean it's useless."
—Thomas A. Edison

*　　*　　*

"Thank you for the privilege of speaking to you in this auditorium. You know the meaning of the word auditorium, don't you? It is derived from two Latin words, *audio*, 'to hear,' and *Taurus*, 'the Bull.'"
—Larry Wilde

"The penalty for success is to be bored by the people who used to snub you." —Nancy Astor

"Doctors said that the test most commonly used to screen for colon cancer doesn't go far enough. They're recommending a procedure that involves photographing the entire colon. I say, don't give CBS an idea for another reality show."

—**Bill Maher**

REALITY BITES

*Reality shows are taking over TV. Here are
some witty (and witless) quotes from some
of the real people who are in them.*

Brian: "What if Helen has an IQ of 25?"
Helen: "Actually, I'm only 23."
—*Big Brother*

"What is Wal-Mart? Do they, like, sell wall stuff?"
—Paris Hilton,
The Simple Life

"There was never anyone called 'Crap.'"
—Jade,
Big Brother,
after being told
by a housemate
that the bathroom
was invented by
a man named
Thomas Crapper

"If there were less people in here, it would be less crowded."
—Dean,
Big Brother

"I'm like herpes, dude. You might lose track of me, but I'm always there."
—Blair, *The Real World/Road Rules Battle of the Sexes*

"I need a Ritalin smoothie to help me concentrate on this disaster."
—Carson,
Queer Eye for the Straight Guy

THE BIG 5-0

Fifty used to be considered ancient. Now it's the new 30.
(That's what all the 50-year-olds say, anyway.)

"Looking 50 is great—if you're 60."
—**Joan Rivers**

"When I was young, I was told: 'You'll see, when you're 50.' I am 50 and I haven't seen a thing."
—Eric Satie,
French composer

"The man who views the world at 50 the same as he did at 20 has wasted 30 years of his life."
—**Muhammad Ali**

"At 50, everyone has the face he deserves."
—**George Orwell**

"Fifty is the age where you stop fooling yourself that if you just eat granola nobody will notice."
—Stephen King

"I have enjoyed greatly the second blooming that comes when you finish the life of the emotions and of personal relations; and suddenly find—at the age of 50, say—that a whole new life has opened before you, filled with things you can think about, study, or read about....It is as if a fresh sap of ideas and thoughts was rising in you."
—**Agatha Christie**

"He that is not handsome at 20, nor strong at 30, nor rich at 40, nor wise at 50, will never be handsome, strong, rich, or wise."
—George Herbert

"Everyone has talent at 25. The difficulty is to have it at 50."
—**Edgar Degas**

ROBIN WILLIAMS

*Here's hoping they never find a cure for
whatever's wrong with Robin Williams.*

"We had gay burglars the other night. They broke in and rearranged the furniture."

"See, the problem is that God gives men a brain and a penis, and only enough blood to run one at a time."

"These people are so rich they don't get crabs...they get lobsters."

On George W. Bush:
"We have a president for whom English is a second language."

On his body hair:
"I've actually gone to the zoo and had monkeys shout to me from their cages, 'I'm in here when you're walking around like that?'"

"Canada's like a loft apartment over a really great party."

"In Dallas a man asked me if I'd been to the book suppository. I told him, 'No, I prefer books on tape.'"

"I've got the fifth sense: I smell dead people."

"Why'd she get her tongue pierced? She said, 'To enhanthe the thekthual thimulathon.'"

"Divorce, from the Latin word meaning to rip out a man's genitals through his wallet"

"I can see it now: Osama bin Laden goes up to the pearly gates where George Washington comes out, starts beating him and is then joined by 70 other members of the Continental Congress. Osama will say, 'Hey, wait! Where are my 71 virgins?' And George will reply, 'It's 71 Virginians, you a**hole!'"

"If you're damned if you do and damned if you don't...you might as well do." —Jay Newman

THE ART OF LIVING

Oh, joy. Oh, joy. Joy. Joy. Joy. Life is wonderful, isn't it?

"Life is like a B-picture script. It's that corny. If I had my life story offered to me to film, I'd turn it down."
—**Kirk Douglas**

"As far as we can discern, the sole purpose of existence is to kindle a light in the darkness of being."
—**Carl Jung**

"Life is a game show where the people who enjoy it are the winners."
—**Orson Bean**

"The art of living is more like wrestling than dancing."
—**Marcus Aurelius**

"Life is the art of drawing without an eraser."
—**John Gardner**

"Change is not merely necessary to life—it is life."
—**Alvin Toffler**

"Life is like a game of cards. The hand that is dealt you is determinism; the way you play it is free will."
—**Jawaharlal Nehru**

"Life is a tragedy when seen in close up, but a comedy in a long shot."
—**Charlie Chaplin**

"The game of life is the game of boomerangs. Our thoughts, deeds, and words return to us sooner or later, with astounding accuracy."
—**Florence Shinn**

"Life is uncertain. Eat dessert first."
—**Ernestine Ulmer**

"The big secret in life is that there is no big secret. Whatever your goal, you can get there if you're willing to work."
—**Oprah Winfrey**

"There is only one basic human right: the right to do as you damn well please. And with it comes the only basic human duty, the duty to take the consequences."
—**P. J. O'Rourke**

"All I can say about life is, Oh God, enjoy it!"
—**Bob Newhart**

"Human beings have an inalienable right to invent themselves." —Germaine Greer

DON'T!

You're thinking of skipping this page? Please don't.

"Don't be discouraged by a failure. Failure is, in a sense, the highway to success. Every discovery of what is false leads us to seek what is true, and every fresh experience points out some form of error which we shall afterwards carefully avoid."
—**John Keats**

"Don't sleep too much. If you sleep three hours less each night for a year, you will have an extra month and a half to succeed in."
—**Aristotle Onassis**

"Don't try to live forever. You will not succeed."
—**George Bernard Shaw**

"Don't worry about people stealing an idea. If it's original, you will have to ram it down their throats."
—**Howard Aiken**

"Don't think there are no crocodiles because the water is calm."
—**Malayan proverb**

"Don't quote Latin; say what you have to say, and then sit down."
—**Arthur Wellesly, first Duke of Wellington, to a new member of Parliament**

"Don't accept your dog's admiration as conclusive evidence that you are wonderful."
—**Ann Landers**

"Don't speak unless you can improve on the silence."
—**Spanish Proverb**

"Don't argue with anyone larger than your van."
—**Red Green**

"Language exerts hidden power, like a moon on the tides." —**Rita Mae Brown**

NEVER...

Uncle John's credo: never follow the advice of experts.

"Never tell your daughter about your sex life—or the lack of it. It's ugly to see pity in a daughter's eyes."
—Joan Rivers

"Never mistake motion for action."
—Ernest Hemingway

"Never esteem anything as of advantage to you that will make you break your word or lose your self-respect."
—Marcus Aurelius

"Never try and teach a pig to sing: it's a waste of time, and it annoys the pig."
—Robert A. Heinlein

"Never, ever go to bed with a man on the first date. Not ever. Unless you really want to."
—Cynthia Heimel

"Never play cat and mouse games if you're a mouse."
—Don Addis

"Never drink black coffee at lunch; it will keep you awake all afternoon."
—Jilly Cooper

"Never confuse cancellation with failure."
—David Letterman

"Never sneeze while leaning your head against a brick wall."
—John Morrison Raymond, III

"Never fry bacon in the nude."
—H. Peter Miner

"Never stand between a dog and the hydrant."
—John Peers

"There are two things I've learned in life: you should never race a guy named Flash and never bring a girl named Bubbles home to meet your mother. Both of which I've done, by the way."
—Burt Reynolds

REEL LOVE

True love. It may or may not exist in real life, but it does in the movies. Here are some romantic moments from the Silver Screen.

"I love that you get cold when it's 71 degrees out. I love that it takes you an hour and a half to order a sandwich. I love that you get a little crinkle in your nose when you're looking at me like I'm nuts. I love that after I spend the day with you, I can still smell your perfume on my clothes. And I love that you are the last person I want to talk to before I go to sleep at night. And it's not because I'm lonely, and it's not because it's New Year's Eve. I came here tonight because when you realize you want to spend the rest of your life with somebody, you want the rest of your life to start as soon as possible."
—**Billy Crystal,** *When Harry Met Sally* **(1989)**

"I've made the most important discovery of my life. It's only in the mysterious equation of love that any logical reasons can be found. I'm only here tonight because of you. You're the only reason I am—you're all the reasons I am."
—**Russell Crowe,** *A Beautiful Mind* **(2001)**

"I might be the only person on the face of the Earth that knows you're the greatest woman on Earth. I might be the only one who appreciates how amazing you are in every single thing that you do, and how you are with Spencer, "Spence," and in every single thought that you have, and how you say what you mean, and how you almost always mean something that's all about being straight and good. I think most people miss that about you, and I watch them, wondering how they can watch you bring their food, and clear their tables, and never get that they just met the greatest woman alive. And the fact that I get it makes me feel good, about me."
—**Jack Nicholson,** *As Good as It Gets* **(1997)**

"I've already wasted my whole life. I want to tell you with my last breath that I have always loved you. I would rather be a ghost, drifting by your side as a condemned soul, than enter heaven without you."
—**Chow Yun-Fat,** *Crouching Tiger, Hidden Dragon* **(2000)**

First movie kiss: May Irwin and John Rice in *The Widow Jones* (1896).

CELEBRITY SECRETS

*When famous people let their guard down and tell
you how they really feel, it can get pretty strange.*

"I wouldn't like me if I had to be around me." —James Dean

"I've been involved in scenes in bathtubs and bedrooms and kitchen tables, but I never even feel comfortable when I have to take my shirt off. That scene in *Dances With Wolves* where I was naked—that was in the book, to show his vulnerability and how comfortable he felt being alone. I found the biggest reeds I could to hide behind."
—Kevin Costner

"The most embarrassing thing is that the salad dressing is outgrossing my films."
—Paul Newman

"I always need a drug to survive. The others did, too, but I always had more—more pills, more of everything—because I'm more crazy probably."
—John Lennon

"I was a horny kid. I fantasized a lot about female vampires."
—Jim Carrey

"I'm basically a sexless geek. Look at me, I have pasty-white skin, I have acne scars, and I'm five-foot-nothing. Does that sound like a real sexual dynamo to you?"
—Mike Myers

"Everyone seems to think I'm very ladylike. That I'm very cultured and intelligent. I drink a lot of Diet Coke and belch. I've been known to use the F-word. I've told a few dirty jokes. I arm-wrestle."
—Helena Bonham Carter

"Someone handed me cocaine at a party in a dish with a gold spoon. I thought it was Sweet-n-Low and put it in my coffee."
—Shirley MacLaine

"I was the worst postman in the history of the post office. I used to start my route at daybreak and I would finish long after dark. I'd stop for doughnuts. I'd play with animals. I'd go home with my bag of mail and just sit around the house."
—Dennis Franz

CELEBRITY TOMBSTONES

More epitaphs of the rich and famous.

The Greatest
Blues Singer in the
World
Will Never Stop
Singing.
—Bessie Smith

Shed not for her
the bitter tear
Nor give the heart
to vain regret
Tis but the casket
that lies here
The gem that filled
it sparkles yet.
—Belle Starr

Thank you for all the love you gave me.
There could be no one stronger.
Thank you for the many beautiful songs.
They will live long and longer.
—Hank Williams

DON'T KNOW MUCH ABOUT GEOGRAPHY

Travel tip from Uncle John: if you're flying to Hawaii from mainland United States, you don't need a passport.

"Every city I go to is an opportunity to paint, whether it's Omaha or Hawaii."

—Tony Bennett

Howard Stern: "What's the capital of New York?"
Tori Spelling: "New Jersey?"

"The only thing I know about it is that it's in New Jersey."
> —Michael Cropuzwel, ex-Dutch national team player and catching prospect for the Phillies when asked what he thought of Philadelphia

"One of those Canadian proverbs."
> —Brewers' Jim Gantner, on being asked where he went on a hunting vacation

"I like most of the places I've been to, but I've never really wanted to go to Japan, simply because I don't like eating fish, and I know that's very popular out there in Africa."

—Britney Spears

"I love California. I practically grew up in Phoenix."

—Dan Quayle

FROM THE MOUTHS OF BABES

*Supermodels make their living by their
appearance...mostly. Unfortunately for them,
they have to talk every now and then.*

"When I'm a blonde, I can say the world is purple, and they'll believe me because they weren't listening to me."
—Kylie Bax

"It was God who made me so beautiful. If I weren't, then I'd be a teacher."
—Linda Evangelista

"What truly inspired and satisfied me when I did my first show for John Galliano is how he explains every moment of the event. He comes to each of us individually to tell us about the part we're supposed to play when we show his beautiful creations. Just like for a play. For example, for a dress that was inspired by a storm or by anger, I have to imagine I'm playing the part of Scarlet O'Hara in *Gone with the Wind*."
—Kate Moss

"I would rather exercise than read a newspaper."
—Kim Alexis

"When I model, I'm pretty blank. You can't think too much or it doesn't work."
—Paulina Porizkova

"I don't know what to do with my arms. It just makes me feel weird and I feel like people are looking at me and that makes me nervous."
—Tyra Banks

"I've always been a little more maturer than what I am."
—Samantha Fox

"Models are like baseball players. We make a lot of money quickly, but all of a sudden we're thirty years old, we don't have a college education, we're qualified for nothing, and we're used to a very nice lifestyle. The best thing is to marry a movie star."
—Cindy Crawford

"Sit by the homely girl—you'll look better by comparison."
—Debra Maffers,
Miss America, 1982

"If men had to have babies they would only ever have one each." —Diana, Princess of Wales

MR. BURNS

He's rich. He's cheap. He's greedy. But Homer Simpson's boss, Monty Burns, still manages to get some of the best laughs on the show.

"Well, that's odd....I've just robbed a man of his livelihood, and yet I feel strangely empty. Tell you what, Smithers, have him beaten to a pulp."

"I could crush him like an ant. But it would be too easy. No, revenge is a dish best served cold. I'll bide my time until.... Oh, what the hell. I'll just crush him like an ant."

"Look at them, Smithers. Goldbrickers...layabouts...slu g-a-beds! Little do they realize their days of suckling at my teat are numbered."

"I'm looking for something in an attack dog. One who likes the sweet gamey tang of human flesh. Hmm, why, here's the fellow....Wiry, fast, firm, proud buttocks. Reminds me of me."

"This house has quite a long and colorful history. It was built on an ancient Indian burial ground and was the setting of satanic rituals, witch-burnings, and five John Denver Christmas specials."

"Why should the race always be to the swift or the jumble to the quick-witted? Should they be allowed to win merely because of the gifts God gave them? Well, I say cheating is the gift man gives himself!"

"I don't like being outdoors, Smithers. For one thing, there are too many fat children."

"Let's keep the laughs coming eh, Simpson? Let's say I make you my executive in charge of recreation. No, better yet, my prank monkey!"

Smithers: "Sir, I'm afraid we have a bad image. People see you as a bit of an ogre."
Mr. Burns: "I ought to club them and eat their bones!"

"Ooh, so Mother Nature needs a favor? Well maybe she should have thought of that when she was besetting us with droughts and floods and poison monkeys! Nature started the fight for survival, and now she wants to quit because she's losing. Well, I say, hard cheese."

Real newspaper headline: "Man Stuck on Toilet; Stool Suspected."

GIVE 'EM HELL, HARRY

*Plain-speaking, straight-talking Harry S Truman
is famous for saying, "The buck stops here."
Here are a few more things he said.*

"All the president is is a glorified public relations man who spends his time flattering, kissing, and kicking people to get them to do what they are supposed to do anyway."

"A pessimist is one who makes difficulties of his opportunities and an optimist is one who makes opportunities of his difficulties."

"A politician is a man who understands government. A statesman is a politician who's been dead for 15 years."

"All my life, whenever it comes time to make a decision, I make it and forget about it."

"I never did give anybody hell. I just told the truth and they thought it was hell."

"We must have strong minds, ready to accept facts as they are."

"Always be sincere, even if you don't mean it."

"It is amazing what you can accomplish if you do not care who gets the credit."

"I would rather have peace in the world than be president."

"The only things worth learning are the things you learn after you know it all."

There is no period after the "S" in Harry S Truman.

"GROOVY, BABY!"

More famous movie lines to keep you busy.

1. "I'll be back."

2. "Yo, Adrian!"

3. "I was born a poor black child."

4. "You can't handle the truth!"

5. "Heeeere's Johnny!"

6. "If you build it, he will come."

7. "They're heeeere!"

8. "I'll have what she's having."

9. "Snakes. Why did it have to be snakes?"

10. "Daniel-san! Show me 'Wax on, wax off."

11. "Say hello to my little friend!"

a. *When Harry Met Sally*

b. *The Shining*

c. *The Karate Kid*

d. *Rocky*

e. *A Few Good Men*

f. *Scarface*

g. *Raiders of the Lost Ark*

h. *The Terminator*

i. *Poltergeist*

j. *The Jerk*

k. *Field of Dreams*

Answers

1. h; 2. d; 3. j; 4. e; 5. b; 6. k; 7. i; 8. a; 9. g; 10. c; 11. f

---

"Have you noticed that all the people in favor of birth control are already born?" —Benny Hill

SNL CLASSICS

More snippets from the "Weekend Update"
segment of Saturday Night Live.

"There was a near-tragedy this week when popular TV personality Morris the Cat attempted suicide. Despondent over the death of close friend Smokey the Bear, Morris chose to call it quits himself, leaving behind a note which read, simply, 'Meow, meow, meow, meow, meow, meow.'"
—**Jane Curtin**

"In a tragic related story, TV personality Speedy Alka-Seltzer came out of the medicine cabinet this week and admitted that he was a bi-carbonate. Fearful over possible criticism, the beloved Speedy threw himself into a bathtub and effervesced himself to death."
—**Jane Curtin**

"Retired Army General William C. Westmoreland stated this week that the advances made in medicine as a result of the Vietnam War have saved more lives than those lost in that conflict. Accordingly, the Pentagon has recommended that the United States immediately begin World War III in the hope of wiping out all disease."
—**Bill Murray**

Jane Curtin: "You're a paranoid schizophrenic, Dan, whose politics are obviously born out of some buried infantile trauma. You hide from reality, constructing a hostile world to justify your own incapacity for love and compassion. Go ahead, Dan, live in your dark, lonely world. The rest of us will extend our hands in friendship to 800 million human beings in China, saying, 'Hi! You do exist. Let's be friends.'"
Dan Aykroyd: "Jane, you ignorant slut."

"The cure for boredom is curiosity. There is no cure for curiosity." —Dorothy Parker

UNCLE JOHN'S QUOTATIONARY

Here's Part 10 of our quotation dictionary.
(Part 9 is on page 374.)

UNHAPPINESS: not knowing what we want and killing ourselves to get it. (Don Herold)

UNDERTAKER: the last man to let you down. (Jimmy O'Dea)

UNHEALTHY: what thin people call fat people—and vice versa. (Sandra Bergeson)

UNDERSTANDING: conception caused by speech. (Thomas Hobbes)

UNIVERSE: a big place, perhaps the biggest. (Kurt Vonnegut)

USER: the word computer professionals use when they mean "idiot." (Dave Barry)

VANITY: other people's pride. (Sacha Guitry)

VEGETARIAN: a person who won't eat anything that can have children. (David Brenner)

VICTIM: a person to whom life happens. (Peter McWilliams)

VIOLENCE: the repartee of the illiterate. (Alan Brien)

VIRUS: a Latin word used by doctors to mean, 'Your guess is as good as mine.' (Bob Hope)

VISION: the art of seeing things invisible. (Jonathan Swift)

VOTING: a way of determining which side is stronger without putting it to the test of fighting. (H. L. Mencken)

WAITING: the opposite of talking. (Fran Lebowitz)

WAR: young men dying and old men talking. (Odysseus, the movie *Troy*)

WEDLOCK: the type of lock that's most easily undone these days. (Mike Barfield)

WEED: a flower in the wrong place. (Bob Hope)

THE WHITE HOUSE: the finest jail in the world. (Harry S Truman)

WHOLE: always less than the sum of its parts. (David Russell)

WINE: bottled poetry. (Robert Louis Stevenson)

WISDOM: knowing when you can't be wise. (Paul Engle)

WISH: a desire without an attempt. (Frank Baur)

WIT: is the lowest form of humor. (Alexander Pope)

WOMAN: the last thing to be civilized by man." (George Meredith)

WOMEN: the peg on which the wit hangs his jest, the preacher his text, the cynic his grouch, and the sinner his justification. (Helen Rowland)

WORDS: the most powerful drug used by mankind. (Rudyard Kipling)

WORK: the only really dirty four-letter word in the English language. (Abbie Hoffman)

WORRY: interest paid on trouble before it falls due. (Hal Roach)

WRITING: the process of staring at a blank sheet of paper until drops of blood form on your forehead. (Gene Fowler)

X: in our alphabet being a needless letter that has an added invincibility to the attacks of the spelling reformers, and like them, will doubtless last as long as the language. (Ambrose Bierce)

XEROX: a trademark for a photocopying device that can make rapid reproductions of human error perfectly. (Merle Meacham)

Y EAR: a period of three hundred and sixty-five disappointments. (Ambrose Bierce)

YEARNING: not only a good way to go crazy but also a pretty good place to hide out from hard truth. (Jay Cocks)

YOUTH: life as yet untouched by tragedy. (Alfred North Whitehead)

Z EAL: a certain nervous disorder afflicting the young and inexperienced. (Ambrose Bierce)

ZEN MARTINI: a martini with no vermouth at all. And no gin, either. (P. J. O'Rourke)

ZOO: an excellent place to study the habits of human beings. (Evan Esar)

*　　*　　*

"If you can't make the putts and can't get the man in from second in the bottom of the ninth, you're not going to win enough football games in this league."

—**Sam Rutigliano, Cleveland Browns coach**

"The wisest men follow their own direction." —**Euripides**

TÊTE À TÊTE

Sometimes the best quotes are exchanges between two people.

Speaker: I have only 10 minutes and hardly know where to begin.
Voice in back: Begin at the ninth.
—Jacob Braude

Michael Curtiz, director, arranging a scene during *Casablanca:* Wery nice, but I vant a poodle.
Prop Master: But you never asked for one. We don't have one!
Curtiz: Vell, get one.
Prop Master: What color?
Curtiz: Dark, you idiot, we're shooting in color!
[A few minutes later, Curtiz is called out to see a large poodle.]
Curtiz: Vat do I do with this goddamn dog?!
Prop Master: You said you wanted a poodle, Mr. Curtiz,
Curtiz: I vanted a poodle in the street! A poodle. A poodle of water!

Isadora Duncan, dancer: You are the greatest brain in the world and I have the most beautiful body, so we ought to produce the most perfect child.

George Bernard Shaw: What if the child inherits my beauty and your brains?

Groucho: You don't mind if I ask you a few personal questions, do you?
Model: If they're not too embarrassing.
Groucho: Don't give it a second thought. I've asked thousands of questions on this show and I've yet to be embarrassed.
—*You Bet Your Life*

Young writer: I don't know what title to give to my book.
J. M. Barrie: Are there any trumpets in it?
Young writer: No.
J. M. Barrie: Are there any drums in it?
Young writer: No.
J. M. Barrie: Why not call it *Without Drums or Trumpets?*

Alison Skipworth: You seem to forget I've been an actress for forty years.
Mae West: Don't worry, dearie, your secret's safe with me.

HOPE FOR THE FUTURE

Ahh, the last page of the book.

"There is nothing like a dream to create the future. Utopia today, flesh and blood tomorrow."
—**Victor Hugo,**
Les Miserables

"Never doubt that a small group of thoughtful, committed citizens can change the world; indeed, it's the only thing that ever has."
—**Margaret Mead**

"If future generations are to remember us more with gratitude than sorrow, we must achieve more than just the miracles of technology. We must also leave them a glimpse of the world as it was created, not just as it looked when we got through with it."
—**Lyndon B. Johnson**

"I have always held firmly to the thought that each one of us can do a little to bring some portion of misery to an end."
—**Albert Schweitzer**

"Tomorrow is the day when idlers work, and fools reform, and mortal men lay hold on heaven."
—**Andrew Young**

"There is no law of progress. Our future is in our own hands, to make or to mar. It will be an uphill fight to the end, and would we have it otherwise? Let no one suppose that evolution will ever exempt us from struggles. 'You forget,' said the Devil, with a chuckle, 'that I have been evolving too.'"
—**William Inge**

"Creating the world we want is a much more subtle but more powerful mode of operation than destroying the one we don't want."
—**Marianne Williamson**

"Better than a thousand hollow words, is one word that brings peace."
—**Buddha**

"Resistance is not futile, we're gonna win this thing. Humankind is too good—we're not a bunch of under-achievers! We're going to get fired up about the things that matter! Creativity and the dynamic human spirit that refuses to submit."
—**Alex Jones,** *Waking Life*

"In the end, everything is a gag." —Charlie Chaplin

INDEX

A Quote From Uncle John

"Membership has its benefits!"

Become a member of the Bathroom Readers' Institute. It's completely free and entitles you to a membership card, an irregular email newsletter, and a discount everytime you order from our online store. The easiest way to become a member is to log on to www.bathroomreader.com and place your first order. Membership happens automatically. If you don't want to buy anything but still want to become a member-in-good-sitting, just send a self-addressed stamped envelope to the address below. Don't forget to include your email address!

The Bathroom Readers' Institute
PO Box 1117
Ashland, OR 97520

Another quote from Uncle John:

"If you like reading our books, visit the BRI's website..."

WWW.BATHROOMREADER.COM

You'll have a blast as you shop at our online store, take our monthly poll, read favorite selections from Uncle John, and much more!

The next book is on the way! Sit tight, and...

Go With the Flow!